CONTEMPORARY JAPANESE CINEMA
SINCE *HANA-BI*

Traditions in World Cinema

General Editors
Linda Badley (Middle Tennessee State
   University)
R. Barton Palmer (Clemson University)

Founding Editor
Steven Jay Schneider (New York
   University)

Titles in the series include:
Traditions in World Cinema
by Linda Badley, R. Barton Palmer and
   Steven Jay Schneider (eds)

Japanese Horror Cinema
by Jay McRoy (ed.)

New Punk Cinema
by Nicholas Rombes (ed.)

African Filmmaking
by Roy Armes

Palestinian Cinema
by Nurith Gertz and George Khleifi

Chinese Martial Arts Cinema
by Stephen Teo

Czech and Slovak Cinema
by Peter Hames

The New Neapolitan Cinema
by Alex Marlow-Mann

American Smart Cinema
by Claire Perkins

The International Film Musical
by Corey Creekmur and Linda Mokdad
   (eds)

Italian Neorealist Cinema
by Torunn Haaland

*Magic Realist Cinema in East Central
   Europe*
by Aga Skrodzka

Italian Post-Neorealist Cinema
by Luca Barattoni

Spanish Horror Film
by Antonio Lázaro-Reboll

Post-beur Cinema
by Will Higbee

New Taiwanese Cinema in Focus
by Flannery Wilson

International Noir
by Homer B. Pettey and R. Barton Palmer
   (eds)

Films on Ice
by Scott MacKenzie and Anna Westerståhl
   Stenport (eds)

Nordic Genre Film
by Tommy Gustafsson and Pietari Kääpä
   (eds)

*Contemporary Japanese Cinema Since
   Hana-Bi*
by Adam Bingham

Chinese Martial Arts Cinema
by Stephen Teo

www.euppublishing.com/series/tiwc

CONTEMPORARY JAPANESE CINEMA SINCE *HANA-BI*

Adam Bingham

EDINBURGH
University Press

Edinburgh University Press Ltd
The Tun – Holyrood Road
12 (2f) Jackson's Entry
Edinburgh EH8 8PJ
www.euppublishing.com

Typeset in 10/12.5 pt Sabon by
Servis Filmsetting Ltd, Stockport, Cheshire
and printed and bound in the United States of America

A CIP record for this book is available from the British Library

ISBN 978 0 7486 8373 4 (hardback)
ISBN 978 0 7486 8374 1 (webready PDF)
ISBN 978 0 7486 8376 5 (epub)

CONTENTS

ACKNOWLEDGEMENTS

Many, many thanks and much love to my family (especially Amelia) and close friends for continued belief and unending support, thanks that I extend beyond the parameters of time spent on this book. Similarly heartfelt thanks to my colleagues at Film Studies and English at Edge Hill University – Dr Jenny Barrett, Dr Andrea Wright, Dr Chris Auld, Dr Jennifer Woodward, Dr David Abel and Dr Peter Wright – whom I am proud and thankful to call my friends as well as (inspirational) co-workers and who have always been more than helpful and supportive. I must also mention and thank Steve Marsh, my partner in (cinema-going) crime for almost a lifetime and someone with whom I have spent literally countless hours, days, weeks and more discussing films and filmmakers, always illuminating and, engaging, and entertainingly so.

Thanks and gratitude to Tom Mes at MidnightEye.com for his help and useful comments and feedback, and to the director Fujiwara Toshi, who has been very generous (both in person and as an interlocutor via email) with his time and replies to my questions and enquiries. My editors and contacts at EUP have been very helpful and supportive, and to my many students and Twitter friends who have provided numerous useful discussions I offer thanks. My gratitude goes also to the friends I made at Sheffield Hallam University and the University of Sheffield (both students and staff), whose help and friendship has always been valued.

ILLUSTRATIONS

NOTE AND GLOSSARY

Japanese names throughout are given in the traditional Japanese order of family name followed by Christian name. The system of romanisation employed in this book is the British Standards Institute Specification for the Romanization of Japanese. Thus when the names of Japanese people, places, production companies, etc. are mentioned in the text they are not italicised and long vowels are not marked (Oshima rather than Ōshima, etc.). However the titles of films, books and less familiar Japanese terms (*giri, ninjō, seishun*, etc.) are italicised and long vowels are marked with a macron. Where English titles include Japanese words long vowels are not marked – thus Japanese *Zatōichi* but English *Zatoichi*, etc.

aimai	*ambiguity:* custom pertaining to the centrality of ambiguity in social interaction as a means of avoiding confrontation or hostility
Aum Shinrikyo	group that carried out Tokyo subway attack in 1995
bakufu	shogunate of the Edo period (1603–1867)
Bunraku	Japanese puppet theatre
chambara	swordplay
chinpira	little pricks (typically a reference to new yakuza recruits)
etchi	sexually provocative soft-core erotica
gaijin	foreigners (used most often to refer to Westerners)
gendai-geki	contemporary drama
giri	obligation
ie	system of family registration

jidai-geki	period drama
jitsuroku eiga	'true account film' – subset of the yakuza genre
kaidan eiga	ghost story
kokusaika	internationalisation
kokutai	national body
koseki	family registration
kurogo	handlers in Bunraku
naniwabushi	traditional song-based entertainment
ninjō	personal feelings or inclinations
ninykō eiga	chivalry film
onnagata	male actor playing female role
onryou	female ghost
oyabun	boss
riaruna eiga	'realistic film' pertainng to the documentary
sakura	cherry blossom
samurau	verb: to serve
seishun eiga	youth film
sempai-kōhai	family hierarchy
seppuku	ritual suicide by disembowelling
shinjū	double suicide
shinsengumi	special police force from end of Edo era working for Tokugawa Shogunate
shishosetsu	I-novel
shiteki dokumentari	personal documentary
shomin-geki	genre of film focusing on ordinary working people and middle classes
tatami	domestic mat
tateyaku	loyal hero
thanatos	death

TRADITIONS IN WORLD CINEMA

General editors: **Linda Badley and R. Barton Palmer**
Founding editor: **Steven Jay Schneider**

Traditions in World Cinema is a series of textbooks and monographs devoted to the analysis of currently popular and previously underexamined or undervalued film movements from around the globe. Also intended for general interest readers, the textbooks in this series offer undergraduate- and graduate-level film students accessible and comprehensive introductions to diverse traditions in world cinema. The monographs open up for advanced academic study of more specialised groups of films, including those that require theoretically oriented approaches. Both textbooks and monographs provide thorough examinations of the industrial, cultural, and socio-historical conditions of production and reception.

The flagship textbook for the series includes chapters by noted scholars on traditions of acknowledged importance (the French New Wave, German Expressionism), recent and emergent traditions (New Iranian, post-Cinema Novo), and those whose rightful claim to recognition has yet to be established (the Israeli persecution film, global found-footage cinema). Other volumes concentrate on individual national, regional or global cinema traditions. As the introductory chapter to each volume makes clear, the films under discussion form a coherent group on the basis of substantive and relatively transparent, if not always obvious, commonalities. These commonalities may be formal, stylistic or thematic, and the groupings may, although they need not, be popularly identified as genres, cycles or movements (Japanese horror, Chinese martial arts cinema, Italian Neorealism). Indeed, in cases in which a group of films is not already commonly identified as a tradition, one purpose of the volume is to establish its claim to importance and make it visible (East Central European Magical Realist cinema, Palestinian cinema).

Textbooks and monographs include:

- An introduction that clarifies the rationale for the grouping of films under examination
- A concise history of the regional, national or transnational cinema in question
- A summary of previous published work on the tradition
- Contextual analysis of industrial, cultural and socio-historical conditions of production and reception
- Textual analysis of specific and notable films, with clear and judicious application of relevant film theoretical approaches
- Bibliograph(ies)/filmograph(ies).

Monographs may additionally include:

- Discussion of the dynamics of cross-cultural exchange in light of current research and thinking about cultural imperialism and globalisation, as well as issues of regional/national cinema or political/aesthetic movements (such as new waves, postmodernism, or identity politics)
- Interview(s) with key filmmakers working within the tradition.

INTRODUCTION: WHY 1997 AND *HANA-BI?*

The cinema of Japan has, over the course of its post-Pacific War history, been an unstable institution. It has been subject to a series of fluctuating fortunes that have in fact contributed significantly to its defining tenets and characteristics, a truly national film industry in that both its fate and its individual products and the characteristics that have defined them have remained closely tied to the socio-political flux of the country in which they were made. Of course one could make similar claims about many national cinemas, but in Japan there is a particularly marked sense in which the fortunes of its filmmakers and studios have been both reflected in and predicated upon the fortunes of the nation. Conceptualisations and histories of Japanese cinema, in both Western and Japanese discourse, have tended to replay several well-rehearsed epithets regarding the highs of its golden eras and the attendant lows that have succeeded them, about marked peaks and troughs regarding economic success and stagnation, technological advancement and problems relating to the same (developments such as the Fukushima nuclear reactor). Successive eras of Japanese history – especially its modern, Meiji-era (1868) development and beyond – can likewise be delineated, suggesting a direct correlation that has endured into the new millennium. However this seemingly perennial paradigm did in some ways begin to erode and to change in the years following 1997, and to understand why 1997 was a significant year it is necessary to elaborate a little on the context.

In many ways the contemporary story of Japanese cinema suggests 1989 as a decisive turning point. Tezuka Yoshiharu (2012) has discussed the late 1980s in Japan as one of three key instances when a national identity crisis resulted from Japan being opened up and/or exposed to the world at large (pp. 9–12). He identifies what has been termed *Kokusaika*, or internationalisation, as part of Francis Fukuyama's infamous 1992 declaration of the end of history, and analyses how 'the essential cultural uniqueness of Japan' began to erode as a result (p. 10). As well as signalling a new social era (the Heisei era), the year 1989 marked an end to a largely stagnant cinematic decade in which hitherto prevalent generic trends (especially yakuza, samurai and *shomin-geki* films) stalled and Japanese films began to wane on the international stage. Such films as did find a receptive audience tended to be those by established auteurs (Kurosawa Akira, Oshima Nagisa, Imamura Shohei, etc.), and many of these were produced with significant foreign investment. Films such as Kurosawa's *Ran* (1985) and Oshima's *Max mon amour* (1986) were made with international (in both cases French) capital, whilst the involvement of American distribution deals helped enormously to secure backing for films like Kurosawa's *The Shadow Warrior* (*Kagemusha*, 1980) and *Dreams* (*Yume*, 1990). This began to change with a new generation of films and filmmakers in the subsequent decade. Rhyming broadly with larger events in the country – particularly the passing of Emperor Hirohito and the collapse of the bubble economy – the films that became significant to the 1990s in Japan established not a commonality of style but a consistent application and extrapolation of socio-political specificity within the sphere of genre cinema. Beginning with Tsukamoto Shinya's *Tetsuo: The Iron Man* (*Tetsuo*, 1989), Kitano Takeshi's *Violent Cop* (*Sono otoko, kyōbō ni tsuki*, 1989) and former editor Sakamoto Junji's *Knock Out* (*Dotsuitarunen*, 1989) a new generation emerged that centralised independent production by demonstrating the viability of genre material to reflect authorial concerns and directorial individuality. Independent filmmaking was by no means a new development within Japanese cinema. Several new wave directors had benefited from the ATG (Art Theatre Guild) that had been established in Japan in 1961 to showcase important foreign films and to produce and distribute Japanese films (many of these directors went on to form their own companies), whilst directors like Ishii Sogo, Masayuki Suo and Kawashima Toru defined 1980s indie cinema and thrived due to the increasing instability of studio production. However these filmmakers remained by and large difficult to classify: they were independent in style and sensibility (Ishii in particular is often referred to as a punk filmmaker) and also committed to cataloguing and exploring social unrest and injustice as a means of distinguishing themselves from the lavish blockbuster productions that had begun to appear around this time. The interest of directors like Aoyama Shinji, Sabu, Iwai Shunji, Yaguchi Shinobu and Hayashi Kaizo in the 1990s arises from an independent or maverick sensibility applied to generic, even at times formulaic material, and this became something of a model throughout much of this decade. If, as Mark Schilling (1999) has argued, there had been in the 1980s a decline of hitherto popular genres alongside an attendant democratisation of the industry – a more open and available means by which prospective filmmakers were able to make their own films without the long-held studio system of serving apprenticeships through numerous subsidiary roles (something that Kitano's route to the director's chair for *Violent Cop* exemplifies) – then these genres began to reappear, and to animate a new generation of directors in the 1990s.

Further underlining 1989 as a significant year, both socially and cinematically (albeit at one remove), is the debut feature by an important director in contemporary Japanese cinema, Aoyama Shinji. His *Helpless* (*Herepuresu*, 1995) is specifically set in that year – over the course of 24 hours on 10 September – and concerns the intertwined stories of a young, seemingly aimless male named Kenji who does little but visit his hospitalised, apparently mentally ill father, and a yakuza just released from prison. The two are old acquaintances, and after their paths cross (seemingly by chance) the latter entrusts to the former the care of his similarly mentally afflicted sister whilst he tries to find out what has happened to his gang's boss. What follows is a distant, largely affectless drama – one shot for the most part in long shots and long takes that drain emotion and spectacle from the narrative – that culminates in a violent showdown in a remote diner, after which the yakuza kills himself and Kenji leaves with his friend's sister.

It is through this de-dramatised sensibility that the relevance of *Helpless* becomes clear. As an independent production, one that was produced under the auspices of the satellite television station WoWow, the film demonstrates the ongoing prevalence and increasing industrial centrality of such a production model following what has been described by some as a decade (the 1990s) that saw the final nail in the coffin of many of the old studios. Moreover setting the film in 1989 (which is in no way facilitated by or relevant to the narrative), the year of Kitano's debut, and its distinctive stylistic register of blank detachment and causal, matter-of-fact depiction of violence, implicitly connects it to the sensibility that *Violent Cop* served to make visible as a narrative and generic style. The story contains numerous features that reflect on some of the specific tenets that may be regarded as important to Japanese cinema and indeed Japan itself in the decade following 1989, when the collapse of the country's economy brought about a severe recession with wide-reaching ramifications, not least for the way it had begun to conceive of itself as a global economic superpower. Most significantly Aoyama ruminates on fathers and sons throughout the film as a narrativisation of past and present wherein problematic patriarchal figures (a missing yakuza boss on the one hand and the protagonist's ill father on the other) bespeak an untenable generation, a bygone age incompatible with that which has superseded it. In other words the characters represent eras in contemporary Japan, the discord and disconnect between the lost prosperity of the recent post-war past and the enforced hardship of a present that cannot define itself against said past but concomitantly has nothing in lieu of such a definition; no tenable history or lineage. At least this remains true for most of the narrative, as ultimately *Helpless* provides a vision of personal over material prosperity when the protagonist makes the symbolic gesture of abandoning his motorbike in order to escort his new female friend on foot, the better to get to know her and to fill in the void in his life. In this the film stresses the validity and viability of relationships over material goods or gain. It is a prescient and pertinent point to make in a film set on the cusp of Japan losing what had been the largest concentration of wealth in the history of mankind before, as Conrad Totman notes, it entered a recession and 'remained stalled throughout the nineties' (2000, p. 530).

This perceived 'lost decade' has more recently been upgraded by some commentators to encompass the subsequent ten years leading up to 2010 (Berra, 2012a, p. 8). However the Japanese film industry managed a certain security, almost prosperity, amidst this ongoing social crisis. The significance of 1997 is perhaps less overtly significant, as the early 1990s had seen the emergence of a new generation of directors whose work was in large part facilitated by the early work of Tsukamoto and Kitano. However this is part of the reason why this year in particular offers a significant turning point in this decade. Jelena Stojkovic has deemed 1997 a key time for the fact that it appeared to signal a decisive end to Japan's cinematic studio system (2010, p. 36). But at the same time there was a marked turnaround in commercial success that in some ways pointed to a rehabilitation for Japanese cinema. At this time studio and independent filmmaking seemed to a degree to merge, to become less mutually exclusive with regard to key genres and sensibilities (something crystallised in the much more mainstream productions directed by Ishii and Suo) and this was further cemented in commercial and critical lionisation. Whilst there was undoubted international success for some of the key films made in 1989 – specifically *Tetsuo: The Iron Man*, which unexpectedly won a prize at the FantaFestival in Rome – these films were by and large national rather than international pictures. By way of contrast, 1997 saw Japanese cinema return to international prominence and visibility. Kitano Takeshi featured prominently when his seventh film, *Hana-Bi* (*Fireworks*, 1997), won the Golden Lion at the Venice Film Festival, whilst earlier that same year Imamura Shohei had shared the *Palme d'Or* at the Cannes Film Festival (with Abbas Kiarostami) for his drama *The Eel* (*Unagi*, 1997) and the *Camera d'Or* at the same festival was awarded to Kawase Naomi's feature debut *The God Suzaku* (*Moe no Suzaku*, 1997). Moreover in this year Miyazaki Hayao's fantasy adventure *Princess Mononoke* (*Mononoke hime*, 1997) eclipsed Spielberg's *ET* (1982) as the most successful film at the domestic Japanese box office, and Suo's *Shall We Dance?* (*Sharu we dansu*, 1997) became the highest grossing Japanese film ever released in the US, taking over $10 million from only a limited theatrical run.

Hana-Bi, then, was notable for its international visibility and success. Its Venice prize and attendant festival screenings at Toronto, New York and Thessaloniki (in Greece) secured its place at the head of a resurgent Japanese cinema. The film in turn performed respectably abroad – earning an initial $59,508 on only nine screen across the US before a three-week run grossed almost $250,000 – and on the strength of this went on to facilitate a number of reviews and essays celebrating the return of Japanese cinema.[1] Indeed when Darrell William Davis stated in 2001 that 'for Western critics Kitano "Beat" Takeshi is the greatest filmmaker to come out of Japan since Akira Kurosawa' (2001, p. 55), he was alluding to *Hana-Bi*'s comparable status to *Rashomon* (*Rashōmon*, 1950) in (re)opening Japanese cinema to the West (a comparison that Miyao Daisuke has reaffirmed (2003, p. 15)), and in Japan the response was not dissimilar. The Japanese journal *Kinema Junpō* ranked the film the best of the year for 1998, and it was greeted with critical enthusiasm from the leading Japanese critics (Otaka, 2003, pp. 234–8). Neither was this an isolated trend; figures in 1997 were the best since 1980 for domestic releases, achieving 41.5 per cent of box office grosses with over 32.5 billion Yen from Japanese films. Audience figures continued to improve in all but one (2002) of the following years, leading to 107 billion Yen and 53 per cent of the market in 2006 and similar numbers in the following five years, whilst the number of films made per year also increased, reaching 356 in 2005 and 417 in 2006 (Bingham, 2009a, p. 162). In addition to *Hana-Bi* Kitano himself helped to spearhead this uptake in audience figures,[2] and this led the Japanese newspaper *Yomiori Shinbun* to declare 1997 to be 'the year of the Japanese film phoenix': the year when an almost moribund national industry rose from the ashes to reclaim a measure of the success and more importantly the visibility it had once enjoyed. Furthermore a book entitled *Japan Movies Now* (*Nihon eiga sangyo saizensen*) discussed in depth the film renaissance of the late 1990s and beyond, something that Murakami Yoshiaki and Ogawa Norifumi relate back to Kitano and *Hana-Bi* (Murakami and Ogawa, 1999, pp. 35–43). Indeed there was so much international cache for Japanese cinema after this film that the producer Sento Takenori established (in 1999) a concern named New Project J-Cine-X that was entirely devoted to films and filmmakers who had made an impact at European film festivals. This was undertaken with an eye to producing works primarily aimed at overseas markets as the Japanese have tended to follow the international canonisation of their films, to value at home what has been successful abroad. As Kawakita Nagamase stated in 1956:

> It must be admitted that the excellent reception abroad accorded many Japanese films in recent years has come as a surprise [. . .] [t]oday, many Japanese are finding attractions in their native films which until recently

they did not realise existed, thanks to the appreciation of these films by audiences overseas. (p. 220)

This practice of celebrating what has already found favour overseas has been retained and echoed in more recent years, and it helps to explain the impact of *Hana-Bi* and of the general upturn in the fortunes of Japanese films in Japan following 1997. However the influence of this film goes beyond purely commercial imperatives. If *Helpless* makes manifest, indeed almost allegorises, its precise place within Japanese cinema of the 1990s, then *Hana-Bi* does likewise with its status as a pivotal film for the late 1990s and beyond. From this point of view *Hana-Bi* served to refract questions and anxieties about identity and self-hood, both personal and national. Aaron Gerow (2007), Darrell William Davis (2001, 2007) and the Japanese critic Kasho Abe (2003, p. 237) have more than once discussed the Japaneseness of the film, the symbolic journey undertaken by the protagonist Nishi through a landscape populated by specifically Japanese signifiers (Mount Fuji, temples, a *ryokan* inn and rock garden, etc.). Davis also stresses the formal and narrative preoccupation with games and puzzles in *Hana-Bi*, ones that 'undermine the uniformity of Japanese uniforms' and show how professional and personal expectations therein can be exploited and manipulated (2007, p. 287). The film's preponderance of encoded surfaces and overt signifiers is also important in reflecting a national dimension to the narrative, a certainty of space as there is a concomitant certainty of time in the repeated mentions made in the dialogue of Japan's recession and attendant economic hardships (and a sense perhaps of an engagement with tradition as a means of negating or overcoming contemporary problems specifically associated with modernity and Westernisation). However another means of understanding its methodology is to say that it is about interruptions. Abrupt tonal and narrative switches predominate throughout the film, fragmenting the narrative with a subjective dimension hitherto unseen in Kitano's work. Even Beat Takeshi is immediately established as a disruptive onscreen presence, with a narratively extraneous moment of violence that intrudes upon the otherwise light, lyrical tone of the credits (quite literally as the music stops when he appears onscreen and restarts following said moment of anomalous violence), and thereafter the film proceeds to perennially undermine any transparent suture or interpellation. Violence intrudes again in the film's dénouement, once again bringing a halt to orchestral music and to a nominally lyrical mood as two gunshots that signal the deaths of the protagonist and his wife ring out across an empty expanse of beach and ocean water and leave only the sombre diegetic sounds of the waves in their stead.

The point of this forceful narrative methodology is to stress a tension between presence and absence, seeing and not seeing, as apparently incidental scenes and moments intervene on what is nominally the main dramatic story. This in turn highlights the elliptical structure of the film, not only making us more aware of what we do not see but also making us question why we see what we do: why apparently extraneous details and events appear to usurp the narrative. As such Kitano in *Hana-Bi* is not only working within a defined lineage – a narrative practice enshrined by Ozu and Itami Juzo in particular – but he is also underlining the significance of that lineage, its contemporary relevance and viability. It is as though the film itself were an interruption, an interjection into a developing trajectory that helped to facilitate a change of direction, which it did at a macro and micro level, for its country as well as its director. It is a nodal film that, as Tony Rayns suggests (1998), consciously summarises and redefines the writer/director's work up to that point (several actors from earlier works appear in minor roles), whilst the fact that it is slyly subtitled 'Takeshi Kitano Vol. 7' is an attempt to retrofit a coherent canon, to place the film within an imaginary oeuvre and thus to both foreground and frustrate auteur study at the intersection of genre and art cinema.

The film's generic identity is also perennially in flux, standing as it does at the confluence of a veritable matrix of ostensibly competing cross-currents. There are actual yakuza in the presence of the gangsters from whom the protagonist Nishi has borrowed money (these figures are in fact almost comedically presented as parasitic businessmen feeding from economic hardships as loan sharks), whilst the fact that Nishi is a cop who literally becomes a criminal when he robs a bank calls to mind the variation of the yakuza film that concerns rogue or outlaw detectives (of which Kitano's *Violent Cop* is a potent modern example). Alongside this is a detailed invocation of family and domestic life that recalls the *shomin-geki* genre of stories about ordinary middle-class citizens. Nishi's life has been ruptured by the death of his child, whilst his partner Horibe's wife and daughter leave him following a shooting that has left him crippled. From this point of view one may even suggest the similarities between *Hana-Bi* and J-horror cinema, as an emphasis on ruptured families rhymes with numerous Japanese horror films, to which end several commentators have stressed the extent to which this genre often examines emasculation and a sense of male disenfranchisement owing to social factors such as the 1990s' economic downturn.[3] In *Hana-Bi*, in contradistinction to Kitano's earlier self-starring films, Nishi is a remote and largely redundant figure. The excessive violence that he metes out is increasingly divorced from any tenable narrative exegesis (as is suggested by its frequent elision), and in meaningful matters such as when he is faced with a deceased colleague's wife he can but sit in motionless silence, unable to communicate with his interlocutor or to offer any comfort or practical aid. This facet of the film is crystallised in the image of Nishi firing his gun into an already dead criminal, a repetitive act of useless masculine spectacle (the criminal has already killed and wounded two of the protagonist's fellow officers) and a sign of its perpetrator's lack of viable social agency. In addition the stylised spectacle of 'Japan' in the film, especially

Figure I.1   Encoding 'Japaneseness': falling camellia (right of frame) signifies a fallen warrior as Horibe (Osugi Ren) is shot in *Hana-Bi*.

sporadic recourse to the imagery of camellias,[4] bespeaks an engagement with at least the iconography of the samurai film (see Fig. I.1), which has several concurrent strands in the film's stylised *mise-en-scène*. Horibe takes up painting as part of his rehabilitation; he paints a portrait of himself as a samurai on the cusp of committing *seppuku* (harakiri) and surrounded by falling *sakura* (cherry blossom) petals, something that resonates with the suicide(s) at the end of the film when Nishi takes the lives of himself and his wife in a variation of a so-called *Shinjū* (double suicide) narrative that is a staple of the classical Japanese theatre (particularly Kabuki) and numerous *jidai-geki*.

Hana-Bi is thus a genre film, an art film, an authored text and an auteurist provocation, as well as a film that questions generic boundaries whilst demonstrating the plasticity of genre as a critical framework. Moreover its emphasis on memory as a key thematic referent, exemplified in its fractured narrative structure that reflects its protagonist's struggles with his past, is echoed in specific works by Koreeda Hirokazu, Sabu and others, and these filmmakers also increasingly turned to more specifically Japanese stories and material. Several key directors in modern Japanese cinema, including those that began their careers in the 1990s as part of this decade's perceived 'new wave', seemed by and large defined by the blank, anonymous, quotidian locations and environments in which the stories play out and that often figure as manifestations of interior emptiness or decay. This is usually either an entirely featureless urban sprawl, an idea of a modern city rather than any recognisable place, or a more isolated rural milieu that offers a point of nominally lush spectacle but is prized for the contrast it proffers to urbanity rather than for any defining characteristics of space or topography. In point of fact Alex Kerr (2001) has argued that the fact that modern Japan has lost much of its once distinctive landscape – the topographical specificity of its traditional cities and countryside –directly represents the loss of that sense of national selfhood that he argues to be pervasive in the post-1989 face of the country. However, whilst this trend by no means disappeared at this time, the years since 1997 saw it begin to diminish, to the extent that Japanese cinema has seen something of a return to earlier modes and models, not simply a return of once-popular and prominent genres but a recapitulation or reworking of their particular generic methodologies. If *Violent Cop* was about rewriting the lineage of the yakuza film as a contemporary *tabula rasa* then *Hana-Bi* is about incrementally filling in, colouring, that blank canvas (hence the narrative emphasis on painting) in order to re-inscribe a sense of history and selfhood (selfhood *in* history), and this served to undermine a hitherto prominent tenet of 1990s Japanese films.

The key directors of the 1990s were by no means the first to undertake this subversion – as Alastair Phillips has noted, Imamura Shohei's *Vengeance is Mine* (*Fukushū suru wa ware ni ari*, 1979) explicitly transgresses a touristic sense of space (2007, pp. 235–6) – but the later films eschew the mission statement that the new wave directors offered. The 1990s' films do not subvert the spectacle of national space so much as overwrite it, meaning that nationhood is more comprehensively undermined. The settings of many films of the early 1990s – most especially *Violent Cop* and subsequent yakuza films – bespeak an abstract urban space. This, however, was tempered in many films made in the wake of *Hana-Bi*. It is not completely overturned, as Kurosawa in particular retained a sense of urban anonymity and desolate ennui, and likewise Miike Takashi, even in his early, V-cinema years, typically located his crime and youth narratives inside specific milieus, often in specific cities that are even denoted in the very titles of films such as *Osaka Tough Guys* (*Naniwa yukyōden*, 1995). Nonetheless, as the new millennium approached and dawned, featureless open space began to be noticeably less visible and pervasive a feature of Japanese cinema. Sabu, for instance, followed his early cartoon-like crime narratives with *Monday* (2000), *Drive* (*Doraibu*, 2001) and especially *The Blessing Bell* (*Kōfuku no kane*, 2002) that are populated by Japanese social and cinematic types such as salarymen, yakuza and men affected by the economic recession, as well as refracting Kitano's almost therapeutic emphasis on problematic violence as a marker of masculinity.[5] Similarly Iwai Shunji followed his pop video-inflected early work with *April Story* (*Shigatsu monogatari*, 1998), a romantic *seishun eiga* (youth film) that, as Schilling notes, is '[f]illed with hypergeneric scenes of cherry blossoms blooming and spring rains falling [...] [that] marked a new, more traditional direction for Iwai' (1999, pp. 36–7). It is interesting from this point of view that in two of his early films Kitano set his stories in large part in Okinawa (*Boiling Point* (*San tai yon ekkusu jūgatsu*, 1990) and *Sonatine* (*Sonachine*, 1993)), an island chain of quasi-Japanese nationality (there is still a strong US military presence in this location) whose as it were knowability as a topographical space contrasts with Japan as presented elsewhere in the narratives. This also applies to directors who began in the late 1990s such as Koreeda and Shinozaki Makoto – directors who 'incorporated elements of classical Japanese cinema into their films' (ibid., p. 38) – and offers an example of the extent to which Japanese filmmaking has returned to earlier modes and influences. And the viability of this return, its concordance with wider social and artistic trends, can be seen both in general terms (a re-found popularity for traditional music and theatre, especially Noh, which now has over 1,500 professional practitioners) and in the work of individuals such as the ceramicist Akiyama Yo, who has exhibited on eight separate occasions since 1998 after only one previous exhibition in the 1990s (in 1991).

This revival was by no means a totalising or all-encompassing feature of Japanese cinema, certainly before the new millennium had begun. Indeed Iwai Shunji said in the mid-1990s that young filmgoers did not really know the work of Kurosawa (Akira) or Ozu and that contemporary films should reflect their lives and tastes (see Schilling, 1999, p. 38). However Mark Schilling noted even in July 1998 that 'I've seen a lot of younger Japanese directors try to make films like Yasujiro Ozu' (ibid., p. 94): a point that reflects a general trend not only today but in the history of the industry. Thus, if it is true that a 'pattern of initial Western influence followed by the development of "purely" Japanese forms has been repeated again and again, not only in individual careers but throughout the culture' (Schilling, 1997, p. 10), then post-1997 Japanese cinema upholds this cyclical model. In other words, following the 1980s and early 1990s (especially the latter, whose perceived new new wave was described in some quarters as the 'Japanese cinema after Mr Pink' generation because of a perceived debt to Quentin Tarantino) there was what Donald Richie terms a 'Japanification' (2001, p. 217), a return to Japanese forms, in the years following 1997. The Japanese critic Yomota Inuhiko, who himself concurs with a significant uptake in audience figures even between 1996 and 1998, has also found Japanese themes and genre material more prominent as of 1999 (2000, pp. 215–21), whilst a new narrative focus on ethnicity, he notes, increasingly helped to frame and refract questions of Japaneseness (ibid., p. 222).

This broad picture offers a starting point for a reflection on post-1997 Japanese cinema as experiencing a significant upturn in its commercial fortunes and a transformation of some of its defining creative tenets. As such, this study will be organised around the ways in which different genres reflect and refract these questions. It will be built around the salient genres, in most cases those that have proliferated across the history of Japanese cinema and that have returned to prominence as part of its contemporary output. As noted there are some (calculated) omissions in the book; in particular the lack of consideration of anime may strike some as notable given its continued international popularity and perceived centrality to the popular face of Japanese filmmaking. However quite apart from the wealth of discourse on this particular subject that has already been written (both in English and Japanese), the breadth of anime – from the variegated realms of Studio Ghibli to the independent contemporary romantic dramas of Makoto Shinkai, the fantasy and dystopian climates of Hosada Mamoru, Oshii Mamoru and Otomo Katsuhiro and on to the niche extremes of hentai and the multitude of pornographic films and the sexually provocative soft-core erotica often referred to as *etchi* – means that in general this diverse field fits less cogently into the thesis of this book. In this, anime stands outside some of the tendencies found elsewhere in mainstream Japanese cinema, and owing to the space required to fully elucidate such tendencies it was decided to omit any consideration of this genre and to concentrate on those genres that confirm and conform to this pattern.

Donald Richie rather broadly noted (2001) that 'the divergence between traditional and non-traditional is much less marked' in the contemporary cinema of Japan (p. 217). However the divergence between studio and independent productions is arguably a more apposite subject for such a statement, one that pertains to a new cinematic millennium wherein a newly negotiated space for tradition and Japaneseness began to emerge amidst a resurgent national, popular cinema. Therein is the subject, the approach and reasoning, of this book.

NOTES

1. See in particular Kehr (1998), G. Allen Johnson (1998) and Scott Tobias (2002) in particular. Numerous Japanese critics such as Otaka Hiroo (2003) and Murakami Yoshiaki (1999) also solidified a response to Kitano at this time based around a perceived return to a once-popular provenance.
2. In 1997/8 Kitano appeared prominently in a nationwide campaign to entice the Japanese public back into cinemas.
3. See McRoy (2005, pp. 3–5), Napier (2005, pp. 63–83), Allison (2000) and Balmain (2008, pp. 128–148) among others.
4. *Camellia japonica* is a flower traditionally associated with the samurai warrior as a metonym because its blossom typically falls to the ground whole rather than petal by petal and is thus regarded as akin to the head of the samurai dropping to the ground following *seppuku*.

5. *Monday*, for instance, is about a salaryman who wakes up in a strange hotel room without remembering why he is there, and then has to piece together the incidents that led to his being hunted by the police, including several instances of extreme random violence.

1. *JIDAI-GEKI* AND *CHAMBARA*: THE SAMURAI ONSCREEN

> The Japanese warrior's powerful hold on the social imagination persists despite the vast and growing temporal, political, and cultural distance between the eras of samurai rule and today.
>
> (Mason, 2011, p. 68)

In 2013, to mark the tenth anniversary of the Japan Foundation's annual UK touring programme of related Japanese films that have not been granted widespread distribution, a catalogue of works collectively entitled 'Once upon a time in Japan' was put together to be played throughout the UK. Concerned with films set in and reflective of a variety of historical periods, this collection underlined what has become an increasingly prevalent feature of contemporary Japanese cinema: namely a pervasive looking back, a re-viewing of the past, with a concomitant sense of the futility that such an undertaking may carry within it, the sub-textual concern with the present as a question as much as an answer. In other words, the past is opened up in many modern Japanese *jidai-geki* for a number of contrastive reasons – in order to reflect on the present and also to probe the past as part of a variously self-reflexive or even subversive discourse on modernity and postmodernity as cultural modes. As such the prominent return to the historical drama that characterises modern Japanese cinema, most often in the guise of the samurai film, frequently engages with a cinematic history as much as (if not more than) a social one, a lineage of the past onscreen rather than a window onto any empirically viable or objective past, and a consideration of the discursive practices of historicity and historiography in place of narrative or generic transparency. Even those films that do not dwell on history as spectacle nonetheless retain a subtly trangressive imperative wherein they deny or frustrate any simple or unitary diegtic suture or illusionist realism. They are often about the respective limits and the possibilities of cinema as an agent for transmitting or representing what Robert Rosenstone terms 'the burden of the past' (1995, p. 4), and as such have broader ramifications for a study of the *jidai-geki* and its popular and populist face in the *chambara* (swordplay) film.

These narrative and stylistic practices, far from animating a series of clearly delineated modernist, postmodernist or otherwise art cinematic texts, are in fact embedded within what are in many ways popular, generic narratives, and it is this tension and interplay that defines a number of post-millennial Japanese *jidai-geki*, even if only as part of a critical enquiry into the socio-cultural treatment of the samurai. The framework of a specifically cinematic treatment of history and the processes and politics of its writing and representation offers a number of possibilities for conceiving of samurai fiction. Rosenstone (1995), Marnie Hughes-Warrington (2007), Thomas Keirstead and Deidre Lynch (1995) and Deborah Cartmell and I. Q. Hunter (2001), to name but a few, have all broadly echoed the work of postmodern commentators like Jean Baudrillard (1994) and Jean-François Lyotard (1984) in conceptualising the historical film as an increasingly amorphous and complex site of play and performance, of a negotiation with the past as it exists in a symbiotic relationship with the present and, as such, one that denies historical veracity or canonisation in pursuit of other goals. It is what Tag Gallagher terms 'myths', which exist only insofar as they serve 'our story' (1998, p. 269). Indeed a recent documentary on the samurai film has stressed the extent to which the films in the eras in which this sub-genre has flourished say more about contemporary concerns than about the past *per se*.

Discourse on the Japanese *jidai-geki* in both Anglophone and Japanese criticism has not tended to follow up on the work of these scholars and interrogate the extent to which period films from Japan may be useful in destabilising illusionist historical narratives. In point of fact if Japanese cinema has, as Donald Richie (2001) in particular has repeatedly stressed, a markedly presentational (as opposed to representational – i.e. narratively transparent) dimension, then the *jidai-geki* can profitably be regarded as a particularly apt discursive arena. But despite this Alain Silver (2005), in what is perhaps the most thorough English-language consideration of the samurai film, makes no mention of its status as a vessel for questioning the past, whilst Patrick Galloway's (2005) collection of reviews and profiles is (perhaps of necessity) not concerned to explore the samurai film's place within the *jidai-geki* or to problematise any individual film's representation of history. Keirstead and Lynch (1995), in a fascinating study of Imamura Shohei's *Eijanaika* (1981) have examined and extolled this film's carnivalesque treatment of history wherein the director explicitly frustrates the official tide of historical 'progress' and development in order to frustrate any popular or comfortable notions of historical lineage and nationality and thereby to centralise nominally peripheral or transitory moments, those incidents that would comment or otherwise cast new light upon the officiousness of historical discourse (pp. 64–76). And whilst the post-millennial samurai film – indeed *jidai-geki* in general – has tended not to replicate this level of explicit self-reflexivity or meta-fictive commentary, and as such has remained somewhat less overt in its frustration of perceived historical verisimilitude, there is nonetheless a strong sense that these works may contribute to a discourse on the past onscreen, over and above the particular representations of samurai life and culture that they variously ponder, parody, subvert, lambast or lament.

The fractious, often symbiotic relationship between past and present, between dramatising the past and commenting on such a dramatisation, offers a correlative here to the extent that the figure of the samurai becomes a metonymical figure. Indeed, whereas the *jidai-geki* was once canonised as, at least in part, a pandering to and a stylised affirmation of occidental perceptions of exotic Otherness and flamboyant pageantry to help secure international visibility and success in the wake of Kurosawa Akira's *Rashomon* (1950) – films like Mizoguchi's *Ugetsu monogatari* (1953) and Inagaki Hiroshi's Musashi Miyamoto trilogy (1954–6) in particular – so in recent years has its generic specificity begun almost consciously to work against such a model. It has begun to call attention to the artifice of this pursuit and frustrate this kind of historicity as a means of questioning such precepts as they pertain to nationhood and historical constructions and perceptions thereof. Much recent discourse has addressed this particular facet of the canonisation of Japanese history. Jonathan Clements (2010) has argued that real historical figures fostered a perception of exoticism and Otherness as regards the samurai in Japan. Sales of heirlooms and artefacts, he notes, helped to create this fetishisation, whilst an increasing Japanese cultural enshrinement of the samurai (of which the aforementioned films were a significant part) underlined and perpetuated it (pp. 299–319), and the arguable over-valuation of martial and warrior aesthetics of notable historians such as Stephen Turnbull (2006) or novelists like James Clavell (1975) or more recently Patricia Kiyono (2013) have further cemented this Orientalist perspective, which has animated much Japanese *jidai-geki* cinema. Indeed, as Miguel Douglas has argued: '[t]hroughout the history of *jidai-geki*, the genre has been a crucial catalyst towards the worldwide promotion of the Japanese film industry as a legitimate and worthy institution' (2012, p. 227).

This revision of history, however, goes hand-in-hand with a recapitulation of generic modes, even of individual films, and it is with this particular tension in mind that any consideration of Japanese historical cinema and the modern samurai film should be explored and understood. This chapter will be concerned with works that engage in various ways in this practice, in this fervent dialogue with Japanese history both social and cinematic. Their dialogism is in fact not only with history *per se* but also with historical verisimilitude and with prevalent notions of the past onscreen. Many of the key films to be examined here – Kitano Takeshi's *Zatoichi* (*Zatōichi*, 2003), Miike Takashi's *13 Assassins* (*Jūsan-nin no shikaku*, 2010), Koreeda Hirokazu's *Hana/Hana – The Tale of a Reluctant Samurai* (*Hana yori mo naho*, 2006) – all take iconic, culturally enshrined genre material as a point of departure, subverting their models or referents as a means of commenting directly on their status as two-fold history: that is, of remaking or reworking older films (a cinematic history) that are themselves depictions of the past, a national history. By way of contrast the *jidai-geki* in particular of Yamada Yoji – his samurai triptych of *The Twilight Samurai* (*Tasogare Seibei*, 2002), *The Hidden Blade* (*Kakushi ken oni no tsume*, 2004) and *Love and Honour* (*Bushi no ichibun*, 2006) – emphasises personal, parochial perspectives on the past as a means of framing an ostensibly more realistic picture. Varied and contrastive as the films under consideration are, they nonetheless all complicate or subvert a certain model of *jidai-geki* and undermine some previous eras' engagement with it. More than ever this so-called 'mega-genre' of Japanese cinema (Wada-Marciano, 2008, p. 44) has become diversified, something Wada-Marciano and Yoshimoto Mitsuhiro (2000) in particular argue to be of particular importance in understanding formations of the nation in historical temporality. Mark Le Fanu (2005) has alluded to this problem from a variant perspective in discussing singular cinematic appropriations of history. In comparing Mizoguchi's *The Loyal 47 Ronin* (*Genroku Chushingura*, 1941/1942) to films such as Eisenstein's *Ivan the Terrible* (1945/1946), Robert Bresson's *Lancelot du Lac* (1974) and Kurosawa's *Throne of Blood* (*Kumonosu-jo*, 1957), he argues that 'the originality of the vision is only allowed to emerge by their directors' finding some [. . .] personal cinematic language uniquely honed to the story [. . .] a language for that very reason unrepeatable' (p. 105). In so saying he draws attention to a tension between genre and auteur, and between perceived neo-classicism and an art cinematic modernity that this chapter will extrapolate in order to analyse how and to what extent postmillennial samurai films contravene or comment upon such facets of history on film.

If the *jidai-geki* has occupied a central place within Japanese cinema it has several different conceptions and ramifications. Historiography is especially pertinent to the Japanese *jidai-geki*, and its samurai and *chambara* subsets in particular. The processes and the writing of history can be held to occupy an especially significant place within Japanese socio-cultural specificity as the seismic changes and transformations that had affected (indeed beset) the country for much of the late nineteenth and throughout the twentieth century disturbed Japan's once clear perception of itself as a nation. Beginning with the forcible opening up of the country to trade by an American delegation in 1853/4, and continuing with the post-1868 Meiji restoration during which time Japan was rapidly modernised and Westernised, there were relatively rapid and successive challenges to the country's sense of its own identity and self-sufficiency. The increasingly right-wing politics of the 1920s, the Sino–Japanese conflict, the Pacific War, the post-WWII occupation (Japan as a coloniser being colonised) and subsequent economic miracle and recession all shaped and reshaped Japanese nationhood. These events served to delimit the country's sense both of itself and of its place within the world, and to foster what Ian Buruma (2003) has termed 'a sometimes obsessive preoccupation with national status' on the part of the country (p. 11). This, combined with competing discourses of both nationalism and transnationalism (globalisation) and modernity and postmodernity that have tended to circulate as essentialist imperatives, have further obfuscated a clear selfhood, as well as inscribing a distance from the relative certainties and social homogeneity of particularly the Tokugawa Shogunate (1603–1868), which latter points make the return to prominence of the *jidai-geki* unsurprising and especially meaningful as this is a common setting for such films.

Darrell William Davis (1996) has extended this paradigm, classifying and interrogating as he has a potential postnationalism as this pertains to narratives intended to map or define national identity. He notes that 'a fixation on the past is the only response to an inexplicable future' (p. 12), before proposing a dialogic model of classifying similarity and difference in national cinematic output that, certainly within Japanese cinema studies, has not been taken up in any extended or detailed way. The condemned-to-die Korean protagonist of Oshima Nagisa's *Death by Hanging* (*Kōshikei*, 1968) dismisses the concept of a nation as an 'abstraction', echoing the imagined communities theorised by Benedict Anderson (1991) or the 'imaginary coherence' posited by Andrew Higson (1989, p. 54). The example of identity as a construction accrued through cultural products rather than an *a priori* fact that is disseminated by them is an important one in this context as it alludes to the variegated new samurai films' emphasis on contested identities, compromised or fallible subjectivity and (mis)remembrance and (mis)perception. A proliferation of narratives told through flashbacks also underlines this precept, whilst the sense of reconfiguring or estranging canonised figures and stories further reinforces the processes of negotiation, of dialogism, that are central to the contemporary samurai film. In point of fact some films have explicitly raised the spectre of historiography and its pertinence to Japanese period cinema. The television drama *Nobunaga's Coffin* (*Nobunaga no hitsugi*, 2006) looks at the aftermath of the famous warlord's death in battle and the mystery surrounding his subsequently missing body, but does so from the point of view of a character who is documenting the warlord's life and exploits in battle. The protagonist is a chief retainer to Nobunaga, a loyal aid whose biographical portrait of the apparently late lord brings him into conflict with his superiors, who do not desire to have the truth told regarding his exploits and attitudes. In so doing this film foregrounds and explores processes of historiography and the narrative of history, underlining the fact that officially sanctioned narratives are at best a partial, and more significantly a biased, record of historical events.

One must thus view Japan's almost incessant canonisation of its past within the framework, the pliable and flexible parameters, of both its contemporary socio-political specificity and within the realm of national and transnational film-making that has increasingly characterised the amorphous boundaries of nation-hood. Many recent Japanese films work through a series of largely circumscribed and clearly defined formulas, but the *jidai-geki* has been open to a number of more complex and interesting narrative and stylistic currents that are, perhaps, due in part to an increase in televisual productions that have re-inscribed a more simplistic vision of the past on Japanese screens in the home. Since the landmark series *Life of a Flower* (*Hana no shōgai*) in 1963, which initiated the so-called *Taiga* phenomenon (Schilling, 1997, pp. 244–8), there has been a staple of period dramas every year from the major television networks NHK (who make the Taigi series) and Fuji. Conversely the genre has had a more adventurous cinematic face. Among the most predominant characteristics of the modern *jidai-geki* in Japanese cinema has been the number of directors making samurai films who have not typically been associated with the genre. Kitano Takeshi, Koreeda Hirokazu, Miike Takashi and Yamada Yoji have all delved into their country's past for the first time in their careers. Moreover the fact that several of these filmmakers have remade or at least reworked earlier material facilitates a sense of connection to their past that had not been apparent in the 1990s in much new Japanese cinema. Miike is foremost in this regard as both of his most notable recent samurai films are direct remakes of earlier works, and furthermore are reasonably faithful to their predecessors, retaining both their narrative outlines and characters. Although neither *13 Assassins* nor *Hara-Kiri: Death of a Samurai* (*Ichimei*, 2011) marked Miike's first venture into *jidai-geki* cinema they did serve as his debut *chambara* films, and as such bear an interesting relationship to the idiosyncratic films that made his name.

When it was released in the Europe and the US in 2011 *13 Assassins* was greeted by some commentators as a neo-classical film, a text that hearkened back to earlier eras when the samurai and swordplay film was among the most prevalent and popular in the Japanese canon. Christoph Huber (2011) notes that '[a]fter the world premiere of *13 Assassins* [. . .] critics hitherto hostile to the work of the prolific Japanese director Miike Takashi suddenly started to rave about the Kurosawa-like classicism of his new sword-fighting spectacular' (p. 52), before himself going on to refer to the film as a 'classical genre exercise' (ibid.), something that Nick Pinkerton (2011a) pejoratively echoes when he calls the film the 'same old epic samurai showdown'. However there are problems here. Huber himself goes on to decry any connection to *Seven Samurai* (*Shichinin no samurai*, 1954) on the part of Miike's film, noting that it lacks the detailed character backstories of Kurosawa's epic (Huber, 2011, p. 52). But if *13 Assassins* does not follow Kurosawa's lead then where can its apparent classicism be found? Kudo Eichii's *13 Assassins* (*Jūsan-nin no Shikaku*, 1963) was produced at a time when the samurai film was beginning to develop beyond the hitherto well-rehearsed confines of the genre. It was made just after *Yojimbo* and Kobayashi Masaki's *Harakiri* (*Seppuku*, 1962) had variously parodied and subverted the traditional Bushido code of samurai conduct. But beside this, both the original film and especially Miike's remake appear to uphold a form of heroism that both James Goodwin (1994) and Donald Richie (1996) have discussed in detail: namely a sense of moral purpose, of didacticism, a humanist impulse where characters teach and live by example. Thus neither film fits neatly into any category: they seem in fact to bridge a gulf between classicism and post-classicism, and Miike uses this tension to underline *13 Assassins*' depiction of the age of the warrior coming to an end. He alludes in particular to the transience of the samurai. A majority of the early scenes in the film take place at night in interiors lit only by lamps, by flickering lights and flames whose transitory nature – bursting into life amidst darkness before being extinguished and dying away – becomes redolent of the lives of the titular warriors. In addition the director has recourse to a very overt (and textually anomalous) point of view shot as one of his samurai dies on the battlefield, replete with a dramatically canted angle as his life gradually ebbs away. It is as though subjectivity only comes to this character in battle, life achieved only in death, reflecting a perceived paradigmatic aspect of the samurai that would become central to their mythical legacy, something that Luke Roberts (2011) in particular has discussed as 'an ideological desire to monopolize in the samurai class certain characteristics of status identity [. . .] [as a] naturalization of a distinctive samurai masculinity' (p. 49).

In other words the politicisation of the Japanese new wave era is not overtly in evidence in Miike's *13 Assassins*. But on the other hand it does not entirely lionise those works more redolent of the so-called golden age of the 1950s. Miike himself has said that his is not an action film (2011), which one may relate to the director's desire to eschew a simple formula, a spectacle of action and period detail, and to engage with the samurai as a socio-historical sign. Certainly the portrait of this supposed warrior class contained within its narrative is not altogether heroic, not a valorisation or celebration. The director is less at pains to stress their nobility and honour than he is to emphasise the extent to which their status as warriors itself becomes a dialogic entity, something that is facilitated in a very specific context and under particular circumstances. The leader of the group, Shinzaemon, has left behind his life as a warrior as the film begins – indeed, contrastive high-angle shots of a samurai committing *Hara-Kiri* and Shinzaemon fishing (the first shot of the protagonist) alludes to the gulf between these men of ostensibly the same caste – and this approach to the material is crystallised in the director's more elaborate treatment than his predecessor of the ostensibly purely evil target for the assassins' quest, Lord Naritsugu Matsudaira. This character appears on the surface to be an embodiment of remorseless, pitiless greed and self-interest, a rampant id, but is in fact a figure who takes the samurai ideal to its ultimate, perhaps logical, conclusion. His monstrous actions – which the film is at pains to depict on numerous occasions and which finds its most extreme example in the image of the girl whose arms and legs he has amputated and whom he has left entirely mute by cutting out her tongue – actually reflect an absolute commitment to samurai ethics and ideals. As he says in response to being questioned over his slaughter of a family:

> What makes a samurai? You men mindlessly chant 'loyalty, duty' like a Buddhist prayer. But if servants are spoiled, then one day,they forget their duty to serve [. . .] [p]unishing one's servants; they are certified as property by the shogun. Dying for one's master is the way of the samurai [. . .] we must protect these 'ways', right?

This directly reflects the rigidity of the samurai class, the fact that appointed roles within a codified hierarchy were expected to be fulfilled and absolute filial piety was demanded. At the end of the narrative, when he has tasted battle following Shinzaemon's attack, Naritsugu tells his chief vassal, the loyal Hanbei that when he rises to power he will bring about a return to the age of civil war that had afflicted Japan several centuries before, prior to the Tokugawa Shogunate, and thereby resuscitate an era when the samurai could fulfil their perceived rightful destiny by fighting and dying in battle. Conversely, the titular thirteen warriors willingly abandon any perceived code when it suits their purposes. Whilst training for their mission the supreme swordsman of the group, Hirayama, exhorts his fellow samurai to disregard any precepts of honour or chivalry, and to fight dirty if it is necessary to triumph over the enemy. In this, Miike in fact amplifies a more or less dormant aspect of the original film by stressing the connection between the leader of the assassins and Hanbei. It is noted that both trained together at the same dojo, whilst one particular long take – a long shot of Shinzaemon and Hanbei facing each other across a corridor – visually alludes to the mirror image that each presents of the other. Again here it is the samurai's life lived in absolute, unquestioned servitude that Miike reflects in Hanbei, as this character raises doubts as to Naritsugu's actions and openly questions his lord but ultimately must follow orders, must take his allotted role as servant (the term 'samurai' in fact derives from the verb *samurau* meaning to serve) and act against his better judgement. In contradistinction Shinzaemon represents a transgression, albeit one officially sanctioned, of samurai ethics and ideals, and the need to forgo such rigorous standards in order to serve a greater good.

Beyond this picture of masculinity there is a contrapuntal consideration of both femininity and of non-samurai that contextualises this humanism and arguable conservatism elsewhere in the film. As is typical of this director, bodily decay, decomposition and transgression feature heavily in *13 Assassins*. Mika Ko (2006) has discussed in depth how the breaking of the body in Miike's work reflects a wider breaking of what she refers to as a national body, and here it is related most forcefully to woman, specifically to the aforementioned mutilated female whose physical defilement becomes a visible marker of doubled Otherness that indelibly inscribes female victimhood as the foundation of the masculine endeavours that define this narrative. Elsewhere, in a subversion of his authorial persona, Miike avoids the exaggerated scenes of violence that had helped make his reputation in his yakuza and horror films. Indeed in two separate scenes of *seppuku* he focuses solely on the faces of the warriors involved, shooting them in identical low-angle medium close-ups that eschew any graphic bloodletting and thereby allow their deaths a measure of privacy and honour so that the self-inflicted violence does not contravene the 'lack of bodily integrity' (ibid., p. 132) that Ko identifies as a central referent in Miike's other films. This also disturbs the apparent reactionary sensibility that this author outlines, wherein the erosion of a homogeneous social and spiritual Japaneseness (its national body, or *kokutai*) is implicitly mourned by Miike – a 'nostalgic nationalist discourse lamenting the loss of *kokutai*' (ibid.). In contradistinction *13 Assassins*' ambiguity over the figure of the samurai questions the roots of this national body (and the perceived classical cinematic idiom that it metonymically represents) and asks that it is not taken at face value.

This particular trajectory returns one to the aforementioned dénouement of the film. In *13 Assassins* it is Koyata (a helper to the assassins) who is (apparently) one of only two of the warriors (along with Shinzaemon's nephew Shinrokuro) to survive the climactic assault and to emerge alive at the film's finish, a key point in that these figures are the two non-samurai among the group. The former bemoans the arrogance of the samurai even when fighting alongside them (his counterpart in Kudo's film offers no such criticism – he is much more openly desirous of becoming a samurai himself), whilst the latter, who had earlier stated how unsuited he was to a warrior's way of life, smiles wryly to himself in the film's final shot. These cryptic climactic moments are rather ambiguous as to their precise meaning, and this in turn complicates responses to the narrative as a whole. The return of Koyata following his apparent death in battle (he is stabbed in the neck by Naritsugu) is a particular case in point. He appears without any apparent injury around his throat or ill effects from such an attack, and he discusses with his fellow survivor his happiness and his plans now that the fighting is over and he can return to his life. Is he an apparition, a spirit who perhaps does not realise that he is dead? Or can one postulate that his appearance is a figment of his interlocutor's imagination, and as such maybe a marker of his elation at surviving, from which point of view it is telling that Miike closes *13 Assassins* on Shinrokuro, fading out on him as he smiles to himself whilst walking away from the burning embers of a now-destroyed village (as opposed to his counterpart in Kudo's film who laughs maniacally). His smile seems to be a recognition that the age of the samurai is coming to an end, and by extension that he is better placed to continue, to live on. Indeed he seems to be mocking his samurai brethren for their over-valuation of death, honour and tradition, their valorisation of death. Certainly the life in death afforded Koyata suggests a commentary on Miike's part on the finality of the insular age of the samurai, the fact that these warriors have sought death as a means of legitimising their lives and in so doing have implicitly reinforced Naritsugu's discourse on their, as it were, unquestioning filial piety. Shinrokuro, the reluctant samurai, appears to recognise this precept, and as such his laughter may be read as a mocking or derisory indictment of the warrior class.

To return to the discourse on classicism, what needs to be clarified is the precise definition of the term in this context. Classical filmmaking in Japan may be understood in a different way to, and as a variegated model from, that which has been perceived to define mainstream cinema in the West. What Miike's film may best reflect is Catherine Russell's (2011) discourse on classical cinema as transnational cinema (pp. 15–18): the notion that any conception of classicism in fact represents a canonisation of the earlier era (the parameters of which may well be divisive or contested) from the perspective or subjectivity of a contemporary space far removed from the era in question. This in turn makes such a canonisation 'uncanny and unstable' (p. 16), a tenuous construction given the contrastive forms of production, distribution and reception within which it is conceived. Kudo's *13 Assassins* is not a canonical text such as *Seven Samurai*, Kobayashi Masaki's *Samurai Rebellion* (*Joi-uchi: hairyo tsuma shimatsu*, 1967) or Gosha Hideo's *Three Outlaw Samurai* (*Sanbiki no samurai*, 1964); Miike's reworking can thus circulate as a text whose apparently classical boundaries or parameters are open to question: where the designation of the film as such becomes a feature of a contemporary imaginary, a mirror held up to a present that arguably needs a classical aesthetic to define and delimit one film from another, one style or era from another. Perhaps in this sense the last laugh that closes the film is on the audience or critics whose misappropriation or indiscriminate use of the term classicism should say more about their own views than about the film they are watching. Miike's *13 Assassins* should thus be understood as a film about classicism rather than a classical film.

After *13 Assassins* came a faithful, almost reverential, remake of Kobayashi Masaki's *Harakiri* (*Seppuku*, 1962). Entitled *Hara-Kiri: Death of a Samurai* the film is notable for Miike's rigorous refusal of spectacle. This is taken to an extreme in several ostensibly minor moments (such as when a dying man looks longingly out over what is described as a beautiful view and Miike refuses to cut to the expected POV shot of this resplendent idyll), but is also reflected in the comparative lack of action set-pieces. A subversive engagement with spectacle is also at the heart of another key modern samurai film – one that in some ways represents both a culmination and a re-contextualisation of its key director's oeuvre. *Gohatto* [*Taboo*] (1999), the final film by Oshima Nagisa, is set among the closed, rarefied ranks of the elite *Shinsengumi*, the special police force formed towards the end of the Tokugawa Shogunate in order to quell insurrectionary uprisings as the Shogun's power was waning. *Gohatto* traces the consequences of a beautiful young male joining the *Shinsengumi*, a teenager named Kano who becomes the object of lustful attentions of several of his contemporaries and superiors and as such who causes significant consternation and private enmity among his peers.

The film engages in a dialogic relationship with its genre's history in that it appropriates a silent *chambara* aesthetic by punctuating the narrative with inter-titles that communicate details of characters' relationships and of life within the *Shinsengumi*. The spectacle of an exotic period *mise-en-scène* had in its earliest incarnations defined the *jidai-geki* and its samurai subset, something that pandered to an extra-diegetic spectatorship who would consume period detail almost as a commodity. Oshima rigorously eschews such spectacular style, such fetish-ised *mise-en-scène*, not only stressing but narrativising diegetic spectatorship and spectatorial consumption. Steve Neale (1983) in particular has written in detail about the ways in which the bodily spectacle of masculinity can offer a challenge to notions of spectatorship and mainstream interpellation. Appropriating and redefining work done particularly by Laura Mulvey and Paul Willemen, he demonstrates how homo-erotic subject positioning is both invoked and disavowed by mainstream texts in Hollywood cinema – through voyeurism and fetishism, wherein:

> [t]he anxious 'aspects' of the look at the male [. . .] [are] both embodied and allayed not just by playing out the sadism inherent in voyeurism through scenes of violence and combat, but also by drawing upon the [. . .] processes of fetishistic looking, by stopping the narrative in order to recognise the pleasure of display, but displacing it from the male body as such and locating it more generally in the overall components of a highly ritualised scene. (p. 17)

Nominally this may well have been written with *Gohatto* in mind as Oshima builds the narrative around violent physical encounters. The opening scene depicts a series of ritualised oppositions designed to test prospective members of the *Shinsengumi*, and thereafter there are numerous physical conflicts leading up to a final scene in which a situation is engineered to facilitate Kano's death (with two characters watching on whilst in hiding). The very first scene eschews an establishing shot to open immediately on a fight, and given the frequent battles between openly desirous men these scenes may at times be read as sublimated sexual acts, something further defined by the gazes of men that are cast onto the spectacle of other males' behaviour – an appropriation of the often festishised period detail of the genre. This is crystallised in a fight between two new members of the militia – between Kano and a man who professes to love him – that is then used as an attempt to uncover whether the pair are lovers by their superiors, at least one of whom openly desires Kano himself. The aforementioned emphasis on the rigidity of this elite force connotes the centrality of conformity and transgression that, importantly, reflects individual actions throughout the film rather than sexual felicity or perceived aberration. Indeed these rigours, which see one warrior beheaded simply for borrowing money, serve to throw into relief the openness to homosexuality within the closed ranks of the *Shinsengumi*.

This engagement with objectivity and subjectivity is not a particularly new phenomenon. Kinugasa Teinosuke's *Gate of Hell* (*Jigokumon*, 1953) is a significant forerunner for the way it treats its narrative visually as a historical picture scroll by beginning with a shot of such an artefact before subsequently cutting to a high-angle shot of movement that looks down on its subjects as they laterally traverse the frame. This film is also of note in that visual spectacle for Kinugasa (who opens *Gate of Hell* with a battle in *medias res* and thereafter refuses to dramatise such exterior action) becomes associated directly with the problematic, obsessive male gaze that is cast onto the heroine by the man who desires her. Oshima broadly replicates this practice, but in *Gohatto* there are a multitude of competing obsessive looks, and instead of the known and knowable courtesan there is Kano – a blank slate who exists at the nexus of the perceptions that accrue around and about him. He becomes what is projected onto him by others, admitting to nothing in the numerous questions he is asked about his sexuality and sexual history, and instead often submitting to the men who want him, becoming the object they all seem to desire and over which they perennially obsess. On the one occasion when he himself becomes a desiring subject the object of his affections is a heterosexual fellow samurai who denies his advances and thus frustrates his subjectivity, reinforcing the idea that this protagonist is less a fully realised character than a symbol, an ephemeral figure whose crystalline, androgynous looks seem to reinforce an ambiguous and indeterminate identity.

What, precisely, Kano symbolises relates to his sexuality and stature. As a practice homosexual relations between samurai, especially between lords and vassals, were far from uncommon, and attitudes towards sexuality in general were not structured around any prevalence of the hetero-normative. Kano becomes associated primarily with this facet of interned Japanese life so that *Gohatto* presents a visual stratification of looks both violent and desirous. In point of fact these two states of mind become almost coterminous, the distinction between the two being progressively blurred as certain characters who are sexually attracted to Kano work to see his beauty desecrated and ultimately destroyed. Men looking, gazing, at men becomes a central referent in the narrative to the extent that *Gohatto* becomes a film about watching, about the distance entailed in this act, the discrepancy between viewer and viewed and the relations of power and control therein, and as such it foregrounds, indeed narrativises, the sadism that Neale discusses. This displacement of fetishisation is crystallised at the end when Kano is equated with the Sakura, or cherry blossom. In the film's final moments, following his murder by one of the *Shinsengumi*, one such tree is destroyed by his superior, and whilst doing so this character states that Kano was 'too beautiful to live' (which echoes Mishima Yukio's 1956 novel *The Temple of the Golden Pavilion* and its depiction of an object so perfect it becomes a Mirror stage marker of the protagonist's ugliness). Oshima often extolled the fact that his family were of samurai stock, and here offers a critique of the image of the samurai as it came to define Japan in the wake of the Meiji Restoration: of the samurai as noble, honourable warriors rather than the bureaucrats and even intellectuals that a majority actually were during much of the Tokugawa Shogunate. The samurai as a metonymic symbol of 'Japan' in the twentieth century (of which the *jidai-geki* sub-genre of the *chambara* became arguably the most pointed example) represented for Oshima an explicit subjugation or disavowal of Japan's hitherto social and religious models, and Kano from this point of view becomes a potent manifestation of what was repressed or denied in Japan's modernisation.

Miike's recent *jidai-geki*, along with Oshima's *Gohatto*, may be contrasted with the ostensibly more conservative films that comprise a contrastive trend in modern samurai cinema. In many ways the nominal antiquation of Yoji's *jidai-geki The Twilight Samurai, The Hidden Blade* and *Love and Honour* was prefigured by films such as *The 47 Killers* (*Shijushichinin no shikaku*, 1994) – a version of the Loyal 47 Ronin – *After the Rain* (*Ame agaru*, 1999) and *Dora-heita* (2000), all works directed or written by established auteurs of earlier generations (*After the Rain* was written by Kurosawa Akira and *The 47 Killers* was directed by Ichikawa Kon, as was *Dora-Heita* from a script initiated decades before by Kurosawa, Kobayashi Masaki and Kinoshita Keisuke). These, in addition to new wave director Shinoda Masahiro's epic *Owl's Castle* (*Fukuro no shiro*, 1999), offer a foundation of quasi-antiquation that bespeaks a popular desire to return to the past onscreen, and perhaps, given the unstable cinematic context in which they were made, to regress to an era of relative (cinematic) certainty and stability and offset such contemporary difficulties (again a contemporary need to lionise a classical canon). Yamada's work is in this regard crucial, as it engages more or less directly with such discourse – with a postmodern nostalgic desire to return to a vanished past – in order to question or reframe the tenets of such a desire. His three narratively distinct but thematically related films feature protagonists who present a nominally concordant picture with regard to their respective scenarios – low-ranking samurai who are drawn against their wishes and better judgement into fighting to serve the interests of their typically base masters in upholding the crumbling edifice of clan power and respectability in a country on the cusp of widespread change and modernisation. However the films are subtly informed by diverse cinematic and narrative cross-currents that makes each story a revision of pre-eminent figures and forebears in the genre.

The Twilight Samurai's protagonist, Seibei, is presented as a mirror image of Mifune Toshiro's Sanjuro in Kurosawa's *Yojimbo* (1961) and *Sanjuro* (*Tsubaki*

Sanjurō, 1962); he is a similarly unkempt, scruffy figure, dirty and unhygienic to the extent that his odour offends a visiting dignitary at his place of work who is a similarly skilled swordsman. However unlike Mifune's iconic ronin he is a very reluctant warrior, working a menial bureaucratic job to make ends meet and admitting to a friend that he would be happy to leave the samurai life behind and become a farmer, such is his unhappiness as a supposed fighter at a time when overt conflict and civil war are all but obsolete (he is a dedicated family man, a loving single father who dedicates his time to his daughters when his colleagues berate his lack of a social life). Yamada ironically stresses this particular context through his depiction of Seibei's clan's seemingly perennial preparation for battle. Scenes in which clan superiors are told about their castle's store of food, or the fact that Yamada stages a key scene in a castle exterior with the constant presence of samurai training as a backdrop, succinctly fill in the tension between a lack of conflict and a readiness for it, more significantly perhaps a popular need for it as a means of defining a way of life.

In Yamada's film this tension between dialectical or dichotomous elements becomes a correlative of the implicit intertextual relationship between its narrative and that of *Yojimbo*, employed as it is in order to structure an interrogation of the idea and the ideal of the samurai: that he should be a morally upstanding individual more than a skilful warrior. Yamada's film has been regarded as offering a more verisimilitudinous picture of the material realities of Tokugawa-era Japan. Indeed Alain Silver (2005) sees the film as representative of what he terms 'the new realism and fatalism that 21st century filmmakers are bringing to *chambara*' (2005, p. 248), and this perceived quality characterises several of the most popular works in the genre. On the surface Silver is correct to note that the film, Yamada's first *jidai-geki* in a career spanning almost five decades, is a sombre picture of the 'vagaries of feudal society' (ibid., p. 252); certainly *The Twilight Samurai* is not as explicitly concerned with deconstructing or destabilising the past onscreen as some of its contemporaries, whilst the picture of Seibei as a petty bureaucrat reflects the lives of a majority of samurai at this time and explicitly counters populist images of a warrior elite. However its narrative structure and technique do not entirely preclude such a consideration as its story is literally framed as an extended flashback, an embedded hypo-diegetic tale narrated by Seibei's now adult daughter in the wake of her father's death soon after the beginning of the Meiji restoration of 1868. It is thus a personal more than a national history, a reflection on individualism in a culture of collectivity and the assertion of a voice, and more significantly a life, amidst a general veneration of death.

The Hidden Blade echoes this with its first-person narration by the protagonist, whilst the comparable *When the Last Sword is Drawn* (*Mibu gishi den*, 2003) refracts Shinoda Masahiro's *Assassination* (*Ansatsu*, 1964) by presenting its central character at the behest of competing diegetic narrators who remember him very differently. The protagonist, Yoshimura, is, like the characters in *Gohatto*, a samurai in the *Shinsengumi*, and his struggle to provide for his family as a low-ranking warrior in the service of clan superiors (as in *The Twilight Samurai*) forms the backdrop of the narrative. There are, as Alain Silver notes, a number of scenes that appear to be beyond the focalisation of either internal narrator (2005, pp. 252–8). However what is ignored here is the extent to which melodramatic excess seems to come to the fore in these scenes, so that they are marked by a sentimental outpouring of emotion and, in many cases (such as when Yoshimura leaves behind his young child to go and fight), a pathetic fallacy, in this case of snowfall. One may read this as underlining the narrator's exaggerated, imagined idea of the subject's life; alternatively one may see Takita as critiquing the imagined individualism and humanism of the historiographic process, what Yuejin Wang (1993) calls the appropriated Freudian 'fort/da' game of historical consciousness: 'first casting it out and projecting it onto the senseless past and then desperately longing to retrieve it back through our melodramatic "representation" of that already transfigured history' (p. 87). *When the Last Sword is Drawn* (its hyperbolic English-language title is already an assumption of narrative and thematic impetus) dramatises a series of slippages in which literal projections on the past fall back on melodrama as a register of 'the aporia of modernity and the melodramatic' (Yoshimoto, 1993, pp. 101–26). It thus foregrounds something of the frustration with said 'representation', in that it alludes to an over-valuation of the exotic aspects of Japanese history in lieu of any viable sense of that history. The diegetic narrators offer a correlative to the extra-diegetic presence of director Takita Yojiro, whose agency as such becomes associated with storytelling, perception, narration and (in part) potential fabrication.

Beside this conception one can place the aforementioned discourses of realism and apparent classicism. The import of such first-person narration can, at least partially, be explicated provisionally by reference to the perceived Japaneseness of the so-called 'I-novel' (or *shishosetsu*) that prevailed in several iterations throughout much of the twentieth century in Japan, and that enshrined autobiography and personal reflection as narrative touchstones. Its formal properties have been claimed to offer 'a truthful expression of actual experiences and emotions [rather] than the fabrications of storytellers' (Keene, 1998, p. 515), so that it resembles annals or chronicles rather than narrativised history: stories where 'art is hidden, whilst honesty and sincerity are displayed' (Miyoshi, 1991, pp. 23). This underlines the realism that so many reviewers have seen as the defining aspect of *The Twilight Samurai*, as well as reinforcing the perceived classicism that has been seen to define the film. However the discourse on classical filmmaking in connection with Yamada's film is another contentious point that has not been explored or elucidated. In his notes to accompany the film's UK Tartan DVD release Tim Robey (2004) notes that Yamada's film is '[c]lassical throughout in its stately plot development and long, attentive takes', whilst Tom Mes and Jasper Sharp (2004) state that 'the film harkens back to the heyday of jidai-geki'. Will Lawrence

(2005) echoes this in his notes on Takita's film when he states that '[a]long with Yoji Yamada's profoundly moving *The Twilight Samurai* [. . .] *When the Last Sword is Drawn* signals the rebirth of a classical genre', all of which statements serve to muddy the already murky water of neo-classical Japanese cinema. There is little commonality between Yamada and Miike's films; even their perceived human-istic qualities have variant effects, and it is difficult to conceive of a common reference point for their stylistic or narrative methodologies. The long takes identified by Robey are not a defining feature of either 1950s' or 1960s' Japanese cinema, only of individual auteurs such as Mizoguchi Kenji or Kobayashi Masaki (one may as well make the same claim of the classical Hollywood cinema on the strength of Welles or Wyler). But even Mizoguchi's famed sequence shots work differently to Yamada's with regard to both movement and transparency. Their more pronounced lateral mobility opens up, cinematises, the frequently theatri-cal pro-filmic space and interrogates it as a means of facilitating a stylistic dialo-gism whose tension bespeaks a world lacking stable reference points. One can but conclude that what is meant by such remarks is that, as Mes and Sharp note, the film looks back to earlier iterations of the genre. But when was this 'heyday'? And do they mean the *jidai-geki* in general or the *chambara* in particular? It is this lack of critical clarity that disrupts any real use value in the term, and this in addi-tion to the aforementioned discourse on classical Japanese filmmaking makes it abundantly clear that the term has been lazily used, without being at all precisely (even perfunctorily) defined.

To return to Russell's point, it is most pertinent that *The Twilight Samurai* represents a contemporary fantasy of what a classical samurai film could (perhaps should) be, especially in the face of such fantastical, frenetic CGI-augmented blockbuster samurai productions as music video director Nakano Hiroyuki's feature debut *SF: Samurai Fiction* (*Esu Efu, Samurai fikushon*, 1998), Kitamura Ryuhei's *Azumi* (2003) and Hirayama Hideyuki's *Samurai Resurrection* (*Makai Tensho*, 2003). In Russell's terms it is a 'repressed memory of a particular story of twentieth-century modernity' (2011, p. 16), where a ground zero for Japanese modernism becomes an exaggerated site of (melodramatic) excess simply by virtue of its popular canonisation. In the cyclical discourses of genre and historic-ity this and other texts become loaded with competing signs that are smoothed out as part of a transparent homogeneity and perceived to cohere in accurately or truthfully representing a past because it appears nominally more authentic. That is, between Yamada's film and *When the Last Sword is Drawn* in particular there is a mediation between realism and melodrama that interpellates its own classicism in the contemporary imagination (Figs 1.1a/1.1b). It is a classicism where history is defined by, indeed reducible to, a vague sense of antiquation so that a contrastive 'vernacular modernism' (ibid., p. 3) that recognises and theorises cinema's inherent centrality to modernity can articulate a discursive practice of mass culture as a perennially changing, transformative entity that

Figure 1.1   The classical imaginary: between realism and melodrama in *The Twilight Samurai* (left) and *When the Last Sword is Drawn* (right).

recognises, even foregrounds, the classical as a ghost of the modern or the con-temporary. The remembrances that are embedded within these films critique such a canonical undertaking, filtering history through individual consciousness and organising the past only (or largely) as a consequence of context, almost of functionality. These films explicitly contravene of Davis' monumental style, in which what he terms the 'furniture' of the films (p. 43) becomes foregrounded in the historical *mise-en-scène* as a means of celebrating tradition for its own sake: a proto-parametric vision. Charles Inoue (2009) has argued that the commercial and critical success of Yamada's triptych can in part be explicated by its appeal to the so-called salary man: its dramatisation of 'regularized labour, drinking after work, putting up with superiors, struggling with finances, (and) trying to raise children' (p. 160). He also alludes to the no less mythic portrait on offer in these films, so that their image of the past remains precisely that: a corrective to melo-dramatic canonisation but, crucially, no less a construction.

This then regulates the historical referent(s) within the films. *Assassination*, like many of the most significant *jidai-geki* of the 1960s, is set during the so-called *Bakumatsu*, the period between 1853 and 1868, between the arrival in Edo of Commodore Matthew Perry's black ships and the final collapse of the Tokugawa Shogunate before the might of the outside world. The socio-political upheavals of this era, as Japan encountered and became internally divided by its attitude to the US, were particularly apt for reflecting on the tensions of the 1960s when the post-war security pact between these countries was the cause of much civil consternation. The reappearance of this decisive, almost discursive period as the context for several recent samurai films refracts the aforementioned internation-alisation; although in fact it can be related as much to its possibilities for auteur cinema as to its contemporary relevance. Rather than a wholesale change of direction for Yamada, this director's recent *jida-geki* tripartite instead represents a different canvas upon which he can paint similar pictures to those that defined his work at Shochiku in the 1970s. Chief in this regard is his interest in antiquation, in traditional but outmoded and precarious lifestyles. Indeed, *Home from the Sea* (*Kokyō*, 1972) is concerned with a vanishing way of life, centred as it is upon a family who make a tenuous living transporting rocks on their fishing boat, but who find their livelihood under increasing threat from modern methods and industrial developments, whilst *The Village* (*Harakara*, 1975) centres on a rural community that is prevailed upon to sponsor a performance by an urban theatre troupe. Similarly Miike Takashi's typical recourse to spectacularly defiled corporeality finds a receptive site of representation in warriors whose bodies remained in thrall to others, indeed in a class whose selfhood resided almost wholly in the materiality of their bodies.

Classicism in this context becomes even more complex: a site of negotiation between the competing projects of industrial organisation, generic demarcation and auteur canonisation, to say nothing of audience taste and consumption. It is thus imperative to recognise the contrastive works that comprise the samurai film and their respective contributions to a historical imaginary. As already noted a contrastive strain of stylised, postmodern, fantastical samurai films have marked out the late 1990s and 2000s, films that Darrell William Davis (2006) refers to with the designation 'pop cultural reincarnation [. . .] [where] [c]onventions like katana *longsword*, *chonmage* topknot, ninja, and seppuku are the stuff of international advertising and video games, rather than a Japanese cinematic tradition, still less an actual historical period' (p. 198). These works help to facilitate the perceived classicism of Yamada and even Miike, with their pasts as fantastical as any conceivable future. However perhaps the most interesting of these playfully revisionist pictures comes from Kitano Takeshi, another director of violence and broken bodies, who moved defiantly into the realms of the *chambara* form of the *jidai-geki* by reworking one of the genre's most formidable and enduringly iconic figures. *Zatoichi*, originally intended as a Miike production (Rayns, 2003, p. 21), follows the blind masseur/ronin as he aids a village of oppressed peasants. The film was released abroad in the same year as *The Twilight Samurai* and proved to be the director's most popular product to date (as it had been in Japan), although it is not merely a *chambara*. As Ken Hall has suggested, it is 'a unique creation' (2005, p. 45) that filters the character through Kitano's own idiosyncratic brand as well as recalling Buster Keaton and even Samuel Beckett. Indeed the director/star in fact works to underline his titular protagonist's status as an elite swordsman precisely by exaggerating it, by separating him out narratively from those around him and in so doing to undermine his centrality, in effect to petrify him and comment on his iconicity. In this sense, beside the copious stylised violence and a tone that invites but stops short of irreverence or pastiche, this work becomes whatever its different viewers want, perceive or believe it to be, an amorphous entity whose ostensibly esoteric detours and deviations (especially the musical passages at the very beginning and end of the narrative) could in fact be said to constitute the fulcrum of the narrative, the thematic heart of the film.

From this perspective the film offers another historical imaginary: one that both Hall and Aaron Gerow (2007) suggest is refracted through an auteurist lens. Here Kitano as storyteller overrides the first-person narrators of Yamada and Takita's films, and in so doing makes historical exegesis an overtly subjective imperative. A pervasive dichotomy between different characters structures and animates much of the meaning of the narrative, with attendant plot detours that destabilise any firm sense of conventional linearity and thus centralise an almost cinema-of-attractions level of pure spectacle. To this end, Zatoichi, as played by Beat Takeshi, remains throughout the film a detached presence, almost as though he was in a different story to those around him. It is a notion that is foregrounded from the very beginning of the film in a series of introductory scenes that, via flashbacks, sketch in the pasts of all the key characters, with the notable exception of Kitano's ostensible protagonist. Following a prologue in which Zatoichi dispatches a series of clumsy would-be attackers he becomes a blank presence, his lack of sight appearing literally to inscribe a comparable lack of subjectivity. Later in the narrative, the character is furnished with a flashback, but it simply offers a further set-piece – a narratively superfluous and redundant scene in which he fights off a horde of attackers during a violent rainstorm. In Kitano's hands Zatoichi, the blind swordsman, thus becomes a signifier without a signified, an incomplete sign whose ostensible centrality is increasingly frustrated through a lack of even a cursory personality or agency beyond the purely functional. Kitano had already approached the concept of a genre as a figurative entity: as, for instance, in *Sonatine* (*Sonachine*, 1993) in which a sense of the circumscribed and ritualised series of actions and encounters associated with a genre film becomes redolent of the protagonist's disillusionment with his existence as a gangster whose life consists of going through overly familiar motions.

In *Zatoichi* this is taken to a more extreme conclusion. The aforementioned and much-vaunted musical numbers are not mere decoration or self-conscious stylisation. Rather, they underline Kitano's specific preoccupation with individual as against collective action and identity. Zatoichi himself remains conspicuously absent from these festivities, concerned as the protagonist is with wrapping up the plot in a dénouement that follows him on a mission to uncover the identity of the local gang boss, a man who had hitherto remained in hiding and pulled strings behind the scenes in another appropriation of vision and blindness. Kitano cross-cuts between these co-temporal events, contrasting the overt business of tying up the plot's ostensible loose ends with the celebration of the villagers, and in so doing he separates out plot from story, causality from pure spectacle, and by extension generic signification from personal expression, *parole* from *langue*.

This the director does to the extent that not only a fracture but, arguably, a hierarchy occurs between the two. That is, the film both liberates and more importantly prioritises this exaggerated carnivalesque through the force of its presentation as a literal usurper of the narrative. The fact that Kitano then proceeds to slyly question the sacrosanct sightlessness of Zatoichi (albeit before appearing to reaffirm it) crystallises further this thin line between generic conformity and subversion that he carefully treads throughout this film, his adherence and apparent blindness towards convention. The musical scene and its inherent spectacle of collective, performative identity and celebration can also be understood along these lines: as an example of conflation and correlation. It collapses distinctions between different genres as a means of destabilising ostensibly clear demarcations and of problematising representation itself, making its titular figure in particular a symbol rather than a flesh-and-blood character, an abstraction and indexical marker of surplus Otherness who remains unrecuperable within the world he moves through. What is interesting from this perspective is the extent to which Beat Takeshi (through his character's diegetic 'performance', his ability) becomes equated with Kitano Takeshi, the latter's filmmaking flamboyance in the staging, editing and heightened, CGI-assisted bloodletting of these particular set-pieces (Fig. 1.2). The film offers a hyper-presence of Kitano that entails a concomitant absence of Zatoichi in a crucial departure for this series. Shintaro Katsu's protagonist in twenty-six films and many more TV episodes incrementally developed a detailed backstory, something that begins with his discussion early in the first film of why he took up sword-fighting (significantly to avoid being looked down upon and patronised), which allows one to read the original blind swordsman

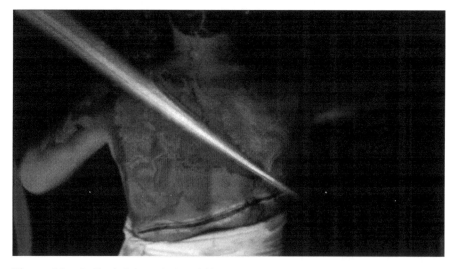

Figure 1.2   Stylised violence in *Zatoichi.*

as a socialist warrior, someone who fights class-based injustice. Kitano offers a critique of this practice; he does not eschew Zatoichi's status as a protector of the weak and oppressed but he foregrounds these oppressed characters much more. His Zatoichi is introduced in action (where Katsu in fact fights very little – only two set-pieces of note in the first film) and as such becomes something like a manifestation of a common or popular desire on the part of the villagers. He stands outside class as he stands outside the story, conjured into being as a present (narrative) absence and thus a veritable performer, an actor.

This also draws on and subverts the humanism prevalent in Kurosawa's (and, latterly, Miike's) recasting of the hero as a type given to 'socialist protest' (Nygren, 1993, p. 138), something Kitano extends to specific characters as agents in the narrative. The subsidiary, comedic figure, whose dreams of being a warrior involve charging around yelling a mock battle cry, becomes a sly subversion of those recurring characters in films like *Seven Samurai* and Mizoguchi's *Ugetsu monogatari* (1953) who are desperate to become warriors as a means of facilitating social mobility and achieving personal glory. Here this character is a narrative non-sequitur, an overgrown child and a comic figure, and he serves to cement the critique of generic types and theatrical *dramatis personae* that Sato Tadao (1987) has likened to the so-called *tateyaku*: the idealised, loyal hero who lives stringently by the code of Bushido above all other personal considerations (p. 38). The fact that Zatoichi here also befriends an elderly woman serves to subvert the recurrent plot device in the Katsu films of having the protagonist awaken 'false hopes in a young woman he chastely befriends' (Rayns, 2003, pp. 22–3), and to offer a further subversion of its forebears as a defining facet of its textual specificity.

Kitano's intertextuality in fact extends further in *Zatoichi* as he positions the titular protagonist within a lineage of Japanese filmmaking that offers an explicit recapitulation of several key works. Most explicitly the ghost of Kurosawa Akira reverberates throughout the film. It can be felt in an opening moment that sees Zatoichi walk by a group of workers harvesting the land in an overtly rhythmic manner, something that Kitano underlines through arranging the sound of their sheathing into a musical motif (with the editing similarly organised in synchronisation) that bespeaks a performative celebration, echoing the ending of *Seven Samurai*. Alongside this is a story taken from Ichikawa Kon's *An Actor's Revenge* (*Yukinojo henge*, 1963) concerning two adolescent siblings who disguise themselves as geishas in order to get close to and take revenge on the people responsible for the murder of their family. Scott Nygren (1993) has talked of this film's own dense intertextuality, wherein its narrative of an *onnagata* (a male actor playing a female role), swearing vengeance on the man who forced his parents into suicide inscribes a veritable matrix of both cinematic and theatrical references. These then carry over by extension into Kitano's film as an embedded cinematic history that uses diegetic performance to underline Kitano's own directorial performativity.

Kitano embeds these intertexts in addition to material retained from the original Zatoichi films. In particular he repeats from the very first film in the series, Misumi Kenji's *The Tale of Zatoichi* (*Zatōichi monogatari*, 1962), the close juxtaposition of the titular blind swordsman and his ostensible antagonist – another expert assassin but one who remains markedly different from his sightless adversary given his desperate personal circumstances. The import of such a myriad of intertextual references is to stress Kitano's engagement with history as canonised onscreen rather than as a tenable entity in and of itself, a representation of a past already represented, in which we see the already seen and comprehend this *déjà vu* through a veritable mirror. Yuejin Wang (1993) has talked in detail of the mediation of history in the modern age:

> [how m]elodramatic representation of history is essentially self-representation. And understanding history is essentially to understand the generic pattern of melodrama, to understand why we spin out this artifact/artifice on which is fixed both our rapt gaze and our anguished and perplexed look. (p. 87)

In other words the 'pathos and emotional rhetoric of excess' that characterise melodrama as history (p. 80) recognise both the aforementioned lack and hyperreal counterpoint to the same that contributes to a paradigmatic postmodernism, and Kitano's *Zatoichi* effectively narrativises this split by offering up the spectacle of performative action that is at times entirely divorced from the exegeses of narrative causality. This action demands extra-diegetic vision to consume its spectacular excesses, but at the same time this very agency is denied the (sightless) protagonist, our gaze on history displaced onto the spectacle of performance that stands in for, and fills in the lack of, any concrete historical veracity. Unlike Miike, Kitano celebrates and revels in this generic landscape of subversive spectatorship, this questioning of generic spectacle, and it makes his *Zatoichi* a particularly complex work – a film about the very negotiation between neo-classicism and postmodern subversions thereof.

Koreeda Hirokazu's carnivalesque addition to the *jidai-geki*, *Hana: The Tale of a Reluctant Samurai*, characteristically subverts both a picturesque approach to Japanese history and, perhaps more significantly, the predilection for *chambara* narratives that stress action-driven stories of revenge. *Hana*, like Yamanaka Sadao's *Humanity and Paper Balloons* (*Ninjo kami fusen*, 1937) or Kurosawa's *The Lower Depths* (*Donzoko*, 1957) and *Dodes'ka-den* (1975), concerns the interwoven lives and stories of the denizens of a poor village, centring on the titular samurai (named Soza) who is determined to avenge the murder of his father. Koreeda's oeuvre has tended to revolve around studies of insular groups of disparate people whose individual stories overlap, remain narratively proximal, whilst at the same time retaining an autonomy that traces individual trajectories as a thematic microcosm. Attendant on this pattern is an interest in questions of personal responsibility and endeavour – of the extent to which personal agency and action should serve wider interests – from which perspective *Hana* is a quietly subversive film for its genre. It is, indeed, a precise mirror of Kitano's *Zatoichi* in that both films pick out their titular 'heroes' from an assorted, knotty ensemble of contrasting characters in a poor village overseen by a tyrannical landlord figure, make thematic play with performance and perception as a central theme, and feature Asano Tadanobu in a key role as a nominal antagonist for the 'hero'. However where Kitano's swordsman is separated from the group by dint of his extraordinary skill and pure, transparent narrative functionality, Koreeda's by contrast remains resolutely unspectacular and effects almost nothing of narrative significance, craving revenge upon the man who murdered his father but seemingly incapable of fulfilling this deed.

That *Hana* is almost self-reflexively concerned with performance and revenge is signalled by the parallel storyline of the 'loyal 47 ronin'. The beginning of the film fills in the details of these vassals, the fact that some of their number are hiding out in the slum dwelling awaiting their legendary, mythical retribution, as a counterpoint to which the denizens of this village stage an annual revenge play that, as one character comments, compensates for the lack of such action in real life during this time of nationwide peace (the time is 1703, 100 years into the Tokugawa Shogunate). Koreeda further underlines this precept when, during rehearsals for the play (in which the protagonist is playing a key role) one character notes that said protagonist has the right looks for the part: in other words that as a handsome young man and a samurai he should adequately fulfil the requirements of such a role, something that he is singularly incapable of undertaking in the reality of the diegesis but which he could perform (i.e. pretend) for others. There also follows a scene when Soza and a young single mother repair to her shack and are summarily followed by numerous men eager to see them having sex, only to be disappointed to find them merely discussing the play – another expected but frustrated spectacle wherein spectatorial edification is buffeted in the face of challenged voyeurism.

These twin themes pertaining to a popular desire to engage in and to see, to consume, action then come together at the end of the film. Here Soza's long-gestating revenge is fabricated as a play, a performance, cementing the primacy of perception and the apparent 'truth' of appearances over the reality that they frequently conceal and even negate. His family, who have long berated him over his apparent procrastination, need to see the retribution, and the play fulfils this imperative whilst absolving Soza of the need to kill. In point of fact it is interesting to note how much of the drama of the narrative revolves around watching and seeing, something exploited by the director as central to people living in such close proximity. Indeed Koreeda employs a diffuse, episodic, almost centrifugal structure in this film wherein the nominally central figure of

Soza acts as a point of departure for the assorted characters that surround him. The writer/director is in fact wholly devoted to the lives of the villagers, and there are several extended digressions away from the central story (as though the protagonist's plight, his inaction, were boring him) where he appears to amuse himself with observations of others, as though he himself had become a casual voyeur. These include in particular a lengthy interlude in which the shanty town's landlord visits each house in turn to collect rent money. Koreeda effectively connects each of the characters within both their peasantry and the mundane realities of their lives (the visit takes place during a severe rainstorm), and as such further undermines any sense of spectacle as a generic determinant, a transgressive imperative that is reinforced elsewhere in the film. If the spirit of Kurosawa is suggested in the setting and theme of *Hana* then another key reference point for the film is Imamura Shohei, whose carnivalesque work was frequently concerned with the lower orders of society and the often animalistic vitality therein. An abiding image from Koreeda's film is of a village whose lifeblood, quite literally, is excrement, with several characters collecting human faeces from their community's communal lavatory with an eye to selling it in order to perpetuate the harvesting of rice. Beyond the obvious allusion here to people who are themselves the dregs, the waste, of society, there is also a pertinent vision of cyclicality. Koreeda construes the natural (bodily) processes of eating and defecating as not only vital but causal actions, against which one may measure the protracted, opaque behaviour that characterise a majority of the (male) characters as they wait, pontificate, and otherwise mark time in anticipation of their perceived fated trajectories of righteous violence. Koreeda even extends this intrinsic norm of juxtaposition into his imagery and *mise-en-scène*. On a visit to his family, Soza watches whilst two people (including a woman) practise their fighting technique with a sword-like implement, hitting and jabbing an inanimate straw figure. Soon after this, a young girl from the shanty town is left angered by a meeting with the former partner of a young man that she is secretly in love with and vents her frustration by furiously beating her washing with a stick in a manner that directly recalls the earlier training. Far from an ostentatious visual mirror image, this ostensibly peripheral visual rhyme highlights a significant aspect of *Hana* – the contrast between the samurai and the peasants and villagers with whom they live and interact. To this end the juxtaposition between the ordered, regimented, channelled aggression of the samurai and the emotional outburst of the girl reflects the fundamental artificiality of the former (especially during a time of national peace), and the humanity of the latter, its relatable universality.

When the moment of revenge for the Ako Clan ronin finally arrives the real import of the earthy, messy reality seen earlier in the film – the emphasis on dirt and excrement – becomes clear, in that it offers a basis in a quotidian natural-ism from which to judge the mythic and generic focus elsewhere in the story.

Koreeda's narrative methodology further underlines this precept. His elliptical approach to the climactic moment when the ronin exact their vengeance is not unprecedented within Japanese cinema; nor is it in fact particularly unusual. Mizoguchi Kenji's *The Loyal 47 Ronin* builds painstakingly through almost three hours to its ostensible climax, only to elide the actual scene of revenge (as it had initially elided the ritual suicide of Lord Asano) and instead present it to us after the fact when a document telling of its completion is given to and read by the wife of said Lord. *Hana* similarly leaves out the actual moment of violence, the long-desired revenge. Instead the director shows his vengeful samurai approaching their victim's residence before singling out one of their number as he appears to hesitate and thereafter to eschew taking part in the group's retributive action. At this point the director cuts away to the village to consider the dissemination of information about the ronins' vengeance throughout the public, thereby alluding directly to the beginnings of its mytholigisation, its separation from reality. Indeed he reverses the typical iconography of the forty-seven ronin attack – the falling snow popularised through cinema, painting and theatre – and displaces it onto Soza's fabricated revenge. In so doing he stresses the sentimental iconicity of this oft-repeated trope, its artificiality, rather than its reality or its historical veracity, so that *Hana* narrativises what may be termed both the weight of the past and its implacable enculturation. Both Soza and Terasaka Kichiemon (the forty-seventh ronin who does not go through with the revenge pact) learn to cope with and overcome their own histories, and Koreeda contrasts their stories in which the heritage of their respective fathers (with regard to their stern expectations) feeds into how they themselves act as fathers, how their sons and stepsons learn from them and continue their teaching – literally so, as Soza begins teaching a class to local children. This individual, personal lineage of parents and children (a theme throughout this film) is then contrasted with the obfuscatory politics of the canonisation of Japanese history, a national lineage, especially where the samurai is concerned. The fact that the ronins' revenge is immediately celebrated, mythologised, even corporatised given that several of the villagers are selling sweet revenge buns and re-enacting the slaying of Lord Kira, underlines this precept, the subtext being that the cultural tradition of this event, and by extension of the samurai as a warrior class, has become both distorted and commodified over time, an object to be consumed (here the fact of only forty-six ronin exacting revenge immediately signals this thematic imperative). Koreeda had already alluded to this motif at the very beginning of *Hana* with the onscreen text telling of the forty-seven ronin presented inside a speech bubble, as if it is an apocryphal story from the mouth of an individual storyteller, something to be told and retold throughout generations and centuries and, then as now, not to be taken at face value. In this, despite its ostensible differences, it takes a key place beside its contemporaries.

This chapter has tentatively posited a series of connections between post-millennial samurai films in Japan, and has sought to elucidate something of their intertextuality and engagement with the past. Remakes and reworkings have become increasingly prevalent in this country; indeed as Fred Shimizu has pointed out, 'there is a peculiarly Japanese penchant for remakes, especially in samurai films' (2012, p. 147), and this has led to new versions of Kurosawa Akira's *Sanjuro* in *Tsubake Sanjuro* (2007) – a very faithful remake – as well as new versions of the same director's *Rashomon* (*Rashōmon*, 1950) entitled *Misty* (1996) and *They Who Tread on the Tiger's Tail* (*Tora no O o fumu otokotachi*, 1945) in *Yoshitsune and Benkei* (*Yoshitsune to Benkei*, 2005). In addition there has been a new retelling of the legend of Miyamoto Musashi in *Ganryu Island* (*Ganryujima*, 2003), another new *Zatoichi* film entitled *Zatoichi: The Last* (2010) as well as significant remakes of popular television period dramas and an anime series based on *Seven Samurai* (entitled *Samurai 7* (2004)). Many modern iterations of the *chambara* are thus fraught with a history that defines their textual and generic identities – a cinematic more than a sociological past whose almost inexorable postmodernism helps to classify Yamada and Miike's films in particular as classical texts and which has led to a problematic classification and canonisation. This history is variously a skin to shed (for Yamada), a semantic field to redefine and reorganise (for Kitano) and a mirror image to question (for Miike); however one pertinent commonality is that its treatment says significantly more, if not about any perceived reality of the contemporary present, then at least about predominant attitudes therein. For this at least they are crucial texts.

2. YAKUZA CINEMA

The main appeal of yakuza to younger people has to be in their ever-intensifying spirals of violence and outlaw behaviour.

(Davis, 2006, p. 199)

Alongside the samurai film the most prominent and popular genre in Japanese cinema in the immediate post-WWII decades was that of the yakuza film. Arguably more than any other generic category in the Japanese canon the yakuza film has been not only perennially visible but also among the most open and responsive to social flux and development, to documenting (explicitly or otherwise) the often dramatic changes that have affected Japan across successive eras of the twentieth century. This ostensibly clearly delineated and narratively demarcated but in fact often amorphous genre thus underlines perfectly some of the issues surrounding the post-millennial return to earlier, popular modes. One can mark out the specific developments within Japan that are, covertly or overtly, reflected within individual films and broader generic trends, even when explicit recapitulations of specific progenitors in the form of direct remakes are not always forthcoming (though there are several such films). However, in a manner comparable to the samurai film, the presence of such reworkings is representative of the general development of the genre that has seen it diversify even as it seems to remain within the realms of established iterations of the form. In other words the modernity or contemporaneous stature of the yakuza drama has tended to go hand-in-hand with its appropriation of a generic antiquation, or at least its adoption of a generic model already introduced and popularised through an extended series of related works.

Taking these features surrounding the yakuza film into account, this chapter will seek to outline and analyse how the modern yakuza films fit into the lineage of the genre, how individual films seem explicitly to engage with its chief tenets and defining narrative and thematic traits. It will attempt to negotiate a space for a dialogical relationship with the prevailing models of both the *ninykō eiga* (the chivalry film) and so-called *jitsuroku eiga* (the true account or actual record film) forms of yakuza filmmaking, and will explore Mark Schilling's assertion that it is a 'disreputable genre' (2003, p. 11) by considering the extent to which it offers a vision of Japaneseness throughout significant eras in the country's recent history. As David Desser and Arthur Nolletti, Jr (1992) have noted, critical engagement with this genre has not always prevailed. Typically it has figured as an adjunct to auteur studies; indeed Kurosawa Kiyoshi (in Richie, 2001, p. 215) has noted the centrality of the yakuza film to the new generation of the 1990s as it formed the most common framework or point of departure for their staking of an iconoclastic populism based on established forms, from both Japan and Hollywood (although earlier auteur-based historical monographs, such as Richie's (1971), had ignored even this), and more than any other genre the symbiosis between auteur and genre has informed the yakuza film. This chapter will consider the significance of this trend in light of new developments in the genre, looking at how theme and variation are pre-eminent, how psychoanalytical precepts are brought to bear on the films' generic landscape and how the known and knowable face(s) of the yakuza film have become an increasingly malleable entity for contemporary auteur directors.

The aforementioned contrastive modes of yakuza cinema each defined a specific era and its contemporary paradigm of the genre. The *ninykō eiga* were often rather simplistic dramatisations of opposing forces; both Schilling (2003, p. 23) and Peter High (2002, pp. 426–7) argue that this schematic was inherited from and informed by the samurai drama, whilst Keiko McDonald invokes the Western as a key dramatic referent (1992, p. 167). As popularised on film and in novels (especially those of Hasegawa Shin – whose work was adapted for the screen many times in the 1930s – and, latterly, Goro Fujita) the heroic protagonists of these stories were clearly delineated from their adversaries by virtue of their personal code of honour and sense of tradition. What is of particular note in this regard, and something that has not tended to be emphasised in Anglophone discourse on this genre, is the yakuza film's place in the reconstitution of Japanese cinema as a vessel for establishing, reflecting on or appealing to popular tastes in the wake of Japan's occupation and the prohibition of images pertaining to the country's feudal pre-modern past. The phenomenal popularity and commercial success of the *ninykō eiga* films in the first wave of the genre in the 1960s (alongside a similar commercial canonisation of the *chambara*) was in part due to the positive picture of a perceived Japaneseness that had for a time been officially denied to the population in both their social endeavours and their cultural products.

Ninykō eiga works like the *Abashiri Prison* series (*Abashiri bangaichi*, 1965–72) thus helped to colour in and counter something of a void or vacuum, and as Darrell William Davis and Emilie Yueh-yu Yeh have noted, its connection to a single studio (Toei) helped to cement recognisable divisions and demographics in the domestic audience in Japan (2008, p. 119). Although it has been argued that there was some continuity between the *ninykō* and *jitsuroku* forms there were nonetheless numerous contradistinctive elements of form and style. The latter model (represented most overtly by Fukasaku Kinji) was a riposte to the *ninykō eiga* in that it typically offered what is perceived to be a naturalistic or sober picture of yakuza life and criminality that dispensed with the romanticised portraits of its forebears; that, in other words, saw any notions of tradition or honour as anathema to a country that had in effect sold its soul in its pursuit of becoming a global economic power. Certainly films like Fukasaku's *Battles without Honour and Humanity* (*Jingi naki tatakai*, 1973), the same director's earlier *Street Mobster* (*Gendai yakuza: hitokiri yota*, 1972) or later *Cops vs. Thugs* (*Kenkei tai soshiki bōryoku*, 1975) were all set in the immediate post-war era and were concerned with broadly allegorising Japan's Westernisation and economic reconstruction, as well as directly reflecting the social turmoil fermented only a few short years before by the student unrest of the 1960s (*Battles without Honour and Humanity* even echoes the credits sequence of Oshima's *Cruel Story of Youth* (*Zangiku monogatari*, 1960) with its bright red characters over sombre black and white images). This was also present in these films' counterparts in *Pinku eiga* – works such as Ishii Teruo's *Female Yakuza Tale* (*Yasagure anego den: sōkatsu rinchi*, 1973) or *Sex and Fury* (*Furyō anego den: Inoshika ochō*, 1973) – which revelled in soft-core sex and hard-core violence as a means of differentiating themselves from televisual products that were at this particular time beginning to make their presence felt by keeping potential audiences away from cinemas.

Thus where the initial surge in the popularity of chivalry films by directors such as Makino Masahiro and Matsuo Akinori can be explained by their simplistic black and white narrative model wherein repositories of tradition and honour fought against paragons of capitalist modernity; and where the paradigmatic conflict of *giri* (obligation) and *ninjō* (personal inclination) structured the protagonists' emotional trajectories, the subsequent *jitsuroku* mode appealed to anxiety over the same. Fukasaku's landmark film *Battles without Honour and Humanity*, a film that formed the foundation of a series that originally went on to number six works, begins with a series of still photographs under the credits, each one depicting the horrors of the atomic bomb and its aftermath. Indeed the narrative is set in Hiroshima, and the fact that the central character emerges from the destruction and the ashes of this national tragedy to rise rapidly through the ranks of a gang presents an alternative history of Japan's own growth following WWII, a contrapuntal narrativisation of rising from the threshold of obliteration to a pinnacle of prosperity that rhymes with the contemporary context in which it is presented. *Street Mobster* also reflects this trend, as it is noted that this film's protagonist (played, as in *Battles without Honour and Humanity*, by Sugawara Bunta) was born on 15 August 1945, the date of Japan's surrender to the Allied forces, signifying unambiguously that its central yakuza's literal birth is coterminous with the figurative death of Japan, and subsequently that the country's exponential regeneration as an increasing economic superpower is a rebirth whose salient subtext is that this development has compromised, even corrupted, the country. Similarly, the style of Fukasaku's film – its urgent, chaotic handheld cinematography depicting scenes of action and violence that typically erupt in public spaces – is a further key to the revolutionary nature of his work, presenting as it does a visual idiom whose pervasive instability reflects a society in turmoil, one unmoored and no longer able to rely on the kinds of certainties that had once anchored its self-definition.

If the yakuza film is a salient aspect of Japanese cinema it is a genre that has been subject to much redefinition and recontextualisation: subject indeed to the prevailing socio-political winds of the successive decades and eras that have marked out Japan's post-war development. The aforementioned allusions to tradition, and by extension the complementary image of modernity, reinforces the aforementioned key antinomy in the genre between the new and the old, the modern and the antiquated, to the extent that the landscape of the yakuza film has become a salient vehicle for understanding some of the tensions, fears and attitudes of the Japanese at various key stages of their post-war reconstitution: 'an excellent example of a genre taking shape, and changing shape, in response to popular culture' (McDonald, 1992, p. 166). More recently the yakuza genre has morphed even more overtly. It remained all but dormant throughout the 1980s, with only a very few titles of significance, which were typically divided between antiquated generic material such as *Tough Guys Behind Bars* (*Kabe no naka no korinai menmen*, 1987) or playful, offbeat variations on the same. However at the end of this decade the marked change of both national and cinematic fortunes that propelled Japan into a new era saw the genre's return to prominence, almost in direct response to events that soon superseded them. In Kitano Takeshi's *Violent Cop* (*Sono otoko kyōbō ni tsuki*, 1989) style is once again to the fore, but Kitano works in diametric opposition to Fukasaku's paradigm. His films are defined by a composed flatness in which the audience are generally kept at an observational distance from the characters and action rather than being cast directly into its maelstrom. It is a style that mirrors the typically detached, disconnected, weary protagonist of the film, and it would go on to define subsequent films by this director as he helped to return the yakuza (and the closely related form of the cop film) to both popular and critical visibility. Going further, there are broader, more literal social ramifications and resonances to these works, extra-textual determinants on their thematic specificity that situate them as definitive products of their time. Chief in this regard was the illness and subsequent death of Emperor Hirohito in early January of 1989. He had been suffering from duodenal cancer, and there had been a perceived intrusiveness on the part of the press and media, who detailed almost every step of his physical degradation and mortality. The emphasis in films such as *Violent Cop* and *Tetsuo: The Iron Man* on the corporeal, on extremes of both bodily decay, transformation and, for Kitano, bodily resistance, is thus charged with a very specific meaning and subtext, one that elevates their narratives beyond their ostensible subjects.

All of this makes the significance of Tsukamoto and especially Kitano's work particularly notable. *Tetsuo: The Iron Man* could well be approached as an overt allegory – of the erosion and corruption of humanity in an advanced technological age – but *Violent Cop* by way of contrast seems a very literal, denotative work. Like its titular figure it appears to exist only on the surface, a character and a film that contravene ostensible depth as a matter of course. The repeated acts of violence both administered and absorbed by the protagonist, Detective Azuma, become indexes of individuality and identity in lieu of any other viable means of constructing or explicating selfhood. He is an affectless figure who frustrates any and every route into conventional constructions of character, and of emotional engagement or involvement therein. Azuma is a blank slate, a *tabula rasa*, who remains resistant to definition, or at least to self-definition. It is perhaps labouring a point to suggest that he is a symbolic figure, that he stands in for modern Japan, but there is nonetheless a tangible sense in which his fundamental lack becomes redolent of a nation devoid of a viable means of defining identity at a time when previous criteria are no longer extant: that is, when the spiritual sense of homogeneous Japaneseness, fostered by the country's almost three hundred years of isolation during the seventeenth- to nineteenth-century reign of the Tokugawa *Bakufu* (Shogunate) had been eroded by Westernisation and the post-war economic miracle.

Violent Cop is, then, something of a ground zero for modern Japanese cinema; it signalled in particular the potential for the yakuza film to reflect and engage with contemporary issues in a way that contrasted with earlier iterations of the genre. One director who drew on his work was Aoyama Shinji, a musician who made his feature debut in 1995 with *Helpless* (*Herupuresu*, 1995), the affectless and dispassionate vision of which can stand in many ways as paradigmatic of the new Japanese cinema and its emphasis on what Mark Schilling terms 'the fantasy of a movie-saturated imagination that sees murder less as a deed with consequences than a kind of stylistic statement' (1999, p. 203). The director followed *Helpless* with *Two Punks* (*Chinpira*, 1996), an offbeat yakuza drama about a pair of lowly gang thugs – the *chinpira*, or 'little pricks', of the title – whose rather aimless existences in the violent, rarefied, hierarchical world of organised crime becomes complicated by their respective relationships with women. On the one hand is Yoichi, a young man fresh into Tokyo from a coastal town who becomes involved with a girl who is similarly on the periphery of the gang (she is courted by a Yakuza). On the other is the near-middle-aged Michio, who wants to leave his urban life behind and ultimately manages to do so with his boss' wife (whom he has impregnated following a brief affair).

As in *Helpless* the director uses the framework of the genre to connotative effect in *Two Punks*. The film is explicit in using the terminology of crime and the yakuza film in order to detail the insularity and hermetic quality of its universe. Time spent within the confines of the yakuza is juxtaposed with that spent beyond its immediate environs, at which moments Yoichi and Michio are depicted as childlike, first in a playground as they jokingly assume the guises of father and son whilst playacting together, and later tussling over who gets to 'pilot' a crashed plane that they come across on the beach. These moments of play, of performance and escape, serve to contrast sharply with the constricting and oppressive nature of life within the gang. The fact that they act out a parental scenario further highlights the figurative familial bond that they form, one offset by the pronouncements by other yakuza in the narrative (typically those who become antagonistic figures) that they are part of what they ominously call 'the family'. Stephen Prince describes yakuza films as built around codes that 'enforce a hierarchical model of human relationships, founded on obligation and sacrifice' (1991, p. 83). However Yoichi and Michio both renege on this apparent obligation where their superiors' women are concerned. But in truth there is little opposition here; neither relationship seems to perturb the more senior gang members whose partners are, as it were, stolen by the titular punks. Michio is only chased by the yakuza when he goes on the run because he has appropriated their money (the gang boss evincing little anger and indeed appearing to give his wife his blessing to have Michio's baby), whilst there is no punishment for Yoichi for his involvement with a superior's girl. Women are peripheral figures here, but Aoyama is sympathetic to their travails, their frustrations within the rarefied masculine world in which they live but from which they are summarily excluded. Indeed the very fact that the boss' wife seduces Michio (a 35-year-old self-proclaimed loser who repeatedly states that he doesn't want to be a yakuza) bespeaks both her desperation and his contravention of any archetypical model of generic masculinity.

From this perspective both 'inside' and 'outside' (in or out) become loaded terms within the film, both denotative and connotative. The protagonists, especially Michio, occupy a strangely liminal position regarding criminality; they are neither part of nor distinct from the yakuza gang, and as noted the children's play area becomes an escape for these characters precisely because they are not inculcated into the rigours of yakuza life. This sense of demarcated spatiality also affects other characters; it is significant that the only time the gang boss is truly vulnerable, indeed the moment when he is attacked, is in a public place, a Pachinko parlour (with this setting further allowing Aoyama a satirical aside on Japanese culture, as none of the boss' fellow players in the parlour notices that anything has occurred even when the boss is stabbed and stumbles through the parlour past a number of machines). In contradistinction the figurative meanings of this dichotomy become pronounced when the film's hapless protagonists both make repeated reference to 'being straight' when referring to leaving the gang behind in order to start a new life with their respective partners. It is as though the strictly homo-social nature of yakuza life, a life marked by intense relationships with men, is broadly equated by Aoyama with (implicit) homosexuality. Certainly, despite the frequent talk of marriage, both Michio and Yoichi abandon their women readily when trouble strikes, and fall back on the comfortable, if at times fraught, relationship they have with each other. Indeed the mother of Michio's baby is almost summarily forgotten when Yoichi follows his friend to warn him of the danger he is in because of the stolen money.

Throughout *Two Punks*, Aoyama is rather circumspect about violence. Tom Mes and Jasper Sharp have described this film as a 'human take on the yakuza genre' (2005, p. 221), and this aspect of its story amply underlines the point. The opening scene features Yoichi attacking a yakuza thug for using acid in a club, and the violence is dispassionately observed by the camera in extreme long shot. Subsequently this thug is brought before the gang boss and tortured by having chopsticks inserted into his ears, to which the camera responds by moving in to frame the victim in empathetic close-up that details his agonising screams. This coldness towards violent behaviour, the typical terrain of the yakuza film, continues when Yoichi confronts an antagonistic superior who has attacked a girl; they fight, and once again the static camera remains at a distance and watches disconsolately, before a cut to a closer shot of Yoichi takes place only after he has been stabbed and left for dead. The camera then tracks in to frame him increasingly tightly as his pain and discomfort grow, underlining once more the film's sympathetic concern with victimhood, with people experiencing rather than dispensing violence.

This latter scene is central to *Two Punks* as Yoichi appears to be close to death; he dreamily states to the girl with him that he would like to be with her and to steal a bicycle to facilitate his freedom. Immediately after this Aoyama cuts to a scene of Yoichi cycling through the streets, the girl now his lover and his place within the yakuza gang apparently secure. No mention is made of how he survived the stabbing; as in Hitchcock's *Vertigo* (1958) its irresolution haunts the remainder of the narrative, with Aoyama suggesting that the subsequent story may be a dying reverie on Yoichi's part. Such a reading helps to explain the loose causality of the narrative – its sporadic reliance on stock characters and situations – as well as to motivate the stark temporal shifts that characterise the film's methodology, the free-form collisions of past and present as Yoichi's formative life in a coastal town is explicated beside his later exploits in the city. Here the almost discursive context of particularly the *jitsuroku eiga* films – what Isolde Standish terms their 'meta-narratives of defeat (and) the occupation' (2005, p. 303) – are effectively negated as individual horizons delimit the film's focus. In other words there are only micro-narratives in Aoyama's narrative; Japan (or 'Japan') no longer seems to offer any tenable macro-narratives, even those against which these characters can react.

The fact that a key scene late in the narrative of *Two Punks* takes place on a beach refers one back inexorably to Kitano, whose preponderance for this particular location became so famous that a 2000 documentary about the director was entitled *Scenes by the Sea*. Aoyama's implicit reference to Kitano is a first real manifestation in the modern yakuza film of the intertextuality that elsewhere marks out much modern Japanese cinema, and the director uses this embedded reference to animate the in-betweenness of the characters. The narratives of both *Sonatine* (*Sonachine*, 1993) and *Hana-Bi* (*Fireworks*, 1997) culminate in violent scenes on a beach, and Aoyama follows suit by having Michio apprehended and killed by the sea. Both Aaron Gerow (1999) and Abe Kasho (1994) have written about the so-called liminal spaces of Kitano's work, those locations in which the characters are typically in a state of in-betweenness, a limbo, an ambiguous space equated by Abe with dying (pp. 105–46). Aoyama appropriates this visual and thematic sensibility quite directly as the beach in this film is a liminal space, a site of escape and of play for Yoichi and Michio (Fig. 2.1). The fact that the former may be mentally playing out this scenario bespeaks the almost culturally canonical status of this locale, reinforcing a vision mediated through the second-hand consciousness of someone whose experience and knowledge of the yakuza comes from popular images and clichés rather than personal involvement. An apposite

Figure 2.1   Liminality and intertextuality: at the beach in *Chinpira*.

foundation for the yakuza film in the new millennium, this character personifies Ian Buruma's dictum that 'the *yakuza* [. . .] in the cinema are creatures of the popular imagination' (2001, p. 167).

The significance of *Two Punks* is the aforementioned focus on protagonists on the periphery of gang life, and as Tom Mes (2005) has noted, this became a key feature of the 1990s' yakuza film. This 'more inclusive yakuza mythology' (Davis, 2006, p. 200) is in fact a reframing rather than a subversion of conventional forms, as traditional yakuza films (both *nikyō* and *jitsuroku*) tend to focus on gang subordinates, and thus on men whose loyalty to a gang and its *oyabun* (boss) is often a defining aspect of their travails (in contrast with their role in mafia films, gang bosses have almost never been central to yakuza pictures). Of the specifically yakuza filmmakers to emerge in the 1990s the two most significant are Miike Takashi and Mochizuki Rokuro, and the latter has frequently depicted the sorry and sordid lives of characters who haunt the fringes of yakuza life – indeed he has claimed to dislike the yakuza (Schilling, 2003, p. 94). Mochizuki began his career in pornography before coming to critical prominence with a quartet of yakuza films that reframed traditional themes, antinomies and narrative patterns. *Another Lonely Hitman* (*Shin kanashiki hitman*, 1995), *Onibi: The Fire Within* (*Onibi*, 1997), *A Yakuza in Love* (*Koi gokudō*, 1997) and *Mobsters' Confessions* (*Gokudō zangeroku*, 1998) are, despite their dramatic tonal and stylistic differences, similarly concerned with protagonists who often feel like manifestations of the repressions of their traditional counterparts. *A Yakuza in Love*, for example, features a protagonist whose *giri*, his fanatical obligation to his boss (as contrasted with a colleague who deserts the gang), does not contravene the *ninjō* of his similarly extreme desire for a waitress, whilst the ageing ex-con protagonist of *Onibi: The Fire Within* lives his life without in any official way becoming obligated to a gang or *oyabun*, acting and reacting as circumstances dictate rather than in any prescribed manner. *A Yakuza in Love* in fact has an emblematic Mochizuki title as its focus on heterosexual relationships (in this case between a low-level gangster and a young waitress and student) is as central as its masculine homo-sociality. The prevalence of the former – where (like Imamura protagonists) men and women seem to physically crave each other like a drug as a respite from their otherwise unremarkable lives – offers a messy, inchoate humanity as a riposte to the subordination of the self inherent in yakuza gang life.

If yakuza films in the new millennium have a long and varied cinematic lineage, the filmmaker who most forcefully and self-consciously pushes the genre into fertile new territory is Miike Takashi – a director like Mochizuki (and unlike Aoyama) in that, as Chris D. has noted, he remains an exponent of genre cinema (2005, p. 189) as well as someone who reshapes and redefines the parameters of the same. His work is frequently not generic, thereby facilitating a tension that characterises his best films as commentaries on genre cinema as much as genre films. Miike's cinematic career (following several years working in V-cinema) was crystallised around his so-called Black Society trilogy of *Shinjuku Triad Society* (*Shinjuku kuroshakai*, 1995), *Rainy Dog* (*Gokudō kuroshakai*, 1997) and *Ley Lines* (*Nihon kuroshakai*, 1999). These studies of social and national estrangement and alienation, writ large in casts of orphans, ex-patriots and/or mixed-race protagonists, refract the yakuza film as a modern form through generic indeterminacy and through explorations of amorphous corporeal identity that effectively heterogenise contemporary Japanese society. Indeed they employ what Theresa L. Gellar has argued is the inherently transnational lens of film noir (2008, p. 173). The title of this tripartite inexorably suggests neo-noir, as does the venal chiaroscuro cityscape and fatalistic masculinity especially of *Shinjuku Triad Society*, in which the circulation of the corporeal as capital (an illegal trade in organs) subverts classical noir's frequent concern with the polarised body as a gendered construct, as does the use of sex and sexuality as a weapon throughout the narrative (one suspect is literally buggered for information). Alongside these concerns the actual family of the cop protagonist stands beside the figurative gang family of his quarry, both problematic amidst what Christopher Howard terms the 'irreversible homelessness' within their lives (2012, p. 339). The yakuza film as transnational neo-noir echoes this lack of a home, this heterogeneous Japan, in its textual indeterminacy, where the Japanese genre's typical recourse to what has been discussed as repressed masculinity (ibid., p. 270) spills out like the blood and internal organs that often figuratively break through the surface of Miike's protagonists (Ko, 2006, pp. 129–37).

Gozu (*Gokudō kyōfu dai-gekijō*, 2003) is even more extreme, presenting as it does what may be termed a meta-yakuza narrative. A surreal thriller that begins as a paradigmatic yakuza narrative before dovetailing into a horror picture, its relationship to the yakuza film is a particularly dialectical one. Its horror elements – which in the main consist of an uncanny setting and a host of strange, dreamlike incidents – grow directly from the initial yakuza scenario, and the crux of this fertile cross-pollination is, paradoxically, to imply the sacrosanct, inviolate status of the genre. It is as though the scenario of the film, in which a yakuza is ordered to assassinate a superior, gives birth to the subsequent horror as recompense for such a contravention of the law that governs the rigid structures of the yakuza film as a genre. This is not, in fact, a wholly original or singular example of this particular generic interbreeding; films like *Yakuza Zombie* (2001), *The Machine Girl* (*Kataude mashin gāru*, 2008) or even Miike's own earlier *Full Metal Yakuza* (*Full Metal Gokudō*, 1997) all seek to place yakuza film tropes and characters in a contrastive context (or in the case of *The Machine Girl* to place an anomalous protagonist inside a typical yakuza framework), and in so doing to comment on the tropes of yakuza filmmaking. The plot of *Gozu*, as noted, begins with a gangster being assigned the job of assassinating a superior who has apparently lost his mind and become deeply paranoid about being killed by innocuous creatures and objects. The yakuza who disappears – a man named Ozaki – is played by Aikawa Sho, a significant feature given this actor's notoriety as a yakuza star in films such as Miike's *Dead or Alive* (*Dead or Alive: Hanzaisha*, 1999) and *Rainy Dog*, Mochizuki's *Onibi: The Fire Within* or Kurosawa Kiyoshi's *The Serpent's Path* (*Hebi no michi*, 1998) and *Eyes of the Spider* (*Kumo no hitomi*, 1998). The fact that he is introduced seemingly as the film's protagonist only to vanish in the second scene bespeaks the film's departure from typical generic norms. His prolonged absence from the narrative is a marker of the film's generic absence, its distance from the mainstream tenets of the yakuza film, following which the man assigned to kill him (named Minami) becomes stranded in the rural town where Ozaki disappeared.

The setting of the film in the rural town of Nagoya further underlines its departure from generic norms. Although non-urban settings have sporadically been employed in yakuza films – Furuhata Yasuo's Takakura Ken vehicle *Demon* (*Yasha*, 1985), for example, is set in a remote coastal village – such films work in a diametrically opposed way to *Gozu*. *Demon* is about an ageing gangster trying to leave his past life behind him and settle down far away from the urban centre of crime and venality associated with the yakuza, but finding that his past life in the city cannot be buried. *Gozu*, in contradistinction, reverses this (common) narrative conceit. Rather than the urban world of the yakuza invading the countryside, here the yakuza, once out of his usual urban environment, is quite literally attacked by the rural milieu to which he repairs. He encounters numerous strange figures who variously conspire to prevent his leaving Nagoya, a surreal trope that evinces elements in common with such Western filmmakers as David Lynch or even Luis Buñuel, given that the protagonist finds himself in a place from which it is increasingly difficult to leave – an echo of *The Exterminating Angel* (*El ángel exterminador*, 1962) in which an upper-class dinner party concludes with no one being able to leave the house in which they are ensconced. This in addition to the mythic allusions at key stages in the film – especially when Minami is told that he will be given aid in his search for Ozaki if he can solve a riddle, or when a demon with a cow head (in Japanese: *Gozu* – a potent urban legend about a story so horrifying that it results in death for whoever hears it) appears before him in a dream – makes *Gozu* a pointedly intertextual construct, and in this Miike alludes to the narrative rigidity, the arguable mythicisation, of the yakuza film as opposed to its once-perceived social realism.

The film's treatment of gender and sexuality remains in keeping with Miike's other work, and is of particular relevance within the context of a yakuza film and this genre's typical depiction of masculinity and male agency. Minami's gang boss is an over-sexed patriarch whom Ozaki criticises for indulging in sex at the expense of anything else (even though the gang boss needs a large spoon inserted up his anus in order to get an erection), whilst the elderly lady who runs the inn at which the protagonist stays attempts to seduce him with her large, perennially lactating breasts. Amidst this plethora of variously aggressive or aberrant sexualities Minami appears a child; indeed it is noted that he is a virgin, one with a large manhood, and he only comes close to intercourse when Ozaki returns as a young woman. However he becomes stuck inside the female Ozaki before she ultimately gives birth to Ozaki – the man he once was. It is typical for sex to be an entirely coldly physical experience for Miike's characters – not without immediate sensory pleasure (though this is not guaranteed) but never connected to any emotional connection or attendant feelings – but in *Gozu* it defines the horizons of all the characters' respective identities. Here, as well as literalising the points implied by Aoyama in *Two Punks* – that the homo-social landscape of the yakuza film carries distinctly homo-erotic undertones (Minami in effect has sex with his yakuza brother in the film's dénouement) – Miike also visualises a proto-Freudian Oedipal scenario wherein the child's consummation of a sexual relationship with a mother figure is literally prevented by the father's prohibitive appearance. It is an overt manifestation of the psychoanalytical subtext of the typical yakuza film, of which submission to the law of the father and the recurrent motif of castration in the severing of the finger are only the most overt examples.

Among Miike's highest profile and best-known films is *Ichi the Killer* (*Koroshiya Ichi*, 2001). This uses a yakuza template of rival gangs and hierarchical power plays in order to pass comment on the yakuza genre, but crucially it does not entirely transgress its intrinsic norms and characteristics. Noted and examined for its extreme violence (Hallam, 2009, pp. 206–16), *Ichi the Killer* concerns a sadistic and masochistic yakuza hitman with a multitude of injuries and deformations due to the severe beatings he has taken at the hands of his beloved boss Anjo. The conflict that arises when said boss is kidnapped structures the inchoate narrative of the film; this act engineers an opposition that is orchestrated by an ex-cop named Jiji (played, tellingly, by Tsukamoto Shinya as an ostensibly slight figure pulling strings behind the scenes), who manipulates a seemingly meek and mild-mannered man (the titular Ichi) into causing friction between rival gangs by summarily slaughtering several of their members.

This generic template is disturbed but not destroyed by Miike. In point of fact both Tom Mes (2003) and Marc Saint-Cyr (2012) have noted how in this film the director probes and challenges the audience to consider both the film itself and, crucially, their responses to it. Mes argues that its apparent excesses are carefully orchestrated to facilitate a reflection on 'the relationship between the viewer and the image [. . .] [and to take] a critical stance towards the portrayal and the consumption of the violent image' (p. 228). This is clear from the prevalence of diegetic spectators throughout the narrative: the opening scene features a woman being beaten and raped in an apartment outside which lurks Ichi, initially only watching but then masturbating to the sexual violence on display. Subsequently Miike cuts from a scene featuring the graphic torture of a gang boss to two drug addicts watching and enjoying this violent act on a TV screen, recalling a similar scene by John McNaughton in *Henry, Portrait of a Serial Killer* (1989) that presents a pro-filmic correlative to the audience themselves. Conversely the obverse image is comically presented when one yakuza underling (one of the gang members earlier seen to be consuming the spectacle of the torture as televisual entertainment) finds his head encased within a television set. The spectacle of the imminent violence to be inflicted on this character is thus diegetically framed as entertainment, something that Miike then undermines by cutting away from the scene just as the torture is about to commence. Here the film establishes a potentially spectacular incident of violence, as well as an anticipation of its specific properties in the viewers, before frustrating such a realisation. In so doing it facilitates a potential reflection on the part of the audience as to their desire to see and to partake in such a spectacle. Indeed Ichi's mirrored opposite in the film is Kakihara, a yakuza hitman who enjoys engaging in (both giving and receiving) extreme violence. His torso is a veritable map of such violence in the scars and contusions that take the place of the tattoos that usually mark out the body of the yakuza and define his identity in both confrontation and commonality, and here such physical defamation singles out this character as an ironic inversion of the typical stoic yakuza protagonist of the *ninkyō* era who courts but condemns violence. Indeed in this pointed duality lies the subversive impetus of *Ichi the Killer*. This figure remains in thrall to violence as both sadism and masochism and as such a marker of the polarised vicissitudes of violent behaviour as it informs the potentially schizophrenic address of the yakuza film.

Miike is subversive here as Kakihara's narrative agency – his definition in action – opposes the voyeurism and frequent inaction of the titular protagonist Ichi, who might otherwise figure as an audience surrogate but whose own proclivities delimit such a construction. He remains distant as a frequent diegetic spectator, thus problematising viewing and the masculine gaze as this distance is central to his being manipulated into exacting violent retribution on a succession of yakuza gang members. He wears a quasi-super hero costume and dispenses questionably excessive violence under provocation, coerced as he is into believing he witnessed the rape of a girl whilst at school and convinced that has to act against those responsible. He later says that he desired to rape the girl himself, being both repulsed and attracted by such acts in a mirror of Kakihara's duality whilst further refracting questions and problems of both gendered looking and of 'the sexualization of violence' (Hallam, 2009, p. 215).

A contrastive feeling – a (natural) sense of reticence around or disgust at such extreme acts – is presented and in a way dismissed in the film when one yakuza is unable to stand listening to a woman being tortured and has to leave the vicinity. Upon doing this he runs into Jiji, who manages to kill him, revealing himself to be a bodybuilder and a man of immense physical strength. It is as though he is punished for his inability to withstand any prolonged exposure to such abuse, particularly as he is killed by an apparent paradigm of perfect masculinity.

Indeed the spectacle of Jiji's body momentarily interrupts, freezes, the narrative, which in turn gives way to a contemplation of nominal masculine perfection, something that specifically counters the apparently depraved, corrupted or otherwise problematic men (with their respective scarred and weak physicality) at the centre of the narrative. Kakihara's open, desirous personality contrasts with Ichi's staid and repressed picture of an apparently typical, average man. Taken together these characters offer a diagrammatic picture of the typical poles of the yakuza film, the excesses inherent in the tension between internal states (the paradigmatic contrast between *giri* and *ninjō*) and indeed between extremes of dispensing and receiving violence (the frequent need to atone for sins or to prove oneself by the cutting off of a finger). This latter point is underlined in a scene in which Kakihara cuts off part of his tongue rather than his finger, Miike underlining the fundamental randomness of this archetypical gesture, its meaninglessness, and in so doing shows how ridiculous all such yakuza film features and characteristics are, how the ritualised extremity of their behaviour has been codified and tacitly accepted only by this route. The aforementioned physicality of Kakihara, his myriad scars and wounds, also reinforces this commentary, as physical pain for him is a pleasurable rather than a punishing experience. They mark his body out as both a battleground and a site of transgressed boundaries and trangressive appetites and desires, again reflecting psychoanalytical precepts. The wounds on his cheeks that allow him in effect to open his mouth much wider than usual reflect this notion, whilst also positioning him as a figurative infant, someone contained within the primary, oral, stage of psychosexual development wherein sexual pleasure and gratification is located around the mouth (see Fig. 2.2).

The particular narrative excesses in the film are matched by a stylistic hyperbole, the saturated colour of whose *mise-en-scène* pushes the naturalism of the *jitsuroku* yakuza film into the rarefied, stylised, anterior universe of the melodrama. The florid costumes and interior sets associated with Kakihara in particular speak of an insular far world removed from a naturalistic landscape, a manifestation of a world divorced from any tenable exterior reality. This also relates to the film's treatment of urban space as a site of what film noir historian James Naremore terms this sub-genre's 'privileged mise-en-scène of the masculine unconscious' (1998, p. 44), from which point of view the vertiginous verticality of numerous exterior scenes (shots looking directly up at Tokyo's skyscrapers) literalises the excesses of hierarchical divisions within and between groups and individuals (Fig. 2.3). Related to this, and to the aforementioned critique of spectatorship and the male gaze, is a narrational aesthetic that privileges a hyperactive space of apparently third-person distance and detached objectivity. As a transitional device between scenes the camera frequently speeds up and darts manically through space, both interior and exterior, as though in appropriation of an agent of storytelling with a physical detachment from the story and characters. The

Figure 2.2   The voracious, libidinal mouth in *Ichi the Killer.*

effect is not only to interpellate but to visualise, literalise, a stylised extra-diegetic
subject position. The aforementioned contemplation of Jiji's aesthetic physical
prowess further underlines this point, helping as it does to interpolate a potentially homo-erotic subject position and in so doing serving to disturb the typical
address to a heterosexual male that Laura Mulvey posited in 1975 as the default
position in conventional Hollywood suture. As noted, the sadism and masochism
of Kakihara may be extrapolated as narrativisations of states of interpellation, in
which sense *Ichi the Killer* is truly a film about its audience, about conventions of
taste and of temperament amidst a wish for the vicissitudes of vicarious thrills. It
is also about yakuza film as a genre, its spectacles of ritualised violence as catharsis
that Richard Tucker in particular has discussed as a central aspect of the 1960s'
films that reflected some of the social unrest during the era in which they were
produced (1973, pp. 122–3).

If *Gozu* represents a subversion of the typical classical yakuza film and *Ichi the
Killer* a commentary on this facet of the genre, Miike's *Graveyard of Honour* (*Shin
Jingi no hakaba*, 2002) is the director's attempt to uphold a more or less generic
template, and it cements his status as arguably the key director in the modern

Figure 2.3   Verticality in *Ichi the Killer.*

yakuza film. A remake of the 1975 Fukasaku film of almost the same name (the title of Miike's film translates directly as *New Graveyard of Honour* where the original is simply *Graveyard of Honour*), the narrative is based on the true story of Ishikawa Rikuo (here named Ishimatsu Rikuo), a yakuza who quickly rose through the ranks of a crime family because of his studied disregard for the typical procedures of gang life and his innate violence and recklessness. In Miike's film he is introduced whilst working as a dishwasher in a restaurant; he inadvertently saves a gang boss from a hitman (he attacks the gunman because he is making too much noise), and thereafter is inducted into a yakuza gang as a senior 'family' member. Miike in his *Graveyard of Honour* both echoes and departs from Fukasaku's film to the extent that a dialogue with the source text becomes paramount, a tension between following and departing from a model that carries particular connotations with regard to the protagonist's relationship to the strictures of yakuza life. He retains the broad outline of his forebear's scenario, its picture of the rise and fall of the wayward protagonist, his problematic exploits within his gang, his murder of his godfather, spells in prison and a fractious but ultimately close relationship with a woman whom he meets and at first violently abuses. There is even a historiography of modern Japan as an adjunct to the typical *jitsuroku* feature of using a specific era against which the exploits of the yakuza act as a counter-history. Fukasaku's *Graveyard of Honour* (*Jingi no hakaba*, 1975) directly apes *Battles without Honour and Humanity* in this regard. It replicates that film's distinctive red characters over black and white images of social turmoil, and appropriates a biographical modality in which Ishikawa's life from birth and childhood through to his career criminality is traced as a narrative of documentary veracity, and Miike updates this facet of his forebear's film. Through the use of an overt extra-diegetic narrator the concentration of wealth in Japan in the 1980s and the economic downturn of the 1990s are explicitly invoked as a backdrop, a national correlative to Ishimatsu's rise and fall – literally so, as the narrative is bracketed by a scene in which he commits suicide by jumping from the roof of a prison.

Ishimatsu as a protagonist is, then, a curiously fractious figure. He is also another psychoanalytical case study, a rampant id made physically manifest. His outbursts of violence know no boundaries even within the stratified hierarchies of the world of the yakuza. In the course of the narrative he succumbs to drug use and rampant gambling, and on several occasions he simply grabs women and proceeds to rape them on the spot, wherever they happen to be. This conceit imagines the rigid rules and circumscribed patterns of yakuza life as a counterweight, as it were a social superego, which makes the scenario a pointed reflection on yakuza culture as a strange marker of normalcy: less a symbol for a nation corrupted than a catalogue of how and why such corruption began (Ishimatsu's superiors in effect facilitating his rampage through their indulgence and fear of him).

Ishimatsu is at once a monstrous yet childlike figure, an index of surplus and excess (himself the symbol for a nation corrupted) and a mirror held up to yakuza lore. The fact that the film makes especially pronounced use of family roles with regard to its key characters is significant from this point of view. It is particularly so given that the unstable protagonist goes on to murder his gang boss (i.e. his father), and in so doing he fails to navigate the Oedipal complex successfully and to ascend to the Lacanian Symbolic order wherein he can take his (perceived rightful) place in society within the law of the father and of language. Indeed he remains especially distant from these precepts given his perennial disregard for any kind of law (be it literal law and order or the codes of the yakuza) and his inability to communicate properly through verbal means. He enters into a majority of situations throughout the film in complete silence, seemingly unable to articulate himself in words, and this becomes increasingly prevalent as the narrative progresses until he remains all but a mute presence. Even when he finds his girlfriend, the one person he comes closest to caring for, almost dead from a drug overdose he can but smile. Not a word escapes his lips, only a mocking acknowledgement of the irony that his culpability in this woman's death appears to literalise and to exaggerate his patriarchal agency even as it makes clear its fundamental monstrousness.

Ultimately, when the narrative returns full circle to Ishimatsu's suicide in prison, it completes, fills in, some details that were elided in the opening scene. Most notably it shows him climbing a large tower in order to throw himself from it, the dramatic low-angle shot that captures the majority of this protracted ascension underlining its symbolic import as a phallic object and by extension Ishimatsu's climb as a struggle to master this phallus, to apparently claim a masculine subjectivity. The prominence of the tower in this particular low-angle shot – a large structure visibly penetrating the clear sky around it – looms over Ishimatsu's comparatively small figure and seems to underline visually the enormity of his task. However the fact that he does reach the top, before subsequently leaping from the tower to his death, appears to secure this mastery. It is an attempt to master his own body, which had previously been assailed on several occasions without being destroyed (he is variously shot and stabbed in addition to poisoning himself to escape prison) and in this his death drive becomes particularly clear. Miike both spectacularises and parodies his death by depicting the protagonist's body hitting successive buildings below him amidst a veritable wave of blood that washes over him as his finally lifeless form drops to earth. This is death, *thanatos*, writ large in opposition to the sex (i.e. life) instinct of *eros* that had earlier been made manifest in Ishimatsu's apparently insatiable desire for sensory gratification. However both states exist for this character as abstract forces or urges, ones that he simply acts on like an animal. They are processes that he does not or cannot reflect upon or understand, to which end he may be seen less as a rounded character than a symbol for a national death drive – of the excesses of Japan's bubble economy and its subsequent collapse.

Having analysed the significance to the yakuza film of *Violent Cop* and *Sonatine* it is ultimately fitting to bring the study full circle and return to Kitano, who after an extended hiatus has begun to revisit the genre that made his name and international reputation as a filmmaker. *Outrage* (*Autoreiji*, 2010) concerns a series of protracted and recriminatory killings and acts of violence that play out amidst hazy talk of open family conflict and gang warfare among Tokyo's major crime syndicates. Largely dismissed upon its premiere (at Cannes) in 2010, and described by Nick Pinkerton (2011b) as looking at the yakuza with 'bemused irony', Kitano's much-vaunted return to the yakuza film may in fact be regarded less as a commercial venture (though the relative lack of success and the critical vilification and dismissal of his work since *Zatoichi* (2004) may have contributed to a desire to return to an earlier model of filmmaking) than an artistic redefinition. In other words it is an experiment in the extent to which the yakuza film, and perhaps more significantly the yakuza film as directed by Kitano Takeshi, is still productive, even relevant.

To this end *Outrage* destabilises its director/star's centrality from the outset, with the film's very first shot visualising this precept through a lateral track along a series of immobile figures of which Beat Takeshi is but one among many, merely a single yakuza like the many others in the film's extended ensemble of characters. Thereafter his protagonist, Otomo, drifts in and out of the narrative, less a centre of gravity than another body in orbit around a different central presence. Or at least that would be the case if such a centre were present in the story. As it is there is no real centre to anchor the film, no clear protagonist whose trajectory and focalisation forms the spine of the narrative and through whose eyes its events are seen and experienced. The story concerns a gang war that escalates when one gang boss is ordered by his superior to sever his ties with a rival boss with whom he formed a pact whilst in prison (the 'outrage' of the title). Action and counteraction mount inexorably as the entire hierarchy of gang life becomes embroiled in what John Berra terms 'the domino effect that can occur within the underworld' (2012b, p. 331), following which Kitano's affectless vision – wherein action becomes meaningful only within a highly ritualised and circumscribed context defined by its relationship to the equal and opposite reactions that it facilitates – becomes paramount. As such he offers something like a metaphor for narrative itself – a pared-down chain of diagrammatic causality – so that the fundamental nihilism that David Desser (1988) has seen within the yakuza genre is foregrounded throughout the film. Violence begets violence beneath a glossy surface of proprietorial control and corporate self-interest. On three separate occasions a request by a superior for a subordinate to behave counter to his best interests is described as a 'formality', something undertaken to appease the status quo, which bespeaks the extent to which a particular façade has to be promulgated. The so-called chairman, who directs operations from a secluded beachfront mansion, pulls the strings like a puppet master, telling an underling that one must always be thinking ahead; yet tellingly he is a perennially remote figure – a distant authority, cut off spatially but also morally in that he wants to keep the yakuza clean from drugs and high-stakes gambling. Beside this the cutting off of a finger is more than once ridiculed as a fanciful and old-fashioned gesture, whilst peripheral characters such as Otomo's wife and the wife of his subordinate (both of whose marriages seem largely harmonious) become collateral damage in the escalating warfare between the gangs.

Kitano has sporadic recourse to a subversion of archetypal yakuza tropes in *Outrage*, and includes characters that disturb the homogeneity of its generic landscape. Sameness and difference is in fact a prevalent dichotomy in the narrative, one that is crystallised around the structural prominence of an African (Ghanaian) ambassador who works for a yakuza gang and who features as an almost comedic figure to the extent that he is perennially put upon by the yakuza. He is forced into a demeaning position of complicity in their various crimes, and is unable to assert any power or agency in response, thus being rather brusquely dealt with as a victim throughout his curtailed time in the story. However this brevity in narrative is itself representative of the film's methodology regarding its thematic precepts. An uncomfortably lingering sense of racism is at least partially offset by the very consciousness of Otherness as a problematic concept that this character instils into the narrative. The yakuza who perpetrate the atrocities and who control the African are themselves reprehensible characters whose actions are in no way held up as admirable or heroic, so that the Ghanaian (a professional man, and moreover a comfortable speaker of Japanese) becomes not simply an anomalous visual and national repository of an Other but rather a prominent problematising of that term as it is often understood to apply to Japan, a character who despite his appearance appears to fit into Japanese society. The fact that he attempts (albeit in vain) to beat the yakuza at their own game and blackmail them, and more significantly that he survives amidst the recriminatory slaughter that sees almost every other character in the film killed, allows one to regard him as a pervasive facet (and fact) of the social landscape of Japan. Although this aspect of the story has led to charges of racism against the film (James, 2010, p. 22), here, in contrast to Kitano's earlier *Brother* (2000), the characters that are explicitly defined as racist are in no way sympathetic or empathetic, are not held up to be identified with in any way. In other words the spectre of racism is overtly raised – most obviously when, after leaving the ambassador in the middle of nowhere after dark, one yakuza states that he will blend in with the darkness because of his skin colour – so that it can be disavowed, displaced onto aggressively antagonistic characters. Kitano has, in the aforementioned *Brother*, reflected on Japan as Other in the popular consciousness of the US (Rayns, 2001, p. 27); *Outrage* in contrast ruminates on Otherness within Japan. And the yakuza film, with its archetypical emphasis on contested space (turf wars), is an apposite framework within which to explore these themes, something Kitano comically underlines by including a recurrent motif concerning drivers parked in inopportune places who need to be perennially moved on.

The sequel to *Outrage* – *Outrage Beyond* (*Autoreiji: biyondo*, 2012) – picks up five years from the point at which its predecessor left off, with the central Sanno family an increasingly powerful force in Tokyo but facing mounting pressure from the police force. Upon being released from prison Otomo is insinuated against his will and better judgement into a conflict between rival gangs, behind which lies the cop Kataoka, and war ensues. *Outrage Beyond* carefully builds its plot around a recondite series of motifs that define the interactions between characters who are throughout the film engaged in nefarious plots and schemes. Appropriately the opening image of a crashed car being exhumed from a river (which is used under the opening credits to contrast with the moving cars that underlined the credits of *Outrage*) establishes the thematic antinomy of the hidden and the visible, of what has been subsumed returning to the surface. Against this backdrop Beat Takeshi's Otomo does emerge here as a clear protagonist. He is by no means central to every scene – indeed he is wholly absent from many scenes following his introduction approximately twenty minutes into the film – but his journey of revenge does structure and animate the narrative. The fact that he joins in a pact of brotherhood with the character Kimura –the man with whom he had a running enmity throughout *Outrage* that culminated in him being stabbed in prison – in order to execute this plan bespeaks the extent to which *Outrage Beyond* works against its forebear. Beyond this clear dramatic arc Kitano concisely fills in the ritualised landscape of the film with a series of minor characters whose lives and fates are elucidated as adjuncts to the main drama of the film. This is particularly true of several ostensibly generic *dramatis personae*: who, like flames, flicker into brief life before being summarily extinguished as part of a universe in which individual actions are coldly circumscribed. An early scene introduces two aggressive, eager young *chinpira* who harass three customers at a baseball batting cage and appear to be mere thugs. However these young men, subsequently revealed to be Kimura's so-called soldiers, his underlings, become almost tragic figures when, desperate to prove their worth, they take it upon themselves to attack a rival gang and are beaten to death in recrimination. Unlike *Outrage* Kitano here elides much of this violence to emphasise its brutality, and even has recourse to an optical POV shot (not typically a central component of his découpage) as a bag is placed over the characters' heads and the screen is darkened prior to their being killed. Their bodies are discovered on a rubbish heap, an apt comment on their sorry status as part of the detritus of society; moreover the fact that a picture of these two characters is seen prominently in a later scene in which Kimuura is killed suggests that he too, despite his ostensible position as head of his own gang, is still subservient to those above him, still a pawn in a game controlled by others and a performer in somebody else's narrative.

This consideration of men on the lowest rungs of yakuza gang life is balanced by a concomitant focus those at the very top. Kato, the gang underling who at the very end of *Outrage* murders his boss and assumes control of the family, struggles to preserve the power that he has accrued, and his increasing uncertainty and desperation reflects the proto-political landscape of the yakuza family as corporate enterprise – of the desire once ascended to power of retaining that power. Kato is only ever seen inside, in his suit; he is a business executive much more than a yakuza and part of a board who talk about redistributing turf only after official meetings, reconfiguring the boardroom rather than the street as the key site of operations. As before, Kitano's *mise-en-scène* elucidates this stark spectrum of narrative oppositions with a series of visual correlatives. He contrasts anonymous, featureless urban sprawl with secluded compounds, offices with homes, business suits with formal kimonos. But crucially the director uses these juxtapositions to adumbrate a narrative in which neither apparent extreme can be understood in isolation or abstraction; it is less a clash of opposites than a series of complementary images that together delimit the face of the modern yakuza film. The most overt pictures of corporate capitalism are precisely those that appear to be the most traditionally Japanese (the gang bosses in their formal kimonos and antiquated homes who reside in Osaka), so that Kitano alludes to the yakuza film as a social barometer in order to negate such contextualism as far as it can elucidate the development of Japan. Joan Mellen (1976) has talked about yakuza films as desirous, through their protagonists, of a return to past values amidst a contemporary 'moral vacuum' (p. 122). *Outrage Beyond* questions this belief, indeed highlights the masochism that underpins it. It is true that Otomo and Kimura hold true to a pact of brotherhood such as was immediately despoiled in *Outrage*; and against the desire by one yakuza to become part of a globalised landscape of stock-broking and hedge-funding they appear to be antiquated figures. But this notion of what Kataoka terms 'old-time yakuza' is used against them to manipulate and engineer their actions. In so doing Kitano implicitly catalogues the development of the genre and even the discursive practices that have accrued around it. The narrative, one may argue, becomes genre cinema as film criticism.

Kitano takes advantage in places of the full dimensions of the anamorphic Scope frame that he employs in *Outrage* and its sequel for the first time in his career (see Fig. 2.4). Both films are replete with rooms full of yakuza 'soldiers': often, as in *Outrage*'s opening scene, with an army of underlings waiting outside beside a fleet of identical cars to connote their collective consciousness and the sublimation of the individual amidst corporate rather than necessarily criminal enterprise. Moreover one prison-based discussion at the beginning of *Outrage*

Figure 2.4   Kitano's use of scope photography in *Outrage*. Note how all characters share the same elongated space but remain disconnected, in small groupings, through being engaged in different activities. Ostensible unity but fractious internal disharmony characterises the yakuza families in this film.

Beyond between Otomo and the corrupt detective Kataoka features a series of shot/reverse shot over the shoulder set-ups that position speaker and interlocutor at either end of the composition. It is a marker of the extent to which these particular characters exist as mirror images of one another (indeed the first shot of this particular scene shows these two figures in a literal mirror, reflected in a door at the opposite side of the room in which they are sitting), and this connotes the uncertainty of their respective identities and places in society. It is a point that is crystallised at the very end of the narrative in a final scene in which Otomo kills Kataoka. Here the yakuza murders the cop for the latter's complicity in the gang warfare that has broken and out and caused the death of almost all the central characters. It is the only point of unilateral action on Otomo's part, and its completion abruptly ends the film (Kitano cuts to black almost concurrently with the gunshot), as though such an incident, such a point of climax, marks the logical endpoint of a yakuza narrative, where action segues from the ritually circumscribed arena of its generic encoding into that dictated only by personal agency and individual desire. If, as Darrel William Davis has claimed, 'the toughness of classic yakuza [. . .] is missing from most contemporary versions of the genre' (2006, p. 199), then Otomo here makes a last stand both for a way of life and a way of cinema. And the very fact of his survival, when his comparable counterparts in Fukasaku's films (the character wedded to the past) would summarily perish as a marker of their anomalous standing in the modern world, is a sign of the (transformed) times.

If *Outrage Beyond* finds the yakuza film in some ways returning full circle back to some of its 1970s' roots in Japanese filmmaking, then a contrastive view of this antiquation has been offered by Sono Sion. *Why Don't You Play in Hell?* (*Jigoku de nazu warui*, 2013) is at once a yakuza film pastiche and a lament for the passing of film, of 35 mm cinematic photography and projection. It regards both (nostalgically) as outmoded forms in its story of rival yakuza gangs whose turf war becomes the subject of a film by a group of amateur filmmakers. Derek Hill has noted that 'the reality of the modern-day yakuza criminal [. . .] is far less romantic than the cinematic image that has resonated for decades in the collective imagination of moviegoers' (2010, p. 267), and Sono's film is a testament to this implacable, idealised model. The iconoclastic director includes a veritable history lesson embedded within the narrative. The proto-*ninkyō* 1920s' yakuza films of Ito Daisuke are alluded to in the final battle. This director's typically stylish scenes of sword-fighting (described by Keiko McDonald as dynamic 'short takes captured by [. . .] running among the fighters') (1992, p. 169) are referenced when a real battle features the young cameramen running amidst the duelling gang members to record their violence. Conversely the music of *Battles without Honour and Humanity* appears over the opening credits of the film, and the sometime prevalence of high-school-based yakuza pastiches – films like *Panic High School* (*Koko dai panikku*, 1978), *Be Bop High School* (*Be bappu haisukuru*, 1985) or

Blue Spring (*Aoi haru*, 2001) – is narrativised in the film-obsessed adolescents who ultimately join in with the fighting in order to complete their dream film. This latter canvas, the canvas of cinema that is the only landscape of the twenty-first century to really feature yakuza films as they are stereotypically perceived and understood, is key to *Why Don't you Play in Hell?* Sono for his part calls attention to this fact, and in so doing laments the death and celebrates the life of the genre as an adjunct to populist imagination.

As a distinct, homogeneous genre the yakuza film has, in the last five or so years, begun to recede from view at the forefront of Japanese popular cinema, even as it continues to be perhaps *the* pre-eminent genre of V-cinema (although this itself is an increasingly problematic term as numerous ostensible video productions are actually released theatrically in one way or another). However the social tableau of this generic form retains its vitality; the yakuza family is a nation in microcosm; its rules and rituals, as well as the emphasis on themes pertaining to the materiality of the body (especially its desecration as a marker of corporeality that becomes the last bastion of personal identity), are all writ large into the fabric of the yakuza film. Miike and Kitano have exemplified this trend, their work ruminating on yakuza cinema as an authorial and social construct even as it does not readily depart from prescribed generic norms. As Alan Tansman has noted with regard to the work of Hasegawa Shin, cyclical narrative patterning is almost endemic within individual works (2001, p. 149), to the extent that a comparable generic patterning should not be unsurprising, a sense of the genre itself returning to feed on its own lore and to canonise its own mythology. The cathartic dimension to earlier yakuza films has largely eroded as a contextual determinant on the popularity and commercial viability of the yakuza film, to which end it no longer counterpoints the nation but has perhaps instead become it, as heroic outlaws give way to corporate businessmen. The title of Miike Takashi's new film, *Yakuza Apocalypse* (*Gokudō daisensō*, 2015), seems particularly prescient.

3. JAPANESE HORROR CINEMA

Of all the commercial genres to have proliferated in modern Japanese cinema, none has achieved the international success and visibility of the horror film. Horror films have long constituted a vital feature of this country's cinema, but since the late 1990s they have become arguably *the* face of Japanese filmmaking, and furthermore the prevalent image of an increasingly transnational paradigm. There are several key and interrelated means of conceiving of the importance of J-horror. Most saliently it seizes on the recent past as a site of tension and anxiety, a textual shadow or even doppelganger of the present that haunts modernity as a spectral repressed or foreclosed. Moreover, as this latter point implies, psycho-analytical imperatives have been writ large – a veritable matrix of concerns with subject formation and problems therein – as a national adjunct to which it is interesting to note the extent to which several films' technical methodology, their means of production, becomes a site of narrative discourse and/or semantic signi-fication. Angela Ndalianis (2010) has analysed in detail the horror genre's influ-ence on associative media, on the extent to which its emotional affectivity lends itself to cultural products such as theme park rides, whilst more significantly Mark Cousins (2004, pp. 475–7) has talked of so-called J-horror (which does technically refer to the Japanese horror canon but seems more often to designate its supernatural cinema, thanks largely to producer Ichise Takashige) as one of the key cinematic genres at the close of the twentieth century, precisely because it proliferated at a time when an apparently global pre-millennial fear, even para-noia, became apparent at the same time as traditional celluloid was beginning to give way to digital forms of cinematic expression and projection. There was a sense in some quarters that authentic film was a dying art (Willis, 2005, p. 1), as though cinema's traditional mechanical means, as well as its capacity to designate or extol a specific, phenomenological dimension, a relationship with a perceived real that offers a potentially verisimilar transparency, was disturbed by this ghost of the machine, and as such that individual horror films themselves are in some way working through problems and tensions that are beyond their supernatural narrative concerns.

Mitsuyo Wada-Marciano (2012) has analysed the pertinence of digital cinema to the J-horror film, analysing its textual features not only insofar as they engage with such technology but also as J-horror film itself reflects or narrativises new forms of exhibition and consumption. Concomitantly Anna Powell (2005) has noted that:

> the horror film's plot, action, special effects and finally, the existence of the film itself, is technology-dependent. Events are recorded, seen and heard through camera lenses and microphones [. . .] [and] [t]he viewer also experiences the film as an event [. . .] we meld with and become part of the material technology of cinema. (p. 5)

The increasing prevalence of digital filmmaking from this perspective serves to implicitly underline the technological development and refinement of socio-political mediation and (interpersonal) intercourse that finds such a potent point of departure in many of the most popular and acclaimed J-horror works. The horror film is the most cinematic of genres precisely because it offers a reflection on cinema's processes – on the experience of filmic performativity in general and on spectatorship (specifically horror film spectatorship) in particular, and Japanese horror filmmaking has for decades engaged directly with this aspect of its specificity. The fact that many such films allegorise the cinematic experience – offering a reflection on, and a mirror of, the pointed duality of filmic performance: that is, of present absences (or vice versa) – means that the horror of ghosts and doubles, of malign doppelgangers, is encoded within the very fabric of the films themselves, in both textual and sub-textual levels of signification. If audiences become part of a horror film's narrative horizons, its diegesis, then the democratisation of its 'material technology' in some J-horror films interpellate or address them further by postulating a media landscape in which they might partake, an almost interactive directivity where agency and control become narrativised as markers of a new means of engaging with the cinematic medium. All of this expands the scope of horror cinema, conceives of the genre as a form that incorporates both direction and spectatorship, production and consumption, realism and representation, into a generically diverse entity, almost a sub-genre unto itself, and one that entails a significant challenge to conceptualisations of horror filmmaking.

Beside this the technological focus of several J-horror narratives is of particular significance; it becomes a means not necessarily of simplistically castigating the modern landscape that it signifies, of reifying and/or allegorising a sense of Japanese victimhood, but rather of challenging the extent to which this sense reflects reality. Modernity and its attendant traumas have been perennial concerns in commentary on Japan over the course of the twentieth century, with a concomitant loss of identity, tradition, spirituality and even purpose being seen as the price paid for the Meiji Restoration on the one hand and (more significantly) Japan's post-war reconstitution as a global economic superpower on the other. In her fascinating anthropological study *Discourses of the Vanishing* Marilyn Ivy (1995) notes how the manifestation of ghosts (in various different guises and concepts) reflects a sense in which Japan has lost much of what once defined it as a nation, and that these variously destroyed or disavowed features can be found as spectres or doppelgangers that haunt the present. The notion of ghosts in this context – as shadows of people, terrible facsimiles that haunt the living as markers of the past – is particularly apposite. Through the explicit juxtaposition of past and present, an emphasis on the lingering presence of history as an inextricable part of the modern world, many J-horror films engage with this aspect of Japan, and this chapter will consider how and to what extent this genre makes meaning from such tensions. It will explore the diverse face of J-horror, looking at both canonical and marginalised films, and in so doing will reflect on both the coherence and the conservatism (or otherwise) of the genre, the nature of its self-reflexive and socio-political discourses and its status *vis-à-vis* the horror genre in general.

Horror cinema has always reflected contemporary concerns, always sought to probe and penetrate the world in which it was born and the context in which it was produced. Christopher Sharrett argues that 'since its glorious inception first in the Weimar cinema, then at Universal Studios, few genres have been as blunt in questioning notions of the monstrous Other, the nature of the family and other elements of received social wisdom as the horror film' (2005, p. 11). Most recent Western discourse on Japanese horror cinema has been overtly concerned with this perspective, exploring the socio-political relevance of the genre's frequent recourse to familial and technological subjects and the gender-based imperatives therein. These points are not a particularly new facet of Japanese culture or its socio-political landscape. The perceived abject nature of Japanese modernity has already been intimated, but Japan's history and tradition have at various times been regarded as a locus of terror in the social psyche of the country, not least following its defeat in the Pacific War when overt references to the country's feudal past and attendant traditions and practices were officially outlawed by the occupying forces and thus forbidden from being seen on Japanese screens. As Linnie Blake has argued, a colonialist agenda began to take hold, an increasingly Westernised, Americanised ideological and sociological model that conflicted with that of the colonised, and as such the ghost in Nakata Hideo's *Ring* (*Ringu*, 1998) in particular can be seen as a repressed past returned to haunt the present, a vision of an earlier Japan risen (literally) to disturb its modernity (2008, pp. 44–70).

The years following Japan's defeat in WWII, surrender to the Allies and, subsequently, the economic prosperity, expansion and incessant globalisation of the miracle economy increasingly frustrated a traditional foundation for a tangible national identity. A climate was created in which nationhood was cheapened as a barometer for individual identity, and as such selfhood itself became problematic, corrupted, lacking any stable points of reference. This has wider ramifications in Japanese cinema than the horror film, being felt for instance in the sphere of everyday family life in the *shomin-geki* (among several other genres and modes). However it is arguably in horror cinema that such implications are most strongly felt and most thoroughly, most potently explored. The direct relevance of a film like Tsukamoto Shinya's *Tetsuo: The Iron Man* (*Tetsuo*, 1989) to the time in which it was made is immediately apparent. It is a film whose dystopian picture of literal (and classless) dehumanisation (Grossman, 2004, pp. 139–40) portends an era when technological fetishism and material commoditisation supersedes human subjectivity and collapses the distinction between man and machine, between organic and Other. Many of the films that followed Tsukamoto's seminal film worked towards a similar socio-political critique, to which end the J-horror boom that began in the late-1990s evinced a profound unease about humanity in a technological age, an anxiety over the precariousness of modern life and the concomitant instability of selfhood as it is imbricated in wider discourses of social stratification. The ceaselessly multiplying and regenerating evils of the *Ringu* and *Ju-on* series, as well as being a sly commercial strategy for an ever-increasing production line of new works, also reflects a world in which horror is an inescapable feature, and in which danger stalks like a shadow and becomes a tangible norm of everyday living, the inexorability of death in life. The specific approach of these works, wherein typical gothic horror iconography (scenes set at night and/or in darkness, sets and locations removed from ostensible verisimilitude, an exotic sense of Otherness) is subverted in favour of an emphasis on the everyday, the quotidian. A majority of scenes, even those that contain set-piece scares and suspense, take place in broad daylight and in typical urban and suburban locations. The films make open, everyday spaces appear strange and foreboding, as though 'normal' life itself contained or gave birth to terror and the uncanny (indeed everyday life is not easily dissociable from any perceived monstrous Other in much Japanese horror cinema, is often in fact responsible for its birth or inception).

As is the case elsewhere in the story of modern Japanese cinema, this is not a new or particularly original phenomenon. J-horror has echoes of several distinct earlier forms, films and filmmakers, some of which feed directly into its generic specificity, but the paradigm can be extended to include not only foreign films and genres but approaches to American and European horror cinema. Jay McRoy (2005a) has noted the hybrid quality of films like *Ju-on: The Grudge*, preoccupied as it is with uniquely Japanese avenging spirits contained within a scenario whose specific details pay broad homage to US progenitors such as *Poltergeist* (1982) and *The Amityville Horror* (1979). Going further, the sense of the uncanny already identified is compounded by an approach to J-horror that recognises a fundamental receptivity to work undertaken on European and American horror filmmaking. Robin Wood (1986) in particular has argued that one of the keys to horror cinema is the return of the repressed, the sense that that which has been buried will return to haunt or terrorise the institutions that have suppressed or otherwise subjugated it. The horror film has often traced personal, social, even national repressions; in recent years one thinks of *Wolf Creek*'s (2004) vision of a popular Australian archetype – here the iconic figure of the Larrikin made internationally popular by *Crocodile Dundee* (1986) – visiting violence back on those who have courted and consumed touristic spectacle in the country's landscape and culture, or of the unconscious mind and suppressed desire of the protagonist made manifest as a serial killer in Alexandre Aja's French slasher film hit *Switchblade Romance (Haute Tension*, 2004). Within Japan this has become a locus of meaning that connects an otherwise disparate series of works. Indeed so prevalent is the practice that some foreign directors and authors have appropriated its tenets. Graham Masterton's 1990 novel *Tengu*, for instance, imagines its titular being (a creature from Shinto religious iconography) possessing a group of warriors created by a secret society in order to avenge the atomic bombings that ended WWII.

There are many faces of Japanese horror cinema, many different subsets that are each comprised of their own narrative patterns and more or less distinct thematic concerns (though some overlap is visible). The popular and populist face of the genre has been the ghost story, or the *Kaidan eiga*, exemplified most overtly the *Ring* and *Ju-on* films. The franchises of these series have spawned numerous sequels and remakes (in different countries) and countless more imitations. Indeed the latter alone now consists of six Japanese features – two features made for cinema, two made-for-television V-cinema movies entitled *Ju-on: The Curse (Ju-on*, 2000) and *Ju-on: The Curse 2 (Ju-on 2*, 2000) from which the first cinematic films draw liberally, and two later films called *Ju-on: Black Ghost (Ju-on: kuroi shōjo*, 2009) and *Ju-on: White Ghost (Ju-on: shiroi rōjo*, 2009) as well as two short 1998 films that began the myth and introduced some of its specific properties (entitled *444444444* and *Katatsumi*). This in addition to a Hollywood, Japan-set remake of *Ju-on: The Grudge* directed by the original director, Shimizu Takashi, and a US-set sequel to this film entitled *The Grudge 3* (2009), directed by an American, Toby Wilkins. There is even a video game based on the films (though this is not unique to the *Ju-on* franchise) and a novelisation of several of the different stories that comprise the early instalments of the series by Oishi Kei.

The supernatural narrative has tended to predominate in Japanese horror film-making, but has worked through a series of transformations that have informed the sub-genre as a series of variations on a theme. Its immediate post-war history is one of generic hybridisation and cross-pollination, albeit with a series of iconic images beginning to dominate. At this time horror filmmaking began to proliferate in the work of specialist directors such as Nakagawa Nobuo and Tanaka Tokuzo, whose films flourished alongside those of more established and diverse directors such as Shindo Kaneto – especially his *Onibaba* (1964) and *Black Cat* (*Kuroneko*, 1968) – and Kobayashi Masaki, whose portmanteau horror narrative *Kwaidan* (*Kaidan*, 1965) was instrumental in popularising several of what would go on to become central tenets of J-horror. The genre as a brand was soon characterised by a generic cross-fertilisation with a series of recondite motifs that frequently merged a *jidai-geki* (period) framework with supernatural narratives, ones in which Ruth Goldberg's definition of 'the nightmare of romantic passion' often leads to vengeful female ghosts (*onryou*) and haunted men (2005, pp. 29–37). In addition to Mizoguchi's *Ugetsu monogatari* (1953), Nakagawa directed numerous films in this vein, especially *The Ghosts of Kasane Swamp* (*Kaidan kasane-ga-fuchi*, 1957), *Ghost Cat Mansion* (*Bōreo kaibyō yashiki*, 1958), *The Ghost of Yotsuya* (*Tōkaidō Yotsuya kaidan*, 1959) and *Snake Woman's Curse* (*Kaidan hebi-onna*, 1968).

In the 1990s there were a number of horror titles that began to broaden the range of the country's horror fiction and to use it as a point of departure, chief in which regard are the films of Kurosawa Kiyoshi. Before moving more or less completely into horror film production (at least for a short time), Kurosawa experimented with the genre in some films that have very little precedent in Japanese cinema, and that in some ways lay the foundations for the directions in which the genre would develop in the late 1990s and immediately thereafter. Foremost in this regard is *The Guard from Underground* (*Jigoku no keibin*, 1992), an affectionate homage to and replication and subversion of the American slasher film model updated as a satire of corporate Japan. Colette Balmain (2008) is all but alone in conceiving of a Japanese slasher film tradition or paradigm, and *The Guard from Underground* remains first and foremost in this regard. Set almost entirely within the building in which the protagonist works (an apt comment on being tied to one's job), the film concerns a new female employee at a large corporation. Her job in the mysterious Department 12 involves evaluating and purchasing valuable works of art. But her job is beset by problems, not the least of which is a security guard, another new employee, who becomes increasingly intent on ridding the department of any and all troublesome figures in and around the office. The value of art is a recurring theme in this film; there are several extended discussions of what different artists and their paintings are worth, what is and what should be their monetary value, and beside this discourse the value of human life appears to be somewhat less inviolate, certainly not sacrosanct. If a painting is worth what anyone is willing to pay for it, then humanity is only safe and healthy to the extent that no one is willing to attack and defile it. The security guard's manner of killing his victims, which is methodically to break bones and dismember limbs, reflects this cheapness of human life, of corporeality as the limit of identity and selfhood. In point of fact two of his victims are disposed of and placed inside cabinets (one is even killed inside an empty locker), with their bodies as it were filed away like mere documents or objects.

The Guard from Underground, like *Tetsuo: The Iron Man*, is an example of how Japanese horror cinema immediately began to reflect and ruminate upon the changes affecting Japan in the years immediately following the erosion of its economy. Another key instance of such socio-political import can be found in what is in some ways a landmark production, one that laid the foundations for much of what became the popular face of J-Horror later in the decade. *Scary True Stories* (*Honto ni atta kowai hanashi*, 1991) is a series of three portmanteau collections of short films allegedly based on first hand testimony that was made for Japanese television in 1991 and 1992. Conceived by the notable horror director Tsuruta Norio – who would go on to direct the Ring Prequel (the third in the trilogy) entitled *Ring 0: Birthday* (*Ringu 0: bāsudei*, 2000) as well as the popular horror films *Premonition* (*Yogen*, 2004) and *POV – A Cursed Film* (*POV: norowareta firumu*, 2012) – this collection spawned a veritable sub-genre of such productions throughout the 1990s. Each film contains three or four short stories relating the experiences of ordinary people with ghosts and strange phenomena, but not all the films are concerned with overtly horrific subject matter. The first compendium contains a story called 'Spiritual Flight' concerning a young girl who, following the death of her beloved grandmother, hears stories of her own ability to commune with the dead, and ultimately comes to realise her powers when a strange dream shows her the location of a hidden graveyard. It is a story of personal empowerment rather than of danger or threat, a narrative in which the benign spiritual knowledge and wisdom of the old is passed down to the young, and as such its theme of productive continuity and lineage – of retaining established or traditional ways and means of self-definition and behaviour – is clearly intended as instructive in a country that was suddenly faced with the severe consequences of its post-war drive towards modernity and economic expansion. In other words it implicitly remonstrates with Japan for contravening what has been perceived to be its traditional national specificity in the face of globalisation, and stresses the salience of retaining this connection to the past.

Subject and Abject; Birth and Death: Law, Language and Patriarchy

> To each ego its object, to each superego its abject [. . .] It is not the white expanse or slack boredom of repression [. . .] Rather it is a brutish suffering that 'I' puts up with on the edge of non-existence and hallucination, of a reality that, if I acknowledge it, annihilates me.
>
> (Kristeva, 1982, p. 2)

Psychoanalysis and horror cinema have long been happy bedfellows in discourse on the genre. Robin Wood's (1986) appropriation of the 'return of the repressed' is perhaps the most significant example, but Barbara Creed (1993), James Iaccino (1994), Steven Schneider (2004) and Linda Williams (2002) among numerous others have all contributed important work on the subject. However, unlike Julia Kristeva's influential application of Lacan to literature in *Powers of Horror*, it is Freud who has remained the locus of psychoanalytical approaches to cinema (both horror and otherwise). J-horror offers something of a contrastive paradigm, a cinema in which Kristeva and Creed's work is particularly receptive and which finds in Lacanian conceptions of subject formation both an individual and a (broad) sociological model of problematic patriarchy – a frustrated Symbolic order – and of disturbed language. As Kristeva argued, the uncanny and the abject are concerned with that which stands not only as perennially outside the realm of 'identity, system, order' (1982, p. 4), but is also fundamentally unassimilable or irrecuperable within it. Many of the key works in modern J-horror explore scenarios built around abject antinomies: a pervasive unease about the boundaries between the corporeal and the technological, for example, or around internal (inside the body) and external, or between adults and children (hence the receptivity to psychoanalytical concerns). Indeed Creed posits as it were an abject distinction between 'the fully constituted subject [and] the partially formed subject' (1993, p. 8), which further situates a discourse on psychoanalysis as a central referent within the application of the concept, whilst attendant notions of representation offer not only a proto-abject challenge to experiential 'reality' faced with an apparently monstrous Other but a challenge to how we consider and conceptualise that 'reality'.

Nakata Hideo's *Ring* and its sequel are paramount in this regard, containing as they do a convoluted history and a past that returns to haunt the present as a narrative framework for a concomitant examination of breached boundaries and ruptures in representation made explicit through a disturbing of language (both social and cinematic). Appropriating the conceit of M. R. James' short story 'Casting the Runes' – previously adapted by Jacques Tourneur as *Night of the Demon* (1957) – Suzuki's Koji's source novel downplays any overt horror in order to stress both a proto-typical detective story and the psychological torment of its protagonist, here a male newspaper reporter rather than the film's female journalist. The novel *Ring* – the first in a linked trilogy of novels that continued with *Spiral/Rasen* in 1995 and *Loop/Rūpu* in 1998 – was originally published in Japan in 1991, and as such may be read as a commentary on AIDS in the 1980s. What is also apparent, if less prominent in critical discourse, is the extent to which the modern face of Japan has eroded and decayed. Suzuki is ostensibly more conservative than Nakata, using as he does a married male protagonist whose wife and son are 'infected' by Sadako's curse and thus in need of him to uncover the mystery of the ghost, offset their impending deaths and come to their rescue. However Suzuki's depiction of this character – a man who clings desperately to the idea of family as a social institution even though he is perennially working away from home and whilst around his wife and child often appears to be distant if not neglectful – reflects a sense in which the corrosion of the social fabric of Japan has left only the vestiges of traditional or reactionary values as a marker of social harmony. It is a façade of synecdochic personal-as-national relations; and in its literal engagement with disease (smallpox) it offers an organic, biological metaphor for a country slowly being poisoned and succumbing to illness and potentially death as the endlessly regenerating curse spreads through its veins.

The film adaptation broadens these thematic horizons to engage with structures (structuralisms) of language and vision as a means of disturbing any clearly demarcated sense of reality or normalcy. Much has been written about *Ring* as the most prominent and popular face of J-horror cinema. Linnie Blake (2008) sees a post-colonialist discourse at the heart of Sadako's curse, her perennial need to return and pronounce her presence figuring as a marker of a past that has been erased in the face of Japan's increasing post-war, post-occupation modernity and drive to Western capitalism. As she notes, the narrative of *Ring*:

> [is] located in a highly Americanised Japan [. . .] a world of baseball games on television, western-style homes, career-driven single mothers, advanced news media and the sophisticated technological mediation of everyday life. But it is also a Japan of far-flung islands, isolated villages, traditional rural dwellings complete with *tatami* mats, futons and paper screens, grand-parental devotion to the family, incomprehensible regional dialects and ancient folk superstitions. (p. 52)

The tension between these narrative features, and the ghost Sadako's breaching of them, then forms the basis of the apparent postcolonial critique: what Blake defines as 'that which will not be eradicated by US colonialism' (p. 54). Concomitantly Eric White (2005) discusses the simulacrum inherent in the narrative's depiction of reproduction and duplication. He argues that the film's 'ubiquitous technological mediation [. . .] [facilitates] the intrusion of "post-human" otherness into contemporary cultural life' (p. 41), and thus regards Nakata's adaptation of Suzuki's novel as allegorising familial life and its agency in the formation of individual identity, which entails a denunciative engagement with the 'media-saturated social sphere' (ibid.) of modern Japan. And Julian Stringer (2007) uses the film as part of a discourse on cross-cultural studies and processes of multi-media recycling, highlighting what he sees as a valuable means whereby 'Japanese cinema studies may be usefully revisited through the prism of film's relationship to other media' (p. 305).

Discussions of Japanese tradition, modernity and transnational textuality have in fact animated a number of J-horror films and critical reactions thereof. With regard to Nakata's film and its sequel what has (perhaps curiously) not been examined in any real detail is the nature of the cursed video itself, something that remains very different in the novel and filmic iterations of the story and that throws the narrative and thematic inquiry of the latter into bold relief. Where Suzuki describes at length the pictures that make up the tape, Nakata's images offer more brevity and an apparently less cohesive rationality; they are less a series of subjective projections, a succession of enigmas or clues to be decoded (at least in this first film) than they are a cryptic and connotative proto-montage. One aspect in particular throws light on the narrative as a whole, and allows one to appropriate structuralism and psychoanalysis as a means of defining its particular project. Rather than the images of a volcanic eruption that are so central to Suzuki's VHS tape the video in the film *Ring* contains the Kanji characters for eruption almost literally erupting on the screen, moving about the frame in an abstract visual approximation of an explosion (in contradistinction to the novel in which the onscreen Kanji is for mountain (see Fig. 3.1)). This is followed by a shot of several people prostrate on the floor being thrown backwards by some kind of unseen force. Suzuki (2004) describes these moments in the novel precisely:

> At one glance he could tell it was a volcano [. . .] [t]he clear blue sky was instantaneously painted black, and then, a few seconds later, a scarlet liquid spurted out from the center of the screen [. . .] [t]he images were now concrete where they had previously been abstract. This was clearly a volcanic eruption, a natural phenomenon, a scene that could be explained. The molten lava flowing from the volcano threaded its way down through ravines. (p. 75)

However as noted the film is more abstract in this significant scene, and its abstractions facilitate a discourse on language and structuralism, on the composition and corruption of the linguistic sign system, in which is inscribed the aforementioned tension or anxiety that disturbs conventional notions of both representation and reality. The aforementioned Kanji characters for eruption almost literally erupt within the frame, and in so doing become a signifier presented as a simultaneous signified, the sign breaking down and its constituent

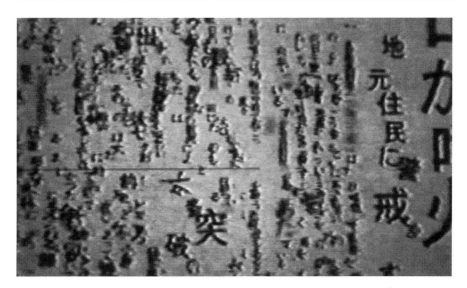

Figure 3.1   Signifiers as signifieds: problematic signs in *Ring*.

elements becoming disturbed or fragmented. The fracturing of the sign here – the presence of a signifier with no attendant signified – reflects a world whose once-familiar and tacitly understood moorings have begun to erode. As a result communication and interaction become curtailed and coldly circumscribed, and if the world cannot be apprehended or represented with any degree of certainty, if meaning becomes openly amorphous as the randomness and arbitrary social codification of signs and signification is underlined, then crucially Sadako's video calls into question modern perceptions and assumptions of what is natural or otherwise. Language is a corruptible facet of modern life in *Ring*; it is used to disguise and deceive, to confound and obfuscate. One of the two girls in the opening scene initially pretends to have seen the cursed video and to be scared of her apparently imminent death, before admitting that she hasn't, only to state again when the telephone rings that she has in fact seen the tape and is deeply apprehensive. Elsewhere the VHS itself is entirely a visual construct, and this is ultimately crystallised when the final clue to the mystery surrounding the protagonist's survival comes in a ghostly visual (rather than verbal) message, when Reiko sees her one-time partner's image reflected in her television screen, pointing out the need to copy the video in order to offset the curse.

Sadako's eruption into the world becomes a marker of a returned foreclosed, so that her appearances (which carry the marker of an apparition or delusion) speak to the victims of their fundamental Lack – the fact that they have not ascended to subjectivity as citizens of a country that itself has undergone a rebirth since its economic collapse. From this point of view the first victims being young characters – and more significantly Sadako's youth – serves to comment upon the figurative infancy that will be made manifest on the part of subsequent victims, and that defines the social landscape of *Ring* as pre-subjective, effectively untethered from the Imaginary. The arbitrary, problematic nature of language that is underlined here also reflects a further Lacanian import, a frustrated Name of the Father wherein Sadako's eruption into the world becomes a returned foreclosed (rather than a repressed due to her external materialisation) whose function is to question the collective subjectivity of a society in a state of figurative infancy and subject formation. This may also be linked to the past that Blake alludes to. In her work on *Ring* Colette Balmain (2008) takes at face value the fact that Nakata's taped images feature, or at least denote, the same meanings as Suzuki's – principally that the victims presented in the shot are struggling in the face of a volcanic eruption. However this is not necessarily the case; the people in the film's VHS tape are lying prostrate on the ground and are having severe difficulty looking forwards as they face some ambiguous off-screen force that is hurling them backwards. The suggestion that a blast of energy is washing over these people seems more prevalent than that they are prey to the effects of a volcanic blast, something that one may link back to the atomic bombings of Hiroshima and Nagasaki and the legacy of this devastating attack on Japan that ended the Pacific War (Fig. 3.2). *Ring* is not alone in reflecting on this very Japanese trauma (as will subsequently be demonstrated), but it is among the most penetrating, its import in this case being to visibly render the historical horrors that have been suppressed, forgotten, through an attack on the materiality of the human body.

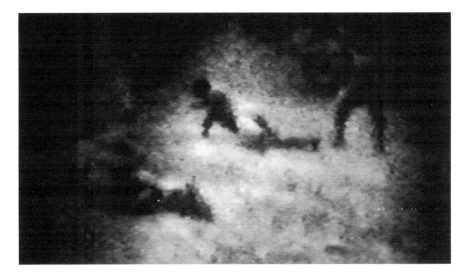

Figure 3.2   Images of a blast specific to Nakata's film of *Ring*.

Nakata appropriates the disease motif from Suzuki but transfigures the novel's global, universal fears (smallpox and in particular AIDS) into the national historical specificity of radiation sickness and poisoning in order to posit Sadako as a particularly Japanese virus, one in which a cyclicality of infection and re-infection (as cure) stands for an ongoing need to face an uncertain future (the protagonist drives down an empty road into an empty landscape in the film's final image) by confronting a corrosive past.

Consequently Nakata's film is significantly more ambiguous than Suzuki's novel, the découpage of its cursed video tape offering a discursive cinematic unit in an almost montage-like collision of shots whose juxtaposition suggests specific connotations where the individual self-contained shots retain a homogeneous and hermetic insularity. The director is thus concerned with employing, indeed foregrounding, the specific properties of his medium as a means of highlighting a key point in the narrative as a whole, the VHS images carrying a metonymic charge that helps to shape and define the antinomies suggested elsewhere as a central referent in the drama. This it does by inferring the centrality of a dialectical methodology wherein ostensible binary opposites or sites of apparent conflict are seen to merge or bleed into one another. In addition these points further reinforce the thematic salience of the climactic use of the breached television screen. It is not only a self-reflexive moment of horror and an allusion to the collapse of the two distinct Japans (past and present) that Blake discusses, it is also a frustration of the boundaries that define the world and its representation, the image becoming 'real' as three dimensions issue forth from two and diegetic and extra-diegetic distance and mutual exclusivity are collapsed. This then comes together only in the eye of the beholder; perception becomes paramount as the victim is seemingly unable to wrest his eyes from the horror unfolding before him as his realm of law and language is literally usurped by this spirit that is birthed from a technological womb. To look is to be seen looking in *Ring*, a punishment (for looking at Sadako's cursed video tape) that engages directly with the precept of the masculine gaze and the socio-cultural stratifications of gender contained therein.

Thus, rather than the socio-cultural specificity of the novel, what Nakata's adaptation stresses is a broader reflection on representation, on the vagaries of image-making as a different means of mediating reality (and not necessarily a less verisimilitudinous one). In this realm of frustrated language, to be perceived, to be seen, is to be under threat, as gazes cast directly back at the characters bespeak their objectification. The director said in 1998 of his rationale for the uncanny VHS images in *Ring* that: 'In shooting the cursed video we didn't want to give to the viewer any reference points, so there is no reference whatsoever as to where the scene is taking place, or where the light and dark are coming from' (quoted in Meikle, 2005, p. 106). In this way does the film further disturb the Symbolic order of patriarchal law, something encoded in the allusion to a fundamentally different, a phantom, POV, a look that cannot be situated in time or space. Like

Kurosawa Kiyoshi in *Pulse* (*Kairo*, 2001), Nakata here alludes to film and digital cinema (to the divergence between pro-filmic transparency and manipulation) by presenting the realism of ghosts, Sadako's specific rupturing of representational distance, as distinct from the overt images (the negative) that beset her victims. Language and images, the verbal and the visual, are both compromised as mediations of the real, leaving the world suspended in a liminal space between direct apprehension and mediation. It is about the reality of representation and the representation of reality, something developed in the sequel, *Ring 2* (*Ringu 2*, 1999), reinforced by the presence of two significant characters whose experiences and apparent paranormal abilities render them unable to speak. These characters' reticence, their fallibility, with verbal communication becomes attendant on encounters with the evil of Sadako, with a reality that is beyond their means of understanding or mediation through the realm of law and language. Again the import is cinematic; digital filmmaking is prized for its ability to be copied with no erosion of quality, for avoiding 'the generational loss experienced through duplication' (Willis, 2005, p. 6). Sadako's link to the cursed VHS tape – an analogue image that has to be perennially copied in order to spread her horror (the multiplication bespeaking monstrousness) – marks out a corruption of a past mode within the specificity of a present terror. It links her to the past, to technological antiquation, whilst locating her inside a reality that stands beyond the potential realm of (digital) manipulation, something finally made manifest when analogue image literally becomes reality.

For these interrelated thematic enquiries *Ring* is rightfully held to be at the forefront of J-horror. Shimizu Takashi's equally successful *Ju-on* films offer perhaps the other most visible face of Japanese horror cinema. Like *Ring*, these films are also concerned with an avenging female spirit and a broken home and family. In a majority of cases the spectral woman is just that, an adult lady rather than a young girl, and this aspect of Shimizu's work places it more comprehensively within a cinematic tradition of the *onryou* than Nakata's work. Much more than *Ring*, one can also place Shimizu's films within the gothic haunted house tradition, as it is through contact with the family home in which the murders took place that the grudge of the title is initially made manifest before being spread thereafter to anyone who comes into contact with it, even indirectly. However unlike the fraught duality of the spatio-temporal setting of *Ring* the narrative(s) of *Ju-on* take place in an entirely contemporary country that has seemingly moved on from (or that at least does not feel overtly encumbered with) any tragic or traumatic past. It is no less a national image in that it alludes to ongoing processes of definition and redefinition that has seen tradition eroded and a specific lineage petrified. Shimizu reconfigures the boundaries of Japanese modernity from the point of view of its pre-modern socio-political specificity in order to problematise the former and the temporal linearity that may be read as defining it. Indeed the critical commentary that has stressed the transnational intertextuality of Shimizu's films – the director's debt to American horror films – offers something of a textual correlative from this perspective, and further contributes to the effect of these most unsettling films.

From almost the very beginning of the Ju-on mythology, in the two made-for-television features *Ju-on: The Curse* and *Ju-on: The Curse 2*, the same overarching narrative events and episodic structure are rehearsed and the thematic emphasis on the nature of the family as an ideological construct in patriarchy is established in embryonic form. These two films in fact lay the foundations for much of what would go on to animate their reworkings in the subsequent cinematic features, chief in which regard is the location itself, the house that remains the locus of the horror and its ever-present ground zero. The haunted house film has been a visible if sporadic feature of Japanese horror; Kumakiri Kazuyoshi's *The Ravaged House: Zoroku's Disease* (*Tadareta ie: Zoroku no kibyo*, 2004) followed Kurosawa Kiyoshi's seriocomic *Sweet Home* (*Suīto Hōmu*, 1989) and Obayashi Nobuhiko's exaggerated postmodern fantasy *House* (*Hausu*, 1977) in offering a playful variation of films such as *The Haunting* (1963) or *The Amytiville Horror* where their lurking psychoanalytical subterfuge was made almost luridly manifest. Barbara Creed has discussed the extent to which the haunted house, particularly in gothic horror fiction, fulfils a succession of functions: as an initial place of refuge, as an uncanny space wherein the repressed is buried, and even as a symbolic representation of the womb in which characters are brought back to a foetal relationship with the mother (1993, pp. 55–8). Obayashi's film more or less explicitly affirms that its haunted house is a direct manifestation of the monstrous, cannibalistic woman who dwells within. This is particularly so given that when she disappears the horrific events begin to increase, as though she had literally become the house, whilst the fact that the narrative traces the experiences of a group of schoolgirls who have gone to the haunted building ahead of the male teacher they all have a crush on underlines a sense of an inverted sentimental education, of progress to monstrous womanhood (literally entailed in the protagonist's trajectory) defined by and inescapable from a desire for a father figure. Even the poster for the film reinforces the connection, with its iconic image of a house whose gaping door (a frequent Freudian symbol of female genitalia) has a row of sharp teeth in a literal representation of the castrating vagina dentata.

The *Ju-on* films offer a pertinent variation on this theme. In the first works of the series Shimizu is careful to depict his haunted house (the same building in every film) as both a typical middle-class residential home and, crucially, as a spatially distinct and discrete abode. The precise topographical proximity of this building to other populous environments, or indeed to anywhere else, is never made clear at any time; on those occasions where characters visit it they are simply shown traversing an apparently busy street in a typical urban centre before the film cuts directly to them arriving at the quiet pedestrian footpath on which the house is located. As a result this apparently normal residence becomes a loaded narrative symbol; it is both any or every house – signalling the fact that this specific home stands in for any such middle-class home (and whose concealed horror could thus have erupted anywhere, in any home or family) – and is also a mirror image of a typical house, a site of death whose horrific excesses amplify and throw into relief the typical tensions within such a family unit, the repressions upon which its ostensibly functional continuance is predicated.

The conceit of doubling or mirroring can in fact be seen at work on a larger scale within this film. Beside a sense of spatial demarcation is the objective correlative of gender and space, as *Ju-on: The Curse* in particular makes specific play with the concept of characters that are directly connected to a particular locale or environment. Kayako is indelibly tied to the house in which she died, to the domestic sphere, and in the first film kills only those within its confines. In this film the son, Toshio, is a harbinger of death inside the house, presaging as he does an appearance by his mother, but only becomes an overt threat in and of himself beyond the domestic sphere. It is telling that the single moment when Toshio does directly attack a victim takes place in a school, in the educational environment that should be a natural milieu for him but which has been lost or corrupted by the events within his family. Furthermore the murderous husband and father, Takeo, is only glimpsed on the outside of any interior space, out in the street following a phone call he makes to a teacher who has gone to his house to check on Toshio following an absence from school. The narrative juxtaposition of these two men is clear in that it is the latter (named, perhaps tellingly, Kobayashi) who became the object of Kayako's romantic affections, something that in turn led to the rage on the part of her husband that facilitated the murders and begat the titular curse. Moreover it is whilst visiting Takeo's home that Takeo himself goes to Kobayashi's house and murders his pregnant wife, the destruction of one family being matched and mirrored by the desecration of another about-to-be familial unit.

The follow-up to *The Curse* expands on its predecessor by contravening the intrinsic norms that its forebear so pervasively established, so that it not only elaborates on the first film but seems to answer it, to extend its narrative and thematic parameters in order to pose questions as to the boundaries that defined that film's characters. Paramount in this regard is the fact that Kayako now appears outside of the family home, becomes a threatening presence beyond the domestic sphere that had earlier appeared to contain her. This spectral female is here not only spatially unrestricted – which has a dual meaning in that she not only now appears in a different space but also transcends physical reality within these locations – but has also undergone exponential bodily multiplication. When she attacks a victim inside a school at the end of the narrative (the sole survivor of the family that was murdered by the ghosts in the first film) there are a number of Kayako facsimiles, ghosts clothed in white with long black hair, as though she has reproduced or given birth to spirits precisely like herself. The fact that birth seems to signify copying here, physical equated with mechanical reproduction, is particularly significant with regard to Kayako's monstrous femininity, her centrality to physical reproduction as the bearer of life extrapolated as an almost technological reduplication that signals its essential monstrousness.

The fact that Kayako multiples exponentially outside the home alludes perhaps to the perceived amplification of the threat posed by women in the social and professional sphere (something underlined by the fact that a young female teacher is a victim in the first *Curse* film). Here it is a quasi-apocalyptic scenario that, like the one already established in *Ring*, constructs and positions female Otherness as a perennial facet (or fact) of her being: irremediable; inexorable, indefinite. This exponential growth on the part of Kayako also affects other characters in *Ju-on: The Curse 2*; Toshio too appears as an overtly threatening presence beyond both the family residence and the school, here featuring as a more directly dangerous entity when he appears in the home of an old couple (the parents of a character from the first film). Furthermore, just as Shimizu extends Kayako's presence, magnifies her body and physicality through her incessant reproduction, so he figuratively curtails that of Toshio. The ghostly child's body is in this film increasingly fragmented, visually dismembered, as much as to suggest the extremity of his physical Otherness, which is amplified here in his first appearance in this location, where only a part of his face is visible through the floor of the living room of the elderly couple. The very sight of the spectral child here is enough to facilitate the deaths of the old man and woman, suggesting the primacy of perception and perhaps the extent of the generation gap affecting their country (the gulf between past and both present and future). Indeed throughout the *Ju-on* series Toshio is the one ghostly figure that does tend to feature as a typically supernatural presence: that is, in a way that transcends corporeal physicality. Scenes such as the one in which a woman ascending her apartment building in an elevator remains ignorant of the child visible on every floor that she passes, or the child suddenly appearing in a car in the opening scene of *Ju-on: The Grudge 2*, demonstrate this, and reinforce the 'neoconservative fear of the body' (Sharrett, 2004, p. 13) that has been proposed as a defining element of some J-horror films. The extreme physical Otherness of the child from this point of view directly expresses an anxious sense of bodily difference, of the young male proto-subject tied directly to his mother in a failed Oedipal trajectory that suggests a potential sexual Otherness to add to and thereby to amplify his perceived threat.

This reflection on the confines of gender in modern Japan is expanded upon in *Ju-on: The Grudge* and particularly its sequel *Ju-on: The Grudge 2*, which both reflect and refract the themes of their forebears. Women become much more overtly central in these films, their narrative situations and trajectories reflective of a more thorough engagement with traditional perceptions of gender. In the first there are three different generations featuring in the film's first two chapters alone. The narrative begins with a voluntary social worker calling at the house of a family only to find an elderly woman, one suffering from Alzheimer's disease, living alone amidst her own filth and squalor. The situation that she has been facing is elucidated in the following story when her family comes into the spotlight; she lives with her adult son, a salaryman, and his wife, who is charged with her care whilst her husband goes out to work in a typical picture of gender division and hierarchy. It has been noted that the horror in this film comes from a contravention of Japanese tradition, most obvious in which regard is the elderly and infirm lady left entirely by herself in the family home. Respect for the old has long been perceived to be a central facet of Japanese society, vertical relationships of *Sempai-kōhai* (the hierarchy of the family over the horizontal relationships with colleagues of the workplace or the classroom) being described by Roger J. Davies and Ikeno Osamu as an ongoing facet of Japanese life (2002, pp. 187–94). And indeed on the surface such a reading would appear to be legitimated by the development of the respective narratives of the *Ju-on* films in which traditional gender roles are taken for granted – indeed in which the breaking or contravention of these on the part of Kayako may be seen to have facilitated or released the horror in the first place.

This reading of the film is, however, a reactionary and limiting one, based as it is on a perception that Shimizu's narrative (either implicitly or explicitly) laments the apparent loss of tradition and continuity in Japan; in other words that the enduring, ceaseless force of the horror in the film arises from the corrosion of the family unit and thus by extension the narrative reinforces its normative status as the centre of Japanese society, its inviolability. There is in truth some validity to this argument, as the disintegration of the family may be seen to result in the terror that spreads throughout all the films, but one may posit that this family, which is destroyed through a contravention of patriarchal social 'law' when Kayako begins to desire another man, is a fallible and perhaps anachronistic institution whose subjugation of women facilitated Kayako's subjectivity in the desirous gaze that she cast beyond the confines of the ideological centrality of the family home. The argument by Robin Wood and others that the horror film has typically maintained a critical stance towards hetero-normative society has animated many of the most significant commentaries on the genre. However for Shimizu both progressive and conservative elements seem inexorably intertwined, almost symbiotically connected, to the extent that a tension between them echoes the fact that Japan is caught or suspended in a liminal space: again a state precariously situated between past and future.

It is this particular ambiguity that reinforces the gothic aspect of many J-horror films. The persuasive arguments by Michael Blouin (2013) that Shimizu's first *Ju-on: The Grudge* film in particular may best be characterised as gothic can perhaps best be exemplified through this facet of its narrative. Clive Bloom (2007) has characterised the gothic as a genre by analysing its frequently unstable, divided, at times almost schizophrenic ontological subterfuge, a dualistic entity in which liberal features can often be found alongside those more conservative or recuperative features (within patriarchal capitalist hegemony). There are certainly several more overtly reactionary J-horror narratives; Tsuruta Norio's *Premonition*, for example, features a male protagonist who (like the lead in Suzuki's *Ring* novel) works incessantly at the expense of time with his family, but who, following the death of his daughter, finds himself in possession of information about tragic events before they occur and must ultimately reconnect with his family to offset impending death. But Shimizu's work typically offers little that is overtly regressive or otherwise, something that is fed by the formal properties of the films. What is meaningful is not necessarily the a-linearity but the way in which the films bluntly jump both forwards and backwards in time with little if any sense of a narrating present from which to demarcate either prolepses or analepses. That is, there is only a nominal present tense in the narratives, and as a result one finds an ambiguity over temporality that works to suspend the respective films in a timelessness and thus stresses the extent to which the characters (and by extension the subject, the corrosive family unit) exist out of time – that is, as a pervasive and ever-present aspect of modernity. The films' abstract pictures of contemporary Japan – with no temporal anchor in any clearly defined present tense and a concomitant lack of any spatial clarity to mark out a concrete or recognisable urban milieu – reinforce this particular aspect of the films. As such the collective picture across the *Ju-on* cycle is one of Japan caught in a cyclical rather than a linear temporality, a progression that is a simultaneous regression, and this sense of time become increasingly important to the series as it moves beyond its first instalments.

Ju-on: The Grudge 2 concerns itself even more overtly with female characters, with victimised and monstrous femininity, and it is through this route that the aforementioned sense of time becomes particularly marked as this sequel narrativises the fractured structural a-linearity of its predecessor. The protagonist here is Kyoko, who as the film begins is several months pregnant, a situation that she seems somewhat less than happy about, looking awkward and snapping back when asked by her partner about whether she has told her employers about her pregnancy. This opening scene sees her and her fiancé driving on a deserted road late at night, and the appearance of Toshio first outside and subsequently inside the car precipitates an accident that causes Kyoko to miscarry and lose her baby. In point of fact it is immediately prior to the aforementioned dialogue that the presence of a ghost is signalled through a washed-out POV shot following the car, following which Kyoko is on the verge of telling her fiancé something important about their baby when they appear to run over a cat and the protagonist first glimpses Toshio. In other words his appearance is directly linked to the emotional state of the protagonist, the spectral child in this particular context becoming a clear marker for and manifestation of this character's terror of children, of her hesitancy, if not aversion, to her impending motherhood. The accident is thus an enactment of her anxiety over her pregnancy, perhaps her unconscious desire not to become a mother, and Shimizu establishes this as a concern of the film as a whole when a shot of blood running down Kyoko's leg as she lies in the wreckage of the car cuts to the film's title page, in which dripping blood (figuratively Kyoko's from the previous shot) incrementally spells out *Ju-on 2*. Blood is at once a signifier of menstruation (and thus cyclicality), of injury and the threat of death, and, given Kyoko's situation, of the promise (or threat) of birth and of life through its connection to the broken water that signifies the beginning of labour.

Fear or anxiety over impending motherhood and the resulting crystallisation of her own nuclear family are then magnified at the end of the film when, following the revelation that she is still pregnant, Kyoko goes into labour and literally gives birth to Kayako. This startling image not only cements the trajectory of Kyoko throughout this particular film but in fact has retrospective ramifications for its forebears in the *Ju-on* films that preceded it. The look of the spirits, their translucent milky-blue colouring and (at least on Kayako's part) the splashes of blood about their person that seem to signify the abjection of death and physical decay, here carry connotations of newly born children, infants covered in amniotic fluid and daubed with the blood of the mother's body. The aforementioned nature of Kayako's peculiar physicality – the fact that she cannot seem to walk but rather awkwardly crawls or drags herself on all fours – in addition to the strange croaking that stands in for her infant-like lack of facility with language, also reinforces this aspect of the film's imagery, and suggests that the perennial rebirth associated with the film's curse is linked directly to the monstrous feminine. *In Ju-on: The Grudge 2* in particular the bodily trauma of childbirth, of the beginning of life, is here combined with that of death and the end of life to create a complex sign whose signification combines nominally contrastive signifiers with an unstable or amorphous signified. Here, as is Sadako in *Ring*, Kyoko and Kayako are joined in being situated further beyond the linear realm of law and language within the regenerative site of womanhood that has not only literally defied masculine power (from the point of view of returning from death) but also male potency, in that Kyoko conceives or is impregnated without the involvement of a man – indeed her fiancé is a notable absence throughout the film, initially comatose and subsequently in an entirely catatonic state that renders him completely inert and unable to act in any way.

This proliferation of abjections all relate to woman's reproductive and maternal functions. Birth is discussed in detail by Kristeva and Creed as a central feature of the abject. For the former the body of woman is already located outside patriarchal and patrilineal normality, and childbirth further draws direct attention not only to what man is not (physically, biologically) but also to the boundaries between inside and outside the body, between the clean and the dirty, and even between human and animal. Creed argues that:

Her ability to give birth links her directly to the animal world and to the great cycle of birth, decay and death. [. . .] The dichotomy of pure/impure is transformed into one of inside/outside [. . .] a more sophisticated perspective in that categories of pure/impure are no longer seen as a simple opposition exterior to the individual. (1993, pp. 47–8)

The locus of Creed's analysis of birth and the horrific womb are those films like David Cronenberg's *The Brood* (1979) or Ridley Scott's *Alien* (1979) in which the mother and/or the womb is an overtly monstrous excrescence, akin to a tumour or cancerous growth, which clearly mark out female difference as an unnatural affront to the normative realm of patriarchy. In *Ju-on: The Grudge 2* there is no such visible deformity or physical anomaly; Kyoko goes into labour in hospital in desperate circumstances but there is no visual marker of abnormality until Toshio appears (chanting 'mother' over and over again in a way that could be addressing Kayako or taunting Kyoko), after which the *mise-en-scène* becomes ominously darker as diegetic lights in particular begin to fail in the face of the abject event about to take place. She literally gives birth to Kayako (the similarity of names a signifier of a commonality of monstrousness) in an ostensibly normal pregnancy that crucially becomes the site of horror and abjection (Fig. 3.3). The natural biological process is transfigured into a foreboding event, following which, it should be noted, Kyoko does find herself a mother to a female child who goes on to kill her in public, begetting a monstrous femininity that perpetuates as the films ends.

Motherhood and maternity are, then, overtly horrific in this sequel, with

Figure 3.3   Giving birth to Kayako and monstrous femininity in *Ju-on: The Grudge 2*.

Kyoko ultimately being punished for her apparently desired eschewal of her traditional gender role and her wish to continue her career – which, significantly and as a correlative, has seen her narrowly, and to her dismay, regarded as a mere horror queen. Moreover it is significant that Kyoko's mother appears as a character in the film, and her death is, uniquely for this film series, not directly situated at the hands of the spirits, remaining as it does entirely undramatised by Shimizu. She is found apparently asleep by Kyoko, and only after glimpsing Toshio does Kyoko think there is anything wrong and find that her mother has passed away. It is thus a representation of a natural cycle of life and death, contrasting with the death and rebirth found elsewhere in the narrative, and this is reinforced by the *mise-en-scène* that places this character in a lineage, a tangible history, as her living room is tellingly full of pictures of the past, of her ancestors. Kyoko's status is juxtaposed against her that of mother, a contemporary womanhood placed beside its traditional mirror image, and given this gender-based imperative, vision and looking become significant thematic cornerstones (of the series as a whole). Drawings of an eye predominate in the scrapbook that Kayako has kept, reflective as these are of the desirous gaze that she bears, the looks that she casts at another man beyond her husband (and which remains only that – her extra-marital feelings are never consummated). More overt are the sporadic visions across space and time, looks into the past and the future when characters in the haunted house bear witness either to another character in the house at a different point in time or to events that have already transpired within. The theme of accursed sight has currency in Asian horror cinema, with films like the Pang Brothers' *The Eye* (*Gin gwai*, 2002) – whose commercial success spawned two sequels – and *The Child's Eye* (*Tung ngaan*, 2010), the Indian film *Naina* (2005), the Thai film *The Unseeable* (*Pen choo kab pee*, 2006) and the Hong Kong horror pastiche *My Left Eye Sees Ghosts* (*Ngo joh ngan gin do gwai*, 2002), and here it emphasises looking as a central aspect of the narrative. The overarching story that structures *Ju-on: The Grudge 2* revolves around Kyoko hosting a documentary that is being made about the house at the centre of the curse, and Shimizu interestingly blurs the distinction between the film and the film-within-a-film that is sporadically shown in production. There is a scene (featuring Kyoko) that appears to be a straightforward set-piece but is subsequently revealed to be a horror film in which she is appearing, and this self-reflexivity calls attention to the mechanical look of the camera as distinct from those of the women within, as though the latter were usurping the typical masculine bias of the former.

Shimizu Takashi has on several occasions had productive recourse to self-reflexive horror. Two of his films revolve around the making of a feature film. In addition to *Ju-on: The Grudge 2* there is *Reincarnation* (*Rinne*, 2005), about a young actress in a horror film haunted by the horrific events that inspired the production, further to which his *Marebito* (2004) explores and indeed narrativises digital technology in its story of an amateur cameraman named Masuoka who is obsessed by capturing human fear on film, a quest that leads him into the bowels of Tokyo and into a labyrinthine underground world. These films variously contrast, correlate, even directly align human and technological looks, and thus engage with the classically sutured notion of the connection between the diegetic and extra-diegetic male gaze(s) in order to mount a pointed reflection on and critique of mainstream cinematic practice and its processes of passive objectification. If the spirit of Michael Powell is inexorably called to mind in such a project, then it is solidified by *Reincarnation* and *Marebito* featuring male characters who, like *Peeping Tom*'s (1960) Mark Lewis, record their own horrific acts, which in both cases entail the murder and/or mutilation of their families. *Reincarnation*'s dual narrative focus sees the 8 mm recordings of real atrocities mirrored by its doppelganger in the form of a 35 mm cinematic makeover, and thus positions the young female protagonist in a liminal space between different iterations of male power: between the murderous patriarch on the one hand and the film's director on the other (whom Shimizu paints as an unsympathetic, bullying figure). *Marebito* in its stead extrapolates from its protagonist's mental collapse, his interior breakdown, to position its fantasy as both a negation and an amplification of the domestic dilemmas that come increasingly to light as the film develops. From this point of view the literal spatial descent that forms the crux of the narrative is clearly a manifestation of a journey into the unconscious as Masuoka's family disintegrates and his vision, his gaze, becomes at times literally indistinguishable from that of his ever-present camera.

The heavily intertextual narratives already implied in both *Marebito* and *Reincarnation* further underline their concern with received images. The former conflates references to Richard Shaver, H. P. Lovecraft (the underground world is referred to as the 'mountains of madness'), Werner Herzog (Masuoka talks of a girl he finds underground as his Kaspar Hauser) and Tsukamoto Shinya (who plays the lead) whilst the latter is set largely in a hotel where both the murders and the filmic reconstruction thereof are taking place in a direct reference to *The Shining* (1980). The effect of this narrative methodology is to inscribe into the films a tension between the known and unknown, knowable and unknowable, the nominally normal and the uncanny. They each presuppose a world that is not only always definable through images but one that is also reducible to them, as though it would not, could not, exist apart from the fact that it is represented: a postmodern post-mortem and a theme that is extrapolated in *Pulse*, perhaps Kurosawa Kiyoshi's key contribution to Japanese horror cinema. Indeed it is arguably the key J-horror film. It both encapsulates and transgresses the paradigmatic face of this genre as represented by *Ring*, Miike Takashi's *One Missed Call* (*Chakushin ari*, 2003), or *Tetsuo: The Iron Man* in that it appears to engage with technological modernity as a locus of terror, and with new technologies, especially the Internet, and the effect they have on the fabric of society. Moreover, as in the *Ju-on* films, the vision here is of a fundamental powerlessness, a helplessness in the face of something amorphous that can barely be defined, much less comprehended. Here however there is no mystery to be solved or overtly evil force to be repelled or expelled, no individual past trauma or tragedy being visited back upon an unsuspecting protagonist; there is, rather, a national repressed, and one may thus read the scenario as a working out of tensions relating to subjectivity in modern Japan. In this sense *Pulse* can be productively juxtaposed not only with its immediate J-horror contemporaries but to such ostensibly disparate predecessors as Hitchcock's *The Birds* (1962), the Val Lewton RKO film *I Walked with a Zombie* (1943) or Lucio Fulci's *Zombie Flesh Eaters* (1979), in which the horror becomes a manifestation of the precariousness of human existence, of the potential chaos underlying the fragile and tenuous order with which humanity lives and against which it must struggle to define itself. All the young protagonists of *Pulse* lead isolated and insular lives; they all live alone, interact at work or university on a largely prescriptive and professional rather than a personal basis, and the perennial presence of mobile phones and the Internet exacerbates personal alienation and disconnection. One of the two main protagonists, a young woman named Kudo Michi, comes from a broken family, only sporadically sees her mother and has no contact any longer with her father, whilst the other, a student named Kawashima Ryosuke, begins using the Internet seemingly in lieu of having any friends, and does this, he says, because everyone else is doing it and he wants to fit in.

Robin Wood has noted of *The Birds* that the unexplained attacks on humans by the titular animals may be conceived of as a manifestation of the tentative nature of the social order that the largely superficial Melanie Daniels blithely ignores: that is, they represent a view of the sudden, not always explicable forces in life that can at any time strike one down, and that can only be (partially) offset or held at bay through the formation of meaningful relationships (Wood, 2002, pp. 152–72). This reading may be seen to have particular relevance to Japan given the country's economic collapse at the end of the 1980s, the abrupt way that its prosperity and stability was eroded to leave the nation suddenly suspended over a precipice, and it is for this reason that the final words of the film, spoken in voiceover by Michi, transgress her uncertain circumstances and refer to her having found happiness with her friend (Ryosuke, whom she meets by chance as both characters attempt to flee Tokyo when traumatic events begin to escalate). The formation of personal friendships and relationships is paramount as a means of survival, of coping with loss and devastation as markers of the unpredictability of modern life, and this devastation is fully realised and of particular thematic import. The impending end of the world in *Pulse*, described by Jay McRoy as 'one of the bleakest apocalyptic visions in contemporary Japanese horror cinema' (2008, p. 161) offers a vision of Tokyo in near ruins, apparently abandoned by its population and with its buildings aflame. It is as though the horrors of the destruction wrought on the capital by intensive firebombing during the Pacific

War were being played out once again – something reinforced by the anomalous image late in the film of an American army cargo plane crashing to earth – or its spectre of national desolation had returned to punish a nation that has failed to progress or move in any meaningful way beyond the horrors of the past. One might even see the film as depicting the ghost of WWII, a notion that is supported by numerous passages throughout the narrative. In particular the strange shadows that are left when people die in *Pulse* – vague outlines of corporeal form seemingly imprinted on the wall or floor where the person died – correspond to an infamous image of the likewise charred remains left following the atomic bombing during WWII when a single man's remains were left following his incineration.

This doubling, this historical doppelganger, further pervades the style of the film. 'Reality' in *Pulse* is constantly mediated through images; the first sound heard in the film is the sound of a computer modem loading, whilst soon after a nominally transparent interior shot is suddenly subject to interruption and distortion as though it were an image on a monitor. Moreover the prevalence of frames-within-frames – most frequently windows – that tend to dominate in the typically long, static takes that are used in a majority of dialogue scenes show the protagonists encased within a figurative image, an internal reduplication that becomes redolent of the potential threat of imagery, of becoming an image in the sense of being removed and distinct from other people. Indeed one scene with Michi and her co-workers employs a *mise-en-abyme* of their deceased friend Taguchi sitting at his computer, and thus presents a series of identical visual replications of reality all contained within the one image. This sense of constricted space not only heightens tension and threat when the characters venture outdoors, where they seem exponentially more open and exposed, but they also bespeak a postmodern 'reality', indistinguishable from images thereof. In a key scene towards the end of the film Kawashima flatly refuses to believe in the material presence, the reality, of a ghost that confronts him in one of the so-called 'forbidden rooms' in which they enter the world. He ultimately charges towards the spirit in the belief that his ghostly interlocutor will dematerialise; however to all intents and purposes his outstretched hands come into contact with a corporeal form, a physical reality. This ghost repeatedly states 'I am real' as he moves in closer to the terrified protagonist, and Kurosawa employs a (for him rare) optical POV shot so that the spirit, in looking directly at Kawashima, also looks directly at the audience, challenging and admonishing both diegetic and extra-diegetic spectators to acknowledge its presence and as such to redefine their horizons of perception and realism (for the latter a realism as defined in cinema and on film). It is a warning about images and unreality, and the boundaries between visually discrete spaces is reinforced through Kurosawa's typical recourse to prominent inter-compositional frames that offer a veritable panoply of figurative screens that divide the pro-filmic space. These demarcated realms then refer one to the discrepancy between image and reality. As the world depicted in *Pulse* is increasingly destroyed there is a concomitant rendering of that world through images, as though the former's erosion was enacted through a proliferation of representations that collapse any clear way of distinguishing said world from that through which it is mediated. In other words the narrative echoes the discursive and practical sphere of digital photography in that the ability of film to render a pro-filmic space (as distinct from a digital production's creation of a diegetic world that is not necessarily tied to a phenomenological referent) was at stake as a site of contestation or challenge. Indeed the fact that the ghosts figure as perennial images – as two-dimensional beings subject to the apparent visual distortion typical of online pictures (something further underlined by the aforementioned sound of a computer modem that aurally accompanies the spirit that assails Kawashima) – underlines Kurosawa's critical engagement with digital filmmaking and its relationship to cinematic realism (as opposed to mimetic reality), and it is in this sense that Kurosawa engages in the technological discourse that many commentators have read into the film: so that it is the cinematic landscape of new technology, of digital filmmaking, that becomes the locus of any perceptible criticism, with the ghosts as analogue beings with an attendant reality and transparency that throws into relief the 'horror' as pertaining to a present that is divorced from the past.

However the film is not just a 'critique of the technologies dominating late capitalist culture' (McRoy, 2008, p. 166); it is, more prevalently, a questioning of the human subjectivity behind such technology. The fact that there is nothing inherently evil in the ghosts in *Pulse* is key in this regard. They are not the malign, vengeful entities that Nakata and Shimizu envision, and it is notable that their 'victims' may well be seen to bring about their own deaths. They all commit suicide rather than actually being killed by the ghosts, and indeed the most common ghostly refrain heard throughout the film is 'help me', so that they not only pose no immediate threat but moreover are reaching out for aid or for connection. Jim Harper (2008) has discussed the extent to which this fundamentally benign nature is more common in Japanese literary and cultural depictions of the supernatural, and in Kurosawa's narrative it is the extent to which people are able (or, more markedly, are unable) to assimilate or accept these beings that leads to a threat to their existence. Ghosts in Kurosawa's work are almost never directly threatening beings; they are arbiters of, variously, guilt – as in *Séance* (*Kōrei*, 2000) or *Retribution* (*Sakebi*, 2006) – of oppressed or subjugated selfhood, as in *Loft* (*Rofuto*, 2005), even of alienation or disconnection, as is the case with the brief appearance of the protagonist's dead best friend in the otherwise resolutely non-horror film *Bright Future* (*Akarui mirai*, 2003) – and in *Pulse* they represent the Lack in the characters' lives that has either been realised or that the characters have attempted to fill in with new technologies.

The stress placed on what is real in *Pulse* then facilitates a psychoanalytical reading of the film, and refers one back almost inexorably to Lacan. In theorising a model of subject formation he designated the first realm of infancy as the Real stage, the stage in which nothing is absent, a world outside of and beyond language that remains without borders and thus without difference, without Otherness and without Lack. It is what Elizabeth Grosz (1990) defines as 'a natural order' but one that is, crucially, 'capable of representation or conceptualisation only through the reconstructive or inferential work of the imaginary and symbolic orders' that follow it (p. 34). From this point of view *Pulse* dramatises a scenario in which pre-Imaginary pre-subjects are made aware through contrastive inference of a world without differentiation, lack or fissure and in which awareness of difference has not been reached. Harue's disillusionment over an apparently alienated population – her assertion that, fundamentally, people and ghosts are the same – crystallises the film's representation of the Real as a site of sameness, of a stage that does not recognise Lack, but does so with the acknowledgement that this is a retrospective delineation undertaken from the perspective of a shattered Imaginary.

The illusory separation of the latter stage – the sense of a distance from the idealised Other – is frustrated directly through encounters with the spirits that are made manifest almost perennially as Othered beings: through their pallid looks, physical two-dimensionality and especially their strange, jerky movements. Figured thus, the encounter with the ghost, the Other, that assaults Kawashima in particular towards the end of the narrative represents a progression towards the Mirror stage wherein the misrecognition of the complete, autonomous ego ideal as a separate being facilitates a tension between the two, following which the child must identify with the image and in so doing establish objectification and an acceptance of Lack and separation. Mastery of the body and particularly entry into the Symbolic law that is language perennially frustrates the characters here; on more than one occasion they stumble backwards and fall to the ground, unable either to speak or to control or coordinate themselves and are as such constructed directly as infants. As Elisabeth Roudinesco (2003) has said: 'when the subject recognises the other in the form of a conflictual link, he arrives at socialization' (p. 30), and it is indeed this 'socialization', or abortive, vain, attempts thereat, that Kurosawa appropriates, with the slippage between the respective states redolent of an absence of 'normal' social subject formation. Russell Grigg (2008) has demonstrated the extent to which certain psychotic subjects can perform what Lacan termed 'foreclosure'; that is, they can abolish aspects of reality, particularly pertaining to his conception of subjectivity, by internalising the signifier of the 'Name of the Father' (pp. 6–10), and through this there can be slippage between the three states that define the path towards subjectivity. Grigg states that, 'when he [Lacan] declares that what has been foreclosed from the symbolic reappears in the real, it is marked by the properties of the imaginary' (p. 10), and it is precisely this inferred presence of the Real that the ghosts draw attention to as the protagonists find themselves frustrated by the Imaginary and Symbolic stages, so that rather than a Freudian return of the repressed one may in *Pulse* theorise a return of the Real. The ghost's assertion that 'I am real' could be amended to 'I am the Real' to the extent that he, they, represent the appearance (constructed from the perspectives of the problematised subsequent stages) of this realm of sameness and need as a marker of frustrated subjectivity. The fact that foreclosed signifiers return as something external to the proto-subject further reinforces the spirits as a manifestation of a compromised subject formation, and posits a world in which the 'Name of the Father' is an anomalous concept (literal fathers, it should be stressed, remain entirely absent from the narrative).

As Lúcia Nagib, Rajinder Dudrah, and Chris Perriam (2012) have argued, the 1990s saw a decentralisation of hitherto academically popular psychoanalytical constructions and conceptions of audience interpellation. However in the context of the new millennium and on the threshold of the digital revolution, Kurosawa here reclaims such a model as a means of understanding and commenting upon cinematic representation both old and new as a key structural antinomy. Interestingly from this point of view Kurosawa went on to almost decry psychoanalysis as a framework for organising salient narrative tenets. His existential thriller/fable *Doppelganger* (*Dopperuganga*, 2003) collates both Freud and Lacan in a playful example of the extent to which cinema is built on the foundations of psychoanalytical theory. It is another Kurosawa film that posits a world in which apparently ordinary people are beset by inexplicable events and encounters (in this case with their exact double), and who in so doing are faced with a world whose surreality becomes an inextricable feature of its reality, a world in which any markers of normalcy against which to demarcate the abnormal or uncanny are almost entirely absent. Doppelgangers in fact have had quite a pronounced presence in Japanese cinema and literature, and Kurosawa's almost meta-cinematic vision here extrapolates from such generically diverse and discrete works in order to distinguish his own genre-less vision. It is, in truth, as much an absurd comedy as a horror film or thriller, and as a textual correlative of such generic indeterminacy there is typically almost no recourse to explanations about where the doppelgangers come from or what their purpose may be. Like the ghosts in *Pulse* they simply appear, are suddenly and abruptly present, and Kurosawa almost parodically alludes to psychoanalytical discourse by, on the one hand, presenting one character's double as a better version of himself (a directly Lacanian Mirror Stage image of a complete ego ideal) and on the other by having the protagonist's doppelganger behave at various moments as though he were a manifestation of Hayasaki's latent desires and frustrations, smashing up his workspace and later attempting to rape the sister of the other doppelganger victim when she seeks his help (a Freudian id as contrasted with the protagonist's superego). There is even a moment that appears to mock the dénouement of David Fincher's *Fight Club* (1999), when Hayasaki vociferously states that his double is a figment of his mind and closes his eyes in order to try and suppress the apparent physical manifestation of his unconscious self, only to find said other self whistling and ignoring him as though the very idea of a split personality perceived as two different people was beyond entertaining or taking seriously.

If Kurosawa – who has actually written a study of horror cinema (along with the director Shinozaki Makoto) – has an international reputation as a horror director then this can be traced back to *Cure* (*Kyūa*, 1997). This particular film helped to establish his international name, playing at numerous festivals around the world and solidifying a perception of him as a filmmaker who was interested in allegory as a mode of storytelling and themes relating to social decay and the limits of individuality and individual selfhood as a coherent construct. *Cure* is a serial killer film, a sub-genre of horror that achieved prominence in the 1990s in Japanese cinema with works like Ishii Sogo's *Angel Dust* (*Enjeru dasuto*, 1994), Aoyama Shinji's *An Obsession* (*Tsumetai chi*, 1997) or *EM Embalming* (*EM enbāmingu*, 1999), Sai Yoichi's *Marks* (*Marks no yama*, 1995) and Iida Joji's *Another Heaven* (*Anaza hevun*, 2000). As in other sub-genres of modern Japanese horror, the influence of comparable American films is significant, in this case Michael Mann's *Manhunter* (1986), Jonathan Demme's *The Silence of the Lambs* (1991) and David Fincher's *Seven* (1995). Indeed, Ishii's *Angel Dust* has a protagonist who, like Will Graham in *Manhunter*, is able to mentally connect to criminals' minds, to think like them and thus to help solve their crimes. However the Japanese films, which Jay McRoy points out form a relatively recent trend in the country's horror canon, offer a distinct variation on this model (2005a, p. 8). Like their American counterparts, they are typically sombre, portentous, morally complex, even morally equivocal pictures that depict crimes from which the ostensible heroes cannot be easily or comfortably extricated (Ishii's protagonist in *Angel Dust* questions her own involvement in the crimes that are committed because she was once personally involved with the perpetrator); however the Japanese films tend to be more ambiguous, wherein social decay is subtly encoded as a by-product of Japan's modernisation, its post-industrial waste. For example the lineage of the atomic bombings that ended the Pacific War and signalled Japan's surrender to the Allied forces, an event of seismic consequence to the hitherto unchallenged nation, plays a significant role in *An Obsession*. The protagonist is a detective whose gun is stolen by a criminal following a shooting in which he is wounded, and the thief suffers from a hereditary illness that can be traced back to the pollution caused by radiation. Similarly, the first three victims of the killer in *Angel Dust* are passengers on the Tokyo Metro, and moreover their murderer is a cult member who has been involved in brainwashing, which directly prefigures the *Aum Shinrikyo* cult's Sarin gas attacks on the Metro in Tokyo in 1995.

These shocking events variously demonstrated a sense of vulnerability within Japan, a feeling that the country was in a precarious state, susceptible to attack, and *Cure* stands out in this regard for its vision of a population who are infinitely fallible. The film is about a young man who seems to be able to hypnotise his ostensible victims, following which they go on to commit murder, the precise reasons or methodology for which is not clear or certain. The perpetrator appears to be suffering from amnesia; he remembers nothing of his own life and identity (not even his name), but he consistently challenges and provokes those with whom he comes into contact by turning their questions back on them, in particular by pressing them to answer 'who are you'? It is a question that perennially confuses his interlocutors but it has several ramifications for the film's thematic inquiry into personal identity, about what precisely defines a person's selfhood. Provocations about what the different characters' names and professions are figure as markers that facilitate an inquiry into selfhood. Is a person's name important to their sense of self? Does their job define who they are, or think they are, and is there a discrepancy involved here, a performance of self? Does a person's family, their city or community, even their country, contribute to how they see themselves and how they are or would like to be perceived by others? In *Cure* – the title of which remains ambiguous, opaque – personal identity is never a stable or unified concept; it is amorphous, elusive and transient as normal, professional men and women behave in ways that would appear to be entirely alien to them. But is this in fact the case? A psychoanalyst who helps the protagonist says at one point in the film that through hypnosis one cannot induce another person to act against their beliefs or morals, that they could not be persuaded to commit a crime if it were not originally in their nature to do so. All of which begs the question to what extent are the nominal victims themselves the true perpetrators of the horrendous crimes they commit? To what extent is anybody capable of murder or of other acts that contravene 'normal' morality, law and order?

Donald Richie has noted, somewhat pejoratively, that *Cure* 'is about a young man with evil supernatural powers', a particularly reductive account of a film that in fact works towards such a narrative schema in order to probe and question its validity (2001, p. 219). Indeed at the beginning of the narrative we are shown a crime being committed in advance of the 'killer' being introduced, complicating immediately any clear demarcation of cause and effect with regard to criminality. Thereafter the fact that he seems to materialise from nowhere – beginning on a beach, like death in Ingmar Bergman's *The Seventh Seal* (*Det sjunde inseglet*, 1957) – cues one to regard him as something Other than merely human, than flesh and blood. Tom Mes and Jasper Sharp have recognised something of this aspect of *Cure*, noting that the film 'explores how we as human beings hide parts of ourselves in order to live in society and how the repression of those feelings only intensifies them [. . .] [with the film becoming a] mirror that forces us to look at our naked selves' (2005, p. 106). It is certainly accurate to describe Kurosawa's film as an allegorical construct. The hypnotist in *Cure*, named Mamiya, is indelibly linked with the past, with the beginnings of hypnosis, both through his studies as a psychology student and in particular through his research into the eighteenth-century Austrian physician Franz Anton Mesmer, whose development of so-called animal magnetism was a forerunner of hypnosis and became a practice for which he was criticised and ultimately exiled from his native country. The repression of natural, perhaps vital instincts that Mes and Sharp suggest is inherent in the film's view of life within modern, 'civilised' society is related in no uncertain terms back to Japan's historical 'development'. This is also something explored by Oshima and Imamura in several of their greatest films: the notion that Japan, in its Meiji-era drive towards modernisation (Westernisation), has denied, repressed, those aspects of its social or religious specificity that distinguished or delineated it as a nation, and it is this primal force that Mamiya represents. He has forgone his name, his occupation, all precepts of personal identity as defined through extraneous factors, and in encouraging his various interlocutors to do the same he is in effect facilitating a connection to something deeper, something more tenable and more important.

Kurosawa's reverence for the processes of particularly American genre cinema (Robert Aldrich and Richard Fleischer are among his favourite filmmakers) is also evident in *Cure* – even as he goes on to undermine, even dismantle, them. He offers enough clues to be investigated, histories to be exhumed (the film is similar to some supernatural J-horror films in this regard) and character arcs to be completed to fill a conventional detective thriller. Indeed Mes and Sharp (2005) note how identification on the audience's part with the detective's plight is secured by Kurosawa, only for him to then follow Hitchcock's lead in *Vertigo* (1958) by showing said character behaving in ways that cast doubt over his state of mind and thus the veracity of his actions (p. 106). Ultimately the search for the 'killer' and for the 'answers' to his apparent crimes comes to very little; the generic trajectory of the narrative is both resolved in a traditional sense – the protagonist kills his nominal nemesis – and at the same time becomes deeply problematic because he destroys that side of himself that speaks to the aforementioned connection to something more salient than surface precepts. The point of this aspect of the film is to posit a world in which no one has fixed or stable points of reference, either as regards their personal identity or with respect to the world in which they live. Like *Charisma* (*Kurisuma*, 1999), whose ambiguous narrative features a contested tree that is said to poison all those around it in order to survive, *Cure* reflects upon, allegorises, Japan heading into the twenty-first century, a country no longer certain of any national selfhood or any clear way of defining itself or its place in the modern world. The country, like the characters, has constructed and relied on a sense of identity based around surface or superficial tenets; selfhood in this film, as in other Kurosawa works, is never a unified or coherent concept but a perennial process, a negotiation and renegotiation. *Cure*, like *Pulse* and *Retribution*, is about genre cinema more than a genre film; it is about those semantic features of narrative, characters and thematic meaning in which we place a presupposition of expectation and faith, so that the destabilising of their centrality not only reinforces a pervasive unease, a textual uncanniness in which the familiar is de-familiarised, but also by extension dramatises a world whose comfortable structures of meaning and ideology have become eroded. In other words they are not only key J-horror films but key Japanese films.

Post-millennial J-horror cinema as a generic entity is at once among the most interesting, representative and in some ways problematic models, as its semantic field has become a site marked by repetition and variation but has done so within wider fields of discourse and popular cognisance pertaining to horror filmmaking. Both Mark Jancovich (2002) and Peter Hutchings (2004) have addressed some of the issues surrounding the horror film as a genre, arguing that historically successive iterations of genre theory (from classical to structuralist and post-structuralist accounts) have typically remained unsatisfying in defining genre, implicitly saying much more about the critics than about viewers and their less stringent generic demarcations or interest in such classificatory systems. Against this the popular canon of J-horror has become such a recognisable brand, its motifs a clearly defined paradigm or syntactical delineation, that films such as Sono's horror pastiche *EXTE: Hair Extensions* (*Ecusute*, 2007) can rely on foreknowledge of its features in order to subvert audience expectations – in this case by imagining hair itself (a defining aspect of many female ghosts) to be a threatening presence, one that literally possesses individuals once they have come into contact with it. However the tension between elements apparently known and definable and those that are unfamiliar, that offer syntactical variations, if not reconceptualisations, of the genre as a whole with regard to its key paradigmatic field, is not only key to J-horror's transnationality but is significant from the point of view of how the genre is received and conceptualised. It allows a space for audience agency between the dictates of industrial regulation on the one hand (something Steve Neale (1980) in particular has written about in detail) and of critical canon formation on the other, a means by which the mass consumption of such films can be an active, inclusive and importantly ongoing process. The fact that it can be a markedly international as well as a national process is a significant point as it reinforces this sense of constant negotiation. As Altman (1999) and Alan Williams (2002) make clear, nationhood, like genre, must be a perennial site of definition and redefinition, and the horror film in Japan stands as a significant, even crucial, means for this ongoing process.

4. THE CHANGING JAPANESE FAMILY
ON FILM

The family plays a significant role in any society determining every-one's psychic and social formation according to changing historical, political, and ideological dimensions [. . .] As an institutional prop of bourgeois capitalism [. . .] the family is extremely dangerous. A case maybe made for abolishing it entirely.

(Williams, 1996, p. 14)

In Japanese studies it has often been argued, at times even presumed, that in Japan the family is a microcosm of the nation, the national body traced in the tissue of intergenerational relations within the domestic sphere. The site of often extended familial units, in which the proximity of elderly, middle-aged and young people bespeaks a cross-section of society, is not as prevalent as it once was in the country. Moreover, as Davies and Ikeno stress, the ideology of the family has become weaker in recent decades, lessening as 'patriarchism has gradually lost its power' (2002, p. 124), and the foundation of the family has shifted from the unit, the collective, to the individual. However this social paradigm, like other aspects of families as an institution, still exists as a contemporary ideal, a perceived repository of traditional values, and as such it still has value for any analysis of both Japan and its often family-centred cinema. Such discourse has increased in recent years, examining several different facets of the family and in particular the fact that it has been undergoing a fundamental transformation as regards its typical formation and the functions of and attitudes to its constituent members. Joy Hendry (2003) regards families as part of a socio-political hegemony, noting that in Japan 'the family has historically been the focus of considerable ideology' (p. 25), whilst in a 2006 study entitled *The Changing Japanese Family* Marcus Rebick and Takenaka Ayumi note that 'it is difficult to understand many of the other changes that are taking place in Japan without some sense of what is happening in families' (p. 12). Yet others have contended that a crisis point has been reached with regard to families in Japan, and concomitantly that it has been (and is still) subject to wider problems such as an ageing population, shifting perceptions and expectations of gender roles and a general decline in the national birth rate that directly affect its composition and social stability.

These often gnomic pronouncements are far from isolated. Indeed as Mike Chopra-Gant (2006) has argued it has been an international phenomenon, with social and national crises like WWII presenting specific problems for the US and the composition of its families as they struggled with absent fathers and newly working mothers. However with regard to Japan they may be taken as emblematic of a general trend that has viewed families in the country as perhaps the key site of struggle in ongoing processes of redefinition and reconfiguration that continue to shape and define the ways that Japanese conceive of themselves, both as a nation and with regard to its individual subjects. Numerous commentators – both cinematic and otherwise – have all attested not only to the centrality of the family within Japanese life but also to its contemporary problems and struggles. Indeed, it has long since become something of a cliché to draw attention to this facet of the country's social structure. Ruth Benedict's (1946) perceived seminal work of post-war socio-cultural anthropology *The Chrysanthemum and the Sword*, written as an attempt to understand 'the most alien enemy the United States had ever fought in an all-out struggle' (p. 1), explains pedantically how the family is a microcosm of the country wherein social etiquette is practised and perfected. Benedict prefigures many of those who followed in her wake when she states that 'In Japan it is precisely in the family where respect rules are learned and meticulously observed [. . .] hierarchy based on sex and generation and primogeniture are part and parcel of family life' (pp. 48–9), before going on to demonstrate how the weight and stature of the family hangs particularly over young boys when they venture out into the world. A supporting view is offered by Sugimoto Yoshio, who has elaborated upon what is known as the 'family system' in Japan, an institution 'which penetrates into the life of every Japanese and controls it in a fundamental way' (2006, p. 146). Named *koseki* (literally: family registration) it is a means by which each household is registered as a family, with everyone therein as part of the household and defined on record as such. *Koseki* information is then required whenever any member of a family enrols in or applies for any important membership, employment, etc., and it is underpinned by an ideological apparatus named *ie*, which represents 'a quasi-kinship unit with a patriarchal head and members tied to him through real or symbolic blood relationship' (p. 147). This ideological system (which bears some similarities with Confucianism) has been regarded by some Japanese – especially Takakusu Junjiro (1906) – as a defining feature both of Japan's success and of its singularity. But it has also at times been seen as a problematic institution, and more recently a potentially reactionary and antiquated model that in some ways facilitates what Timothy Iles refers to pejoratively as a recourse to the family in defining 'the root of national malaise' (2008, p. 81).

Ian Buruma concurs in finding familial life, especially the bond between mother and son, a relationship that 'seems to foster passive dependence' (2001, p. 20), and similarly describes how Japan's families remain primers for the ways in which children are indoctrinated into 'social graces' (ibid.). It can feel as though families (along with schools) offer a production line of ready and willing young adults who can take their alloted role in the workplace and indeed in society, and such is the pervasive nature of this received wisdom, its widespread comprehension and acceptance, that Izuhara Misa has been eager to challenge it as a means of defining the modern face of the country. In a study of the chang-ing relationship between families and the state she notes that 'there is no such thing as a universal type or structure to describe "family"' (2006, p. 162): that, in effect, there is no longer (if ever there was) any tenable model of family life and relationships in Japan, any single means of conceiving of, and by extension of representing, Japanese families.

One must also contend with the fact that life for the Japanese has typically remained unstable. The country has been, and continues to be, open to wide-spread fluctuations and disasters (both natural and otherwise), which is why the 'patterns' described by Donald Richie as a central facet of Japanese life and culture have been so pervasive (1962, p. 42). In a country that was in the 1990s already undergoing its most significant changes in almost half a century (the bursting of the bubble economy and death of Emperor Hirohito in 1989 in addition to the sarin gas attacks by *Aum Shinrikyo* on the Tokyo subway of 1995 that followed the Great Hanshin earthquake in January of that year), it is little wonder that fami-lies have returned to something like a social lionisation. As such the (arguably) less overt but far more fundamental shifts in family and domestic life already noted began to be felt as a destabilisation of hitherto hegemonic structures that impinged upon personal and national identity. The more recent tragedy of the Tohoku earthquake, Tsunami and the resulting disaster at Fukushima in early 2011 (something that has been the subject of more than one family film already) further crystallised the tenuous nature of Japanese life as at the mercy of larger forces that could strike at any time and throw it into turmoil. And with this in mind the attendant need for familial structures to offer some measure of respite or stability becomes especially pronounced and important, and accounts to some extent for the recent upsurge in these films, the fact that they have once again begun to make their presence felt in Japanese cinema.

A forthright statement such as Izuhara's begins to cast light on the ways in which family life has been conceptualised in Japan. As noted it also underlines the potentially problematic nature of many of the broad historiographies on Japanese cinema that have typically drawn on such familial narratives in order to examine how Japanese filmmakers have engaged with the society and culture in which they were working. This discourse appeared in the earliest accounts in Anglophone criticism as a marker of the extent to which it was deemed necessary to open up and explain Japanese cinema as a product of Japan, not only of the country's socio-cultural specificity but also of the Otherness of its artistic landscape. Those studies of the 1970s that are often taken to be seminal texts – especially Noel Burch's *To the Distant Observer: Form and Meaning in the Japanese Cinema* (1979) – variously describe and examine this manifest cultural standardisation whereby so-called 'bulwarks of tradition' (p. 75) remain steadfastly in place even after significant prolonged exposure to the West and to post-war, post-occupation American ideological imperatives. Several such books position the family as a sacrosanct entity, microcosmic in make-up and cinematically salient as a means of defining Japan onscreen, of situating daily life in the country as a site of representative tension and socio-political anxiety. Joan Mellen's *The Waves at Genji's Door* (1976) reads a simple binary opposition of conservative and radical precepts within competing classical and new wave visions where the family is the chief point of departure. Mellen relies on a socio-political anthropology to contextualise her work on the major directors, themes and subjects to have defined the country's filmmaking, prefiguring her study of familial representation with introductory remarks about the lineage of familial relations in the country. She notes that 'filial piety in Japan dates from the Chinese *Hsiao King* and has always involved much more than reverence of one's parents or ancestors' (p. 313), and goes on to define the national imperative of such discourse, of the family replicating and working to uphold the government in power. The problem of these kinds of assertions, especially as they go on to inform the author's analysis of such diverse directors as Ozu, Ichikawa, Susumu Hani and numerous others, is that it tends to preclude any sense of a potentially complementary or contrapuntal interest in the material realities of family life in Japan. It offers an essentialist perspective wherein aforementioned perceptions of the singularity of the Japanese – both their pronounced difference from other nationalities and, concomitantly, their commonality within and across the country – becomes an *a priori* fact or received wisdom.

With very few exceptions (the outstanding example being Robin Wood's (1998) detailed work on Ozu's Noriko trilogy), Mellen and Burch have remained largely unchallenged and uncontested. In marked contradistinction to the former, and despite a section of his book *Currents in Japanese Cinema* being devoted to 'The Family', Sato Tadao (1987) tellingly refuses any such sweeping pronouncements; indeed he draws attention to ways in which particularly masculine behaviour within families directly contravenes any image of the father's status as a microcosm of the Emperor and thus of the family as a synecdochic symbol or construct (pp. 124–60). And herein can be found some of the key changes or embellishments that throw light on contemporary iterations of this form of the *gendai-geki*, or contemporary drama. According to Keiko I. McDonald 'Japanese cinema had fixed its attention on family relations from its earliest days' (2000, p. 221). However there have been particular eras in which it has predominated, in which the *shomin-geki* genre of predominantly middle-class domestic life (Bingham, 2012, p. 304) has become predominant in Japanese filmmaking. Traces of this patterning can be found in the 1930s, 1950s and 1980s in particular, and 1990s' and post-millennial films in many cases carry the weight of this intertextual lineage. Perhaps most overtly the late Ichikawa Jun consciously set out to echo Ozu Yasujiro with films like *Dying at a Hospital* (*Byōin de shinu to iu koto*, 1993), *Tokyo Siblings* (*Tōkyō kyōdai*, 1995), *Tokyo Lullaby* (*Tōkyō yakyoku*, 1997), *Osaka Story* (*Ōsaka monogatari*, 1999) and *Tokyo Marigolds* (*Tōkyō marigōrudo*, 2001), the very titles of which clearly signal their debt to the director of *Tokyo Story* (*Tōkyō monogatari*, 1953) and *Tokyo Twilight* (*Tōkyō boshoku*, 1957). In these films Ozu is in fact a structuring absence, the ghost of his cinema being invoked in order to define the frequently family-less social landscape of his narratives – his common pictures of young protagonists in search of meaningful relationships – as a contrastive face of contemporary Japan.

At the opposite end of this spectrum one finds Yamada Yoji's remake of *Tokyo Story*, which connotes the ongoing significance of this particular filmmaker. *Tokyo Family* (*Tōkyō Kazoku*, 2013) is a reasonably faithful, at times reverent, reworking of Ozu's most famous and acclaimed film, the impetus behind which arises from updating the documentary aspect of his forebear's work, wherein the resolutely contemporaneous settings record events, attitudes, emotions, relationships and socio-cultural ephemera as a by-product of a narrative focus on everyday lives and domestic tensions. The landscape of Yamada's film contains details both peripheral (the May 2012 opening of a new landmark in the Japanese capital) and seismic (one character talks about volunteering during the clean-up operation following the Fukushima disaster) to locate its narrative firmly in Tokyo circa 2013. This offers a potent backdrop to a picture of family relations in Japan that is tied directly to their milieu at a specific juncture, both in negative and positive ways. The elderly mother, Tomiko, is comfortable with her mobile phone, yet when she and her husband need to take a taxi to their son's home after their youngest child Shoji has gone to the wrong train station to collect them she is entirely unfamiliar with the driver's satellite navigation and begins to direct him via a hand-drawn map. At the same time Shoji's ignorance of where the bullet train stops proves that Tokyo can defeat its younger residents as well as its elderly visitors, suggesting something of its development over time. More seriously, the journey to Tokyo for the elderly parents still contributes to the wife's death, but Shoji also says that he met his fiancé whilst helping at Fukushima, whilst a poster for the aforementioned landmark (the Tokyo Skytree) features prominently in the home of the eldest son Koichi, suggesting not only a pride in Tokyo, in their home city, but also perhaps a postmodern imperative where this household (about whom the youngest son complains because they never go on trips anywhere) consumes images in lieu of 'reality'. In this the portrait of the city becomes predicated on an imaginary contiguity. Yamada tellingly eschews Ozu's scene during Shukichi and Tomi's touristic tour of Tokyo in which their guide points out from a high vantage point the different directions in which their children live. In *Tokyo Family*'s titular city its contours cannot be mapped as clearly as its people, to which end its social landscape appears to have changed in the sixty years since *Tokyo Story*. However the gulf between city and countryside is still prevalent, as is the attendant disconnect between generations, the inconvenience of the visit amidst the busy professional lives of middle-class Japanese and the apathetic disinterest of the new generation. The elderly parents are here less sentimental and naïve than their counterparts in Ozu's film, particularly the more obstinate and temperamental Shukichi, but in replacing the widowed daughter-in-law Noriko with the engaged son Shoji Yamada finds prospective families more readily available and visible than Ozu.

That Yamada also copies some (though by no means all) of Ozu's singular cinematic style is also a defining feature of *Tokyo Family*, though potential problems also stem from such an approach. The director – who like Ozu has spent almost his entire career at Shochiku studios – retains the elliptical narrative structure, eschewal of transitions other than straight cuts, frequent low camera height, pillow shots (though these are less frequent and offer more cutaways to narratively salient details) and compositions of his progenitor. Unlike Ozu, though, the inexorably second-hand sensibility of Yamada's film can but make it feel like a self-reflective rumination on cinema rather than a direct engagement with Japan or its contemporary social landscape. From this point of view, references to Fukushima in particular seem a little forced, cheap, or even offensive, there to offer a parallel to Ozu rather than to engage with the crisis itself. Yamada does, however, include enough small changes and minor details to avoid appearing slavish and thus antiquated in his depiction of familial relations. He even has fun misleading those in his audience who know *Tokyo Story* by heart. The first scene in both films in which the elderly couple stay with their middle child, the daughter Shige, features said daughter and her husband pondering over where to take her parents. In Ozu's narrative the husband suggests a *Naniwabushi*, a traditional song-based entertainment, and Yamada (who eschews this suggestion) cuts from the scene at Shige's to a classical theatrical performance, apparently facilitating a belief that the parents have been taken to a performance only to reveal that rather than an outing for them this is in fact a dress-rehearsal and that Shoji works as a set designer at the theatre. Here Yamada complicates any clear demarcation between tradition and modernity as exemplified by older and younger generations, something reinforced later in the film when Shukichi's reunion with an old neighbour leads to their getting drunk in a bar and making so much noise that they disturb all the younger clients, who promptly leave the establishment in disgust. He thus shows that social roles are not fixed, even as those pertaining to the family appear inviolate, and it is the slippage between the two that defines the narrative here. Donald Richie has said of Ozu that his 'characters are family members rather than members of a society' (1974, p. 1), a remark that seems even more pertinent to *Tokyo Family* and its immediate context defined by apparently secure familial units amidst a more amorphous and divisive social space, a literal topographical uncertainty born from such technological advancements as satellite navigation.

If, as Ozu himself said (quoted in Masazumi and Yamane, 2003, p. 146), *Tokyo Story* is one of his most melodramatic films then the aforementioned postmodernity of Yamada's aesthetic affirms *Tokyo Family*'s demonstration of the extent to which the cinema of Japan has become an arbiter of familial relations as a social barometer. This almost meta-cinematic (meta-Ozu?) film lays bare the prevalence of images of families as offering an inherently fictive picture, an ideological construct and a means of mediating rather than reflecting reality. This is in fact a key point that other filmmakers have implicitly exemplified as part of their intertextuality. Koreeda Hirokazu has similarly enshrined Ozu, domesticity and the quotidian practices of daily routine. His fourth feature, *Nobody Knows* (*Dare mo shiranai*, 2003), marks his first direct engagement with literal family life, as well as with insular young protagonists and their complex relations with older generations – something that has gone on to characterise such recent films as *I Wish* (*Kiseki*, 2011) and *Like Father, Like Son* (*Soshite chichi ni naru*, 2013). *Nobody Knows* is built around children left alone by their parents, in this case around four young children who are all but abandoned when their single mother leaves the family home to be with her new partner. The oldest of the children, 12-year-old Akira, assumes responsibility and becomes the nominal head of the household, taking care of and providing for his three siblings (who are all by different fathers) by whatever meagre means are available to him. Unlike the aforementioned films, however, Koreeda's style and narrative register in *Nobody Knows* is resolutely naturalistic. It is, paradoxically, comprised of an almost magniloquently observational style that matches the exaggeratedly quotidian aspects of the story and indeed that serves to implicitly highlight its director's somewhat complex relationship to the family drama. The younger children remain encased within the apartment whilst Akira ventures out to obtain money and to haunt the city outside his door as a figurative ghost, someone wrenched from the world before his time and left to fester as a nobody, a boy whose transient identity is accrued from fragments and external sources. In this he is a typical Koreeda protagonist; he is, like the characters of *Maborosi* (*Maboroshi no hikari*, 1995), *After Life* (*Wandāfuru raifu*, 1998) and *Distance* (2002), removed spatially from a secure environment (his 'family' has only just moved into the apartment where he is to live as the film begins) and as such is abstracted from any known or comfortable space. Almost all specific-ity is drained from the narrative, from places as much as people, and similarly the family becomes an increasingly abstract entity, the point of which narrative methodology is to locate the film within a tension between specificity and univer-sality. *Nobody Knows* is based on a real incident that made national headlines in Japan, yet Koreeda stresses its status as pure fiction from the outset (in a caption that is among the first things to be seen and which presents a paratextual sign of unreality and of artistic licence). Moreover with its emphasis on urban anonym-ity and observational aesthetic it seems to offer a picture that could be taken as any family in any Japanese city, but at the same time the vagaries of its depiction of masculinity and femininity – its inattentive, irresponsible fathers and neglect-ful, selfish mothers – present a very specific picture of dysfunctional parents that amplifies the discourse concerning the erosion of the traditional family unit.

This, in addition to Mitsuyo Wada-Marciano's (2012) argument that Koreeda deftly conflates feature and non-fiction modes of filmmaking, means that *Nobody Knows* occupies a fault line between competing signs and systems. From this perspective one may underline what could be termed the ordered disorder of Koreeda's structure, which throws his portrait of familial relations into bold relief. The entirely character-driven story seems to depict a world thrown wholly out of orbit, one populated by protagonists who remain in a state of transience and instability, yet the careful construction embeds an abundance of rhyming moments throughout the narrative that serve to instil a formal patterning. For instance the youngest children at the very start of the film are smuggled into their new house in a suitcase so as not to alert the landlord to their presence, and this portends a darker moment at the very end when the youngest girl, Yuki's, death necessitates the removal of her body in precisely the same manner in which she arrived, whilst the framing event of a journey to the airport to bury her lends a circularity to the narrative, of arriving full circle and completing an arc where one family unit is replaced by another as Akira and his new girlfriend seem to become surrogate parents to the former's siblings. Moreover the freeze-framed final shot of all these characters works like Truffaut's in *The 400 Blows* (*Les quatre cents coups*, 1959) – another story of a young boy tenuously held between child-hood and adulthood – to petrify time's inexorable forwards march into a future that remains resolutely uncertain, untenable and impossible (see Fig. 4.1).

This pervasive sense of opposing or contradictory forces held in (tenuous, tentative) check relates to the precariousness of the family both within *Nobody Knows*, an institution caught between fragmentation and an attempt to negotiate a space for continuation, expression and growth. Like the flowers that the chil-dren try to grow on their tiny balcony their family needs nourishment and care, needs individuals to play their allotted role in order to sustain it. Indeed to this end, rather than a film about the complete obfuscation of the family unit, *Nobody Knows* is about childhood negated but a family tentatively and problematically

Figure 4.1   The freeze frame that ends *Nobody Knows* and that recalls *The 400 Blows* (note the youngest sibling tentatively looking back toward the camera) by capturing a liminal moment between a problematic past and an uncertain future.

upheld, or at least the concept or idea of a family, of a guardian taking care of younger charges who cannot look after themselves. The younger children's fundamental adaptability – the fact they seem to carry on with their lives without overtly or continually questioning their predicament – connotes something of the familial foundation that survives even their abandonment by their mother. Similarly significant is the fact that as a protagonist Akira finds himself thrust into a role that negates his adolescence, just as his mother negates the role of parent that she is (by society, by her family) expected to fulfil. Indeed her behaviour around her children is often akin to that of a friend or sibling rather than a parental figure, and in particular she often abdicates responsibility to spend time with her daughters. The weight of the familial in this regard is something that she ignores, as though she is an adolescent herself, and it is this that Koreeda's narrative methodology underlines. It amplifies the ordinary, domestic details of everyday life as they appear to the children, where the space of the (family) home defines the horizons and the limits of their world. Cutaways to close-up shots of activities like washing clothes or dishes, dialling the telephone or turning on a light bespeak the domestic sphere and the actions that regulate day-to-day existence in this space that now for the first real time fall to the children, who thus have a new weight conferred upon them. At the same time they also foreground such daily amenities that are generally taken for granted but are ultimately denied the children when their money begins to run out and the household bills cannot be paid, resulting in a loss of electricity and water services. Koreeda juxtaposes these activities, along with an attendant use of generally tight interior compositions, with a preponderance of long and extreme long shots (often taken from a high angle) when Akira goes outdoors, a stark contrast of interior and exterior space that is at once a means of delineating this character's anonymity once away from the home environment and his fundamental inability to ascend to the position of social subjectivity that is thrust upon him.

Koreeda's work as a whole exists in a particularly marked relationship with Japan's cinematic past. At times in *Nobody Knows* the faint ghost of Ozu is discernible in the director's (infrequent) recourse to broadly definable pillow shots that bridge scenes and allow a measure of both distance from and contemplation of the unfolding drama. There are also moments when, as was typical of Ozu's methodology, non-diegetic music accompanies only the transition shots, helping to make of them an almost narratively autonomous unit, a discrete, transitory schema whose status as such helps define the stasis of the children's lives. Akira himself finds his own natural path as an adolescent becoming more marked – he befriends a group of boys and enjoys playing computer games with them, and later he meets a girl with whom he begins a close friendship – and with this he becomes caught between two worlds. As, indeed, does his mother, although the shockingly casual manner in which she deserts her children, apparently seeing little if anything wrong in her actions, bespeaks her lack of reflection on or misgivings about her situation, about her parental responsibility. On the single occasion when she briefly returns she berates Akira's father for not giving her eldest son enough money, as though her family's well-being were not really her primary concern. Motherhood in this context is at once a particularly heavy burden, a cross to bear, and a nuisance to be cast away, familial responsibility falling (at least in the mother's eyes) upon the typical, traditional social agency of masculinity rather than the perceived domestic site of the feminine. This is not really designed to openly challenge traditional gender roles on Koreeda's part; there is no special pleading or overt moral imperative, little if any tangible sense that the director is presenting a synechdochic narrative. Rather the point of the film is that this particular situation exists as an extreme potentiality in modern Japan, a litmus test for the viability of the familial in modern Japan as opposed to a complete or representative negation of it.

More recently the aforementioned *I Wish* may be seen as a lighter, seriocomic mirror image of *Nobody Knows*. It is similarly concerned with a broken family as seen from the point of view of young children – in this case one with two estranged siblings who live in different cities following their parents' separation (one with each parent) – and there is a comparable emphasis on the potential childishness of adults and the attendant adulthood of children. The title of the film relates to a perceived miracle that is rumoured to occur at the precise moment when two bullet trains cross paths at a particular location. If a wish is made at this time it is purported to come true, and the two brothers and their friends make a pilgrimage to this site in order to cast their various desires to the wind in the hopes of securing their realisation. One of the brothers has always desired the reunion of his mother and father and thus a rebuilding of his broken family, but he ultimately accepts the situation as it stands and refuses to wish for change. It is a story of growth and maturation, of discarding unrealistic dreams and desires not only as an intrinsic part of growing up but also of being a member of a family, an institution that does not necessarily exist as an ideal but which is not therefore to be negated or destroyed.

The contrast between *Nobody Knows* and *I Wish* – between an extreme scenario presented with a documentary veracity and a more common, everyday picture developed within a lighter, ostensibly fictive narrative register – is reflective of a spectrum of representations of Japanese families by Koreeda wherein a clash of nominally dichotomous elements underlines the fact that families in Japan are not of a piece, not adherent to a homogeneous model. To this end perhaps his pre-eminent contribution to the family drama is a film that reconciles these apparently contrastive poles and that in so doing seeks to offer a thorough consideration of families in modern Japan. *Still Walking* (*Aruitemo aruitemo*, 2008) served to establish a model that Koreeda has followed in most of his subsequent films: namely a depiction of familial reunion following a period of distance or estrangement. The film concerns a fraught family meeting over the course of a single day and night (a ritual in memory of a deceased relative) and almost immediately signals its concern with the past through its pervasive intertextuality, its references to Japan's cinematic lineage. Most overtly Koreeda appropriates the scenario of Itami Juzo's *The Funeral* (*Osōshiki*, 1984) whilst at the same time making broader references to the work of directors such as Ozu and Naruse as representative of successive generations of family drama and *shomin-geki*. The latter can be seen not only from the fact that Koreeda's scenario concerns a wake but also in that one of its concerns is tradition and modernity, which accrues here around a generational contrast and malaise, the clash of an older generation living in rural Japan with perhaps a limited understanding of their city-based offspring, whose lives are perceived to be fundamentally different. The device of the wake also refers one back to Itami's film, from which Koreeda lifts almost wholesale a comedic scene concerning the annual visit to the parents' home paid by the young man whose life the dead son, Junpei, saved at the expense of his own. After paying his respects at the shrine in the living room, which necessitates a formal pose on a *tatami* mat, he rises quickly and immediately stumbles and falls due to the lack of feeling in his legs from the uncomfortable material beneath him. This directly echoes a moment in *The Funeral* when, after sitting for a prolonged period of time in a cross-legged position listening to a Buddhist sutra, one man abruptly stands to answer a telephone and promptly falls due to cramp. For Koreeda, though, the point is less about the incompatibility of tradition and modernity, the anomalous place of the spiritual in the materially oriented present. Rather, given the contrastive context and the character's young age, coupled with the fact that he is in this instance respectful of the ceremonial tradition of which he partakes, the implication is that such a tradition retains a use value, that modernity must be reconciled with tradition. Moreover this comedic point is enlarged upon and potentially complicated elsewhere in the narrative when one middle-aged female character remarks that the design of her house is such that it precludes having any rooms for *tatami*. She is in fact desirous of moving her family in with her parents and in so doing of remodelling the house, but her mother is resistant to the idea, wanting to live out her life with her own space and not, as she suspects, as someone beholden to the domestic whims of her daughter. The elderly couple here are more circumspect, less naïve and sentimental, than their counterparts in *Tokyo Story*, with a practical outlook that bespeaks their more comfortable position, their harmony within their own lives, which are distinct and separate from those of their children.

The fact that the story here sees the city-bound children visiting their rural parents rather than vice versa marks the extent to which Koreeda uses *Tokyo Story* as a point of departure in delineating his own particular thematic space. There is, as in Ozu, a tension here between parents and children, something that is especially pronounced between the middle-aged Ryo and his father, but it is of a different order to the subterfuge of distance and disappointment in Ozu's film, more pronounced and sharply focused around the notion of patriarchal succession wherein the latter bemoans his lack of an heir to his small family practice as a doctor (the allotted role of Ryo's deceased brother). The father's desperate desire to bequeath his profession to a new generation offers a less positive view of the negotiation with and continuation of history and tradition – a sly nod to Koreeda's own position *vis-à-vis* Ozu – and of the need for a life, an identity, away from that defined by the collective of the family unit. At the same time Ryo's professional uncertainty and insecurity, the struggles he is having as an art restorer, negate any clear sense of an easy or comfortable alternative to the almost gravitational pull of the family.

Stylistically *Still Walking* provides a sharp contrast to *Nobody Knows*. The film is characterised by a preponderance of largely static long shots and long takes that in effect offer an ostensibly stable frame. However this stability is frequently offset by a pervasive sense of often chaotic movement within. There are frequently several different generations engaged in contrastive actions across all planes of the image, and the camera's stasis is implicitly marked as incommensurate to either following or focalising the drama that unfolds within its borders. The sanctity of the frame that one finds in Ozu, something often retained through the use of frames-within-frames designed around the then-prevalent Shoji screens of the traditional Japanese home, is not observed by Koreeda. Instead several of his characters rupture said frame through their incessant movement through and beyond its confines, with the camera's often observational distance suggesting its fundamental inability to capture or elucidate the full subjectivity of the protagonists. As a mirror to the aforementioned individual tensions the effect of this methodology is to frame the family and all its myriad, disjunctive constituents as a protagonist in and of itself whilst at the same time not disavowing its fractiousness, the messiness that seems to be its chief characteristic. That is, by refusing any analytical découpage the film effectively refuses any point of view other than its own, refuses to privilege any particular character or centre of focalisation. These characters, when in proximity to one another, are defined primarily by their familial relationships. But it is implied that this is a different state wherein their respective actions, interactions, emotions, attitudes – indeed their very selves – are curtailed, where they seem to become different people.

In a further echo of Ozu the sense of limitation and restriction inherent in the static camera makes it possible to productively break from such self-imposed strictures and thereby to infer meaning through a creative breaching of intrinsic norms. There are several instances in *Still Walking* where an overtly mobile camera becomes a means of thematic signification, paramount in which regard are those moments associated most clearly with the deceased family member Junpei. On an outing to visit his grave the scene begins with a static establishing shot before cutting to a lateral tracking shot that takes in the cemetery before coming to rest on the family members tending the gravestone. As in Ozu's *Early Summer* (*Bakushu*, 1951), the moving camera here calls attention to itself through a concomitant lack of pro-filmic motion; its movement is untethered, autonomous, contrastive to its earlier immobile observation of the chaotic physical trajectories of the various family members and now motivated to move by other than purely functional means and in a way that contrasts with the stasis of its subjects. It becomes a motif, one that is subsequently repeated when a butterfly enters the home that the elderly mother believes to be the reincarnated spirit of her dead son. Here Koreeda employs a handheld camera that follows the mother as she moves haphazardly around her living room trying to apprehend the insect and catch the soul of her beloved deceased child. The camera's more personal, intimate and sympathetic treatment of this character at this particular time, as it were when she is at her most vulnerable, most obviously removed from her otherwise practical self, attests to the need for interpersonal relationships and structures to support and nourish individuals: in other words the need for a family, although once again this ideal is not sentimentalised as the elderly woman's relatives here do not really attend to her so much as they remove the butterfly from the house without paying her too much mind.

Narrative motifs also abound in *Still Walking*, ones that further underline the film's antinomy between idealised and actual family relations. Chief in this regard are those of cooking and eating. Like another significant modern family drama from Japan, Kawase Naomi's *The God Suzaku* (*Moe no Suzaku*, 1997),

Koreeda's film opens with the readying of food prior to being cooked – in this case the elderly matriarch and her daughter preparing a meal. The almost metronomic sound of vegetables being peeled and scraped precedes any images, establishing an insistent tempo or pulse that offers an aural counterpoint to the stark emotional violence to come, before the very first shot details this action in close-up, isolating it in lieu of an establishing shot as a means of underlining its significance, both its denotative and metaphorical import. Thereafter at several junctures either the preparation or the consumption of food becomes a narrative kernel, facilitating the coming together of the family members and thus providing a platform for airing their various contrastive views and perspectives. It is at once a marker of the quotidian detail in the film, of Koreeda's desire to root his drama in the recognisable routines and rituals of everyday life, but it also becomes redolent of the contrast between constituent parts, as it were ingredients, and the whole. Just like the meals whose careful and attentive preparation is repeatedly dwelt upon, a family unit with its often disparate constitutive individuals must similarly be taken care over, attended to, even though the rules for preparing the latter are entirely lacking, the recipe in this case an impossibility.

Junpei, the deceased member of the family at the heart of *Still Walking*, the son and brother of the chief protagonists, is a key figure in the film. A present absence, his shrine in the living room of the parents' home is a central feature of the drama not only to the extent that it facilitates the gathering but also in that he is a barometer against whom other characters are judged, especially by the elderly couple. It is as though death has perfected as well as petrified him. Unlike everyone else (i.e. those still living), he remains the ideal, the already idolised son and heir to his father's surgery who cannot disappoint or frustrate his family. They worship him and treasure him even over his siblings, something made explicit in a scene in which the whole family gather in the garden to be photographed. As they all make their way out of the house the camera remains focused upon the aforementioned shrine in a static shot through which the family members pass as they leave the living room (Fig. 4.2). The fact that Junpei is frozen in time, as it were static and immobile, throws into bold relief the concept of still photography as a means of capturing, crystallising or immortalising a single moment. It is an attempt to overwrite or negate the inexorable ebb and flow of time, but even this relatively small moment becomes unattainable as the already irascible father becomes even more frustrated with being manoeuvred around the frame and storms off in protest. In this way Koreeda contrasts movement and stasis, the petrified perfection of memory and the messiness, the instability or chaos of living and of perennially coping with frustration and disappointment, with the fallibility of being alive and being human, of still walking. Being a family for Koreeda in this film means reconciling oneself to imperfection and to failure, to accepting others as they are and not demanding that they be other than themselves. The film's insistence on what are comparatively petty problems and frus-

Figure 4.2   The still centre of a storm of movement. The perfected and petrified memory of a deceased son/sibling at the heart of *Still Walking*. Note the apposite title of the film.

trations over and above grand traumas – something highlighted when the elderly mother casually tells her husband that she is aware of a past instance of marital infidelity on his part (something that she seems to have accepted and moved on from and which plays no further part in the story) – reflects a sense of family life as a site of daily struggle rather than of grandiose melodrama or a preponderance of life-changing events.

It is here that the aforementioned complex temporality of the film becomes especially marked, where the present as an uneasy coalescence of problematic past and uncertain future becomes particularly prevalent. Ultimately, when the main drama of the film is revealed to be in the past tense, when Ryo notes in voiceover narration that his father and mother passed away only a few years following the events in the narrative, the concept of flux and impermanence becomes central, pertaining as it does to the need for harmony in the here and now in order to better guard against and deal with the uncertainties and travails of (modern) life. The fact that Ryo has in the final scene of the film cemented his own family unit by having a child with the woman he remarried attests to the extent to which he has taken this on board. Moreover it is significant that the setting of this dénouement is once again Junpei's grave, and that it sees Ryo repeat a gesture performed earlier by his mother, that of pouring water on his brother's gravestone to cool him in the summer heat. He honours and indeed appropriates the actions of his family, synthesises his past into the present (much as Koreeda does through *Still*

Walking's cinematic intertexts) and steps into a more secure future, coming full circle as signalled through the bracketed panoramic shots of the town replete with a train, a paradigmatic Ozu motif, moving steadily across the frame. Alan Tansman has discussed the significance of the train in Japan and its cinema, stressing its significance for 'social linkage and cohesion' but also for facilitating social disconnection through allowing physical movement and spatial displacement (2001, p. 157). This tension is recalled at the end of *Still Walking*, as the train hints at both coming together and separation, unity and dislocation, and in this way points forwards to the inevitable future for Ryo's own family, indeed for any and every family, as time flows inexorably forwards and children grow and move on with their own lives. If the film is about 'rebirth and reconciliation' (Osenlund, 2011, p. 55) then it also acknowledges that to reconcile oneself to a family and a heritage is a difficult, if potentially unavoidable and necessary, experience. In this it is about more than simply individuals, it is about Japan.

The canonical position of Ozu is a demonstrably central feature of the family drama. This is reflected not just in films like Ichikawa's, Yamada's and Koreeda's but in those works that react against his style and methodology, something that became evident in the increasingly thriving independent cinema of the 1980s that, like the new wave before it, used the golden age filmmaking of Ozu (and others) as a point of departure. Films such as *The Family Game* (*Kazoku gēmu*, 1983), Ishii Sogo's *Crazy Family* (*Gyakufunsha kazoku*, 1984), *The Funeral* and Suo Masayuki's *Abnormal Family: Older Brother's Bride* (*Hentai kazoku Aniki no yomesan*, 1984) all worked variously satirical and parodic variations upon their forebears in order to narrativise the gulf between modern Japan and the country that was documented by Ozu and his contemporaries. Indeed as Kirsten Cather (2010, p. 133) has noted, Masayuki intended his film to be a sequel to Ozu's *Late Spring* (*Banshun*, 1949), whilst Itami's debut examines the weight and implacability of a Japanese spiritual tradition, something exemplified by the aforementioned scene in which the ceremonial formalities are presided over by a Buddhist priest (played, tellingly, by Ryu Chishu) whose protracted and apparently rambling sutras make proceedings increasingly difficult for the mourners who find it all but impossible to sit still in the standard kneeling position. This decade's subversive exaggeration of the *shomin-geki* had been prefigured in the by a series of darkly comic films by Ichikawa Kon – especially his adaptation of Tanizaki Junichiro's *The Key* (*Kagi*, 1959) – and this trangressive alternative tradition of the family drama is reflected in some of the more esoteric post-millennial films. Indeed, as with the *jidai-geki*, some of the most significant additions to the family film have been made by directors not typically associated with the subgenre, and chief in this regard is Kurosawa Kiyoshi and his *Tokyo Sonata* (*Tōkyō sonata*, 2008). The lack of literal, certainly complete and stable, families in this director's films is an important aspect of their textual and narrative make-up; they figure as structuring absences that throw into relief usually a personal, existential odyssey, and the protagonists of *Tokyo Sonata*, despite belonging to a nominally complete household, are no less alienated, especially the father Sasaki Ryuhei. This character's recent unemployment (something that he conceals from his wife and children by pretending he still has a job and leaving the house every day as though to go to work) is a humiliating and emasculating experience. Masculine agency and attendant notions of patriarchal control are significant aspects of the film, something that has ramifications with regard to the ideology of *ie*. Ryuhei increasingly begins to act irrationally, even violently, at home when he thinks that he is being defied by his sons, especially the youngest, Kenji, who has to take piano lessons in secret following his father's refusal to allow him to learn, whilst Kenji's older brother Takashi similarly defies his father when he decides to enlist to fight alongside America in the war in Afghanistan in the Middle East (an important signifier of masculine agency defined in and by violence, something that affects Ryuhei in the domestic context).

The individual trajectories of each member of Ryuhei's family are traced by Kurosawa but, like *Nobody Knows*, the film is far from random in its narrative structure. From its telling, symbolic opening moments inside the family house when a storm begins to encroach on the domestic space, the film traces the diverse narratives of the father and his two sons but perennially returns to the home in order to anchor the drama and orient it around the domestic space and thus to draw a contrast between their respective lives outside the home and their lives within it. Each character faces a specific crisis pertaining to their individual need to define themselves *vis-à-vis* their family. The lack of agency and authority that characterises Ryuhei's travails outside the family home feeds into the aggressive, even violent, temperament and actions that he displays whilst with his family, the defiant assertions regarding the law of the father that he ostensibly assumes but cannot live up to. The fact that he further demands to be recognised as an authority figure for his sons underlines this aspect of the narrative, and seems to be a displacement of or a substitute for the lack of power and control in his professional life. This then dictates the perceived rebellions of his sons, whilst his wife Megumi – who is kidnapped following a failed robbery on the family home by a man not unlike Ryuhei (a professional man recently left unemployed) – is made to question her commitment to the family and the expectations of her domesticity therein. Kurosawa then goes on to compare and contrast these characters and their actions. The aforementioned juxtaposition between Ryuhei and the burglar is extended and refined subsequently in the film. After the former has lost his job at the beginning of the narrative he sneaks into the family home through a window rather than using the front door, an allusion to his shame and perceived failure, and this action is later performed by the criminal when he attempts to rob the same house. Indeed Kenji also sneaks into the house at a crucial juncture – following a piano lesson that he believes he should not have attended – thus extending this motif to encompass a variety of variously transgressive actions that together contribute to a view of masculinity as inexorably tied to sites of work and profession, to spaces outside the home. Now however, in post-bubble economy Japan, they are incommensurate even to these spheres of identity and subjectivity, linked to Kenji in order to stress their status as figurative children as well as their fundamental homelessness within their country.

Here, then, unlike the closed and corrosively insular families depicted in the 1980s, in which the family was typically assailed from within, it is especially vulnerable to attacks from without, from outside its borders. The family remains at the behest of wider social structures, and Takashi's involvement in the US war in the Middle East is from this perspective a national correlative, Kurosawa slyly commenting on the perception of the family as microcosmic nation that has often fed the *shomin-geki* genre. These separate threads come together in the final act of the film when several temporally concurrent and dramatic stories, each one distinct from anything that has gone before (and each one a self-contained micro-narrative), begin and play out beside one another. Kurosawa's editing during these scenes, cross-cutting between them, takes on a different sensibility, separating them formally from the rest of the narrative in order to stress the challenge these stories and actions present to the collective (however tenuous) that was depicted earlier in the narrative. The film is edited such as to make the stories collide into each other, cutting abruptly from one to the other at key moments (typically directly on action when a character is involved in physical activity) in order to underline their commonality and explicitly to present them as contrastive actions, variations on a theme. Moreover the fact that each of the stories concerns criminality in one way or another – Sasaki finds an envelope of money in a public toilet, Kenji tries to help a friend run away from home before attempting to do likewise himself and being caught hiding in the luggage section of a coach and arrested, and Megumi is taken hostage – bespeaks a sense of transgression, of denotatively breaking the law but more perhaps more significantly of the erosion of the Lacanian law of the father. The men commit crime here whilst the woman is a victim of crime; however it is Megumi who becomes a narrative agent, becomes proactive rather than simply reacting to what befalls her (as the males each do). Both Ryuhei and Kenji are stopped in their tracks by the intervention of others – the former being knocked down by a car in the street as he aimlessly flees with the money he found, whilst the latter is apprehended and arrested by the police – whereas Megumi is faced with a situation in which she herself takes control. She at first willingly acquiesces with her kidnapper in driving away from the house, and ultimately they arrive at a beach apparently some distance away. By this stage the criminal has broken down emotionally and Megumi is free to ponder her situation and her fate, and she makes the unilateral decision not to continue to run away but to return to her home and her family, to dedicate herself to working through her problems rather than taking the easy way out.

She usurps the primary narrative agency, and in so doing she both re-inscribes the centrality of the family and asserts its validity, or at least its continuance, on her own terms.

Against Kurosawa's other, more overt, manifestations of the apocalypse in such films as *Pulse* (*Kairo*, 2001) and *Charisma* (*Karisuma*, 2000), the sense in *Tokyo Sonata* is that the continuation of everyday life, of the minutiae that comprises day-to-day existence, remains the most potent struggle. The musical terminology that is lent to the title of the film finds an obvious point of narrativisation in Kenji's prodigious talent for the piano, and further in the final scene in which he performs Debussy's *Clair de Lune* as an audition for a school of music. However it carries a charged and thematic meaning if one considers that it is a solo performance, a mark of (positive) individuality that stands beside and indeed against the enforced communality that elsewhere seems to define the horizons of life and identity for the characters. The fact that we do not learn how his performance was received, whether or not Kenji was granted admission to the school, reflects a sense of playing for its own sake, for pleasure rather than for pragmatism or profit, a means to a potential future end and a career. In this the film further undermines the capitalist aesthetic depicted pejoratively elsewhere in the film, particularly in the vast numbers of men sporadically seen at the job centre and at the soup kitchen frequented by Ryuhei. It also points to a positive masculinity not tied directly to work and capital but rather attached to pleasure and creativity, although at the same time it also links him to his teacher, Kaneko, who is a recently divorced woman working to support herself by giving piano lessons to local children. This then provides another objective correlative, this time to Megumi, the housewife contrasted with a woman whose enforced professionalism seems to offer a picture of a viable alternative to traditional family life and the agency of the male. Kenji and Kaneko together offer a surplus of meaning that is not tied directly to patriarchal authority, and it is thus significant that they both be invoked directly in the film's open ended dénouement as it means that their stories seem free to develop as they are, to remain uncontained within the traditional familial and patriarchal model; to find a measure of personal space away from its strictures.

Koizumi Kyoko, who plays the put-upon housewife Megumi in *Tokyo Sonata* features prominently in a comparable role in another key modern family drama. Toyoda Toshiaki is another director not associated with the *shomin-geki*; however *The Hanging Garden* (*Kuchu teien*, 2005) directly prefigures *Tokyo Sonata* in that it is also built around a nuclear family variously struggling with a wife's problematic domesticity, her husband's professional dilemmas and two children who are in different ways discontent. In Toyoda's film this messy reality is pervasively ignored by the mother, Eriko, who is obsessed with cultivating the perfect family. She remains preoccupied with smiling perennially in the face of adversity and believing in lies until eventually they become the truth, so that her happy family becomes akin to the title's Babylonian namesake – a myth, and it is this particular tension – between façade and apparent reality – that structures *The Hanging Garden*. The narrative begins with an assertion that the Kyobashi family keep no secrets from one another; its opening scene shows mother, father and teenage son and daughter sitting around the breakfast table talking about the places in which the latter were conceived, whilst subsequent mealtime discussions include the father, Takashi's, habitual consumption of pornography and his sex life with Eriko. Reinforcing this tension, as D. J. White (2011) has recognised, are the mirrored spaces of the family home (especially the dining room) and the love hotel. The latter (the same one in which the children were conceived) is frequented by Takashi and, at different times, both his teenage children, though neither of the latter engages in sexual intercourse whilst there, so that it becomes a space of secrets in contrast to the enforced yet obfuscatory truth-telling of the family home.

Attendant on this spatial demarcation is the insular, artificial milieu in which the narrative takes place. Ko, the family's teenage son, is interested in computers and virtual reality, and on two separate occasions we see a computer generated appropriation of the family's home town, its rather sterile suburban landscape comprised of an upmarket shopping district (a space of capitalist consumption) and the strange, angular building in which the family live (Figs 4.3a/4.3b). It is a postmodern paradigm of hyperreality – a social topography of depthlessness – that is further reflected in the façade of a happy family promulgated by Eriko and underlined by Toyoda's typically excessive cinematography. The camera swoops into and out of the diegetic space and appears to float beside and observe the characters; at one point it tellingly rotates to frame the family's apartment building upside down, as though trying to probe its subjects, to view them from a myriad different perspectives in order to penetrate the veneer of their lives. *The Hanging Garden* is, then, concerned with the typical, clichéd, apparently unrealisable composition of the nuclear family. Unlike Kurosawa, however, Toyoda traces its corrosive interiority more than its victimhood. Takashi's sexual frustration means that he has two mistresses, one of whom perennially refers to him as a wimp and engages with him in sadomasochistic sex acts in which his social emasculation becomes enacted in a performative private arena. In an echo of Morita Yoshimitsu's *The Family Game*, an intruder into the family appears in the form of a tutor for the teenage son; this character is also the other mistress of the father, conflating the two spaces and identities that animate the narrative and pointing to the vulnerability of the home and the family. This reinforces the aforementioned point that personal identity as delimited in a familial context is a problematic concept, but Toyoda denies a reading that pertains only to contemporary Japan. Eriko's mother is a key character in the film; she is dying of lung cancer and has a particularly fractious relationship with her daughter, perceived as she is to have been a corrupting influence during the latter's formative years (Eriko's obsession with the perfect family is a result of this corrosive past). Generational

Figure 4.3   The postmodern city (and family): 'reality' and reproduction in *The Hanging Garden.*

discord from a matriarchal perspective is not a common narrative focus, and the fact that the mother is perennially dressed in a formal kimono appears to position her as representative of a problematic national lineage, one that destabilises a traditional patriarchal impetus and instead both connotes and undermines the family as a feminine sphere.

In contradistinction Sono Sion has recently changed his usual exaggerated register to make a restrained and largely naturalistic family drama. His work has often placed family life and the home drama in the midst of other, contrastive generic entities – variously the melodrama, detective film, crime thriller and film noir – as a means of overtly juxtaposing the insular, everyday domesticity of the home drama with the often violent iconoclasm of the other genres. These genres' exterior action and/or stylistic and emotional excess acts as a manifestation of the tensions and repressed emotions of the protagonists in Sono's so-called hate trilogy – *Love Exposure* (*Ai no mukidashi*, 2008), *Cold Fish* (*Tsumetai nettaigyo*, 2010) and *Guilty of Romance* (*Koi no tsumi*, 2011) – which, along with his earlier *Strange Circus* (*Kimyo na sakasu*, 2005), place families within a stylised, often proto-Freudian context in order to stress their unstable, uncanny nature. Indeed if we accept, as Tony Williams (1996) does, that 'Freud's definition of an Oedipus complex, generated within a family situation, still usefully explains psychic mechanisms operating within an exploitative patriarchal capitalist system' (p. 15), then Sono's early work offers a useful test case for such an approach.

In direct contrast *The Land of Hope* (*Kibo no kuni*, 2012) is a transparent drama that was based (controversially, as it transpired) on real-life victims' testimonies. Like the same director's earlier *Himizu* (2011) it is a direct response to the Fukushima Daiichi nuclear disaster of March 2011 that followed in the wake of the Tohoku earthquake and resulting Tsunami, and centres on one extended family of farmers affected by a similar tragedy (clearly a reference to Fukushima, although in fact the diegesis in the fictional town of Nagashima concerns an event that is described as similar to the actual incident rather than a direct dramatisation of it). The film thus depicts a family being assailed by forces from outside, and indeed the director initially portrays them as a happy and harmonious unit, comfortable in one another's company and largely fulfilled in their work. The old couple at the head of the family are close to their adult son and his wife, who live and work alongside them on their farm. However estranged families are common in Sono's work, and so it is in this film that three generations of the family are forcibly separated when an official government line demarcating the nuclear fallout radius is placed between the neighbouring homes of the elderly couple and their children, a seemingly arbitrary act and a signifier of the redundant (if not harmful) attempts of those in power to control the terrible situation. Images of the bisected landscape divided by fences demarcating areas of radiation become replete with connotations regarding the fissures in the fabric of Japanese society. Indeed in one of the subjective inserts that sporadically peppers the otherwise undemonstrative naturalism of the film, the middle-aged Yoichi is told by his father that the disaster has driven a stake through the country, something that Yoichi visualises as a literal series of wooden posts across his living room, separating him from his parents. This also highlights the divisions in reactions to the disaster. The elderly head of the family, Masuhiko, remains largely practical and pragmatic, urging his son and daughter-in-law to leave the family home, although in so doing at times he appears cynical and embittered, forcefully telling Yoichi not to trust the government or the Prime Minister but to look out only for himself.

At the opposite end of this spectrum is the daughter-in-law Izumi, who also comes to believe something that she is told, in her case that the radiation from the nuclear meltdown is still in the air in the town to which she and her husband have moved and that it will directly affect her unborn child. These moments often play out in a landscape of media saturation, either on television or in the books that Izumi begins to take to heart (against Yoichi's better judgement). A variety of different, often quasi-parodic broadcasts discussing the disaster form the backdrop to several different scenes – from news reports and talk shows to an abrasive stand-up comedy routine – which bespeaks a Baudrillardian hyper-reality (Baudrillard, 1995). This philosopher's diatribe regarding the Gulf War not taking place in reality but only as mediated through media saturation is extended by Sono to encompass official reactions to the disaster. And from this point of view the perennial reaction of the characters – to turn their television off – suggests not only how seriously this officiousness should be taken but also the fundamental difference and discrepancy between ostensible reality and representations thereof.

Past and present are in many ways central to *The Land of Hope*. The film is not without apparently surreal moments that punctuate its otherwise naturalistic veneer and that further probe or question the apparent 'reality' of the disaster. Of particular note is a haunting scene in which a young couple searching for the girl's parents visit the disaster zone, and amidst the wreckage they encounter a little boy and girl who, after talking about a lost Beatles record from their youth, appear to vanish before their eyes. It is a quasi-supernatural moment and an allusion to the fundamental sense of unreality that becomes attendant on such a tragedy, the sense in which normality, and by extension reality, is fractured or suspended as an experiential sense of the world is overturned. A key character from this point of view is the elderly mother of the family who suffers increasingly from dementia and as such is someone who has in a way become divorced from 'reality'. Her behaviour, particularly towards the end of the film when she disappears from her home in order to attend a festival parade from her youth that she imagines is nearby, offers a regression to the past that is also inherent in the apparently spectral children seen earlier in the film. Beside this the unborn child of Yoichi and Izumi becomes a tentative symbol of the future, of hope in a devastated land and potentially one of the single steps being taken by Japan (represented, as in *Himizu*, by young characters) at the film's end.

The notion of taking steps, indeed of walking, is a motif throughout *The Land of Hope*, first raised when the elderly Chieko is prevented from going near the barrier demarcating the radiation zone outside her house, to which she replies curtly by asking if Japan now gets mad when a Japanese walks in Japan. Subsequently the youngest couple in the film are reprimanded by the ghostly children they meet amidst the devastation for walking in a showy manner. Instead, they are told, all Japanese should walk one step at a time; in other words that the country must develop slowly and carefully, from a strong foundation, rather than the explosive (showy) steps of the miracle economy that Sono implies has led to this present crisis. Images of the young couple following suit and walking in said orderly manner close the film, suggesting the tentative steps to rebuilding a shattered nation now underway, and given the elderly couple's suicide this country may be said to be definitively unmoored from its past. As in *Tokyo Sonata* the family here is a victim of the state as much as anything else; they are harmed by their country as much as by the natural disaster that has struck it. The 'moral crisis of alienation' that Timothy Iles (2008, p. 79) has identified in several contemporary family films is effectively externalised in *The Land of Hope*. Unlike in *Himizu*, Sono here avoids any reductive sense of the disaster as a manifestation of interpersonal tension and anxiety; it is, rather, a tangible physical sense of estrangement and division that is felt by the characters. The young couple have to evade official police cordons in their search for her family, with the girl lamenting how she has to become a criminal just to visit her hometown. The tragedy here is felt strongly in the domestic sphere, where 'the dissolution of the family is a catastrophe because in Japan [. . .] [a]n identification with family [. . .] is necessary for a complete identification of self' (Richie, 1974, p. 4). Sono, in addition to Yamada Yoji, demonstrates this precept amidst a postmodern landscape so that they present their own catalogues of the historical spectrum of representational registers and in so doing encompass a cinematic historicity of the family drama.

The preponderance of the post-millennial family drama is far from a Japanese phenomenon. Countries such as China, India, Italy and Iran among others have all had recourse to films featuring families. Indeed Ginette Vincendeau (2008) has analysed a contrapuntal trend in recent French cinema that has seen a preponderance of extended family-reunion narratives that conform to national cinematic generic trends and reflect wider social developments and patterns, whilst the ongoing centrality of the family to the horror film is, as both Robin Wood (1986) and Tony Williams (1996) imply, a point of particular interest. Indeed the latter connotes a blurring of generic boundaries – the fact that the family remains salient within a range of diverse, nominally contrastive forms (something that Sono Sion's work exemplifies particularly well) – and this points to the complexity of Japanese cinema, the respective overlaps and distinctions between super-genres such as *gendai-geki* and *shomin-geki*. The specific properties of the Japanese family drama as a sub-genre of the *shomin-geki* have remained largely recondite over time, with (sometimes dramatic) variations on themes rather than complete revisions or transformations of material. Contemporary iterations carry this weight, at times self-consciously, even self-reflexively, but the very fact of such of weight bespeaks the extent to which this genre has remained salient within Japanese filmmaking.

5. POSTMODERNISM AND MAGIC REALISM IN CONTEMPORARY JAPANESE CINEMA

The modes of magic realism and postmodernism are among the few recent generic trends in Japanese cinema that one could identify as a legitimately new phenomenon, a development in genre filmmaking that owes less to extant and established modes of (national) storytelling than to a broader interaction with and response to cultural paradigms and artistic practices. Of course, there are significant precursors to this sub-strata of Japanese filmmaking, both literary and cinematic – the novels and short stories of Murakami Haruki or Yoshimoto Banana for instance, or several early films by Itami Juzo, most especially *Tampopo* [*Dandelion*] (1986). However, the recent iterations of cinematic magic realism have worked towards a different model that actually bespeaks cross-fertilisation with postmodernism, a cultural condition with which it has not typically been perceived as coterminous by those few commentators who have written about and theorised both practices. This has resulted in a distinct, discrete cinematic form that has increasingly permeated Japanese cinema since the turn of the millennium, one that has incorporated facets of several different genres into a heterogeneous whole whose constituent parts or elements are often placed in opposition or tension in order to problematise representation and encourage an active spectatorship to question and interrogate the text. Self-reflexivity is typically understood to be a key feature of postmodern art, the calling attention by a text to its own artifice being a means of frustrating diegetic transparency and suture and thus potentially of disturbing dominant ideology and the implied empiricism of its prerogatives. However if it is true, as Max Weber notes, that 'the highest ideals [. . .] which move us most forcefully [. . .] are always formed only in the struggle with other ideals which are just as sacred to others as ours are to us' (Harvey, 1990, p. 1); and if we consequently accept that postmodernism by its very definition allows for (indeed facilitates) a refusal of any totalising theories or meta-narratives, then it must follow that it is not incompatible with other registers or frameworks of representation, that it can productively breed with other modes – as a means, perhaps, of better categorising and analysing the features of increasingly transnational cinematic products.

There is, then, at least a potential space for the productive contrast or cross-pollination of these forms, if only as a means of throwing (much-needed) light on their respective projects, their particular arenas of interest, engagement and emphasis. There has in fact always been a measure of ambiguity and uncertainty surrounding their usage and artistic or socio-cultural designation(s). The lack of clarity particularly over cinematic iterations of magic realism is a critical commonplace; however postmodernism has also been rife with division and contestation, its boundaries and parameters perennially open to redefinition and remapping. As Cristina Degli-Esposti (1998) has argued it can be a term that resists precise definition, but it may be said to incorporate not only a frustration of grand narratives but also of historical verisimilitude, as well as a prevalence of pastiche and parody, an intertextuality or self-reflexivity, a sense of depthlessness wherein the world goes no deeper than its sensory surface and a preponderance of simulation, of copy, and of artificial bodies and experiences losing the boundaries pertaining to the relationship to a perceived original. Within the context of Japanese culture these factors may be held to be particularly relevant. As Miyoshi Masao has argued, 'the description of postmodernism began to fit the Japanese conditions remarkably well, as if the term were coined specifically for Japanese society (1991, p. 15).

Magic realism has been an even more problematic concept, one whose cinematic parameters are particularly ambiguous. Indeed, as Anne C. Hegerfeldt has noted, the label 'instead of growing more rigorously defined and restricted in application [. . .] has evaded critical demarcation and today enjoys a usage more diverse than ever' (2005, p. 11). There is a notable lineage of literary criticism that has seen magic realism employed in several different and contrastive forms. One need only consider the fact that the form has enjoyed a significant provenance as regards so-called 'third world' and/or postcolonial literature for evidence of its vitality, the centrality of a postcolonial (typical South American and West African) magical realism to which is such that it is at least potentially problematic to talk about a first world iteration of the form, one based in a capitalist country such as Japan. Thus where the typical imperatives of a postmodern cultural condition are born of advanced consumer capitalism, those of magic realism are fundamentally opposed. Authors such as Gabriel García Márquez, Jorge Luis Borges, Mário de Andrade, Isabel Allende, Laura Esquivel and the Nigerian novelist and poet Ben Okri and his fellow countryman Amos Tutuola have worked within a narrative modality that explores real, often historically verifiable people and incidents but does so within the framework of a pervasive spiritual or religious imperative. Whilst these authors do not necessarily always remain consonant with the salient tenets of postcolonial discourse (at least to the extent that the colonised subject is not necessarily a central aspect of their work, at least denotatively so), they do nonetheless present a framework that juxtaposes ostensible reality and those abnormalities or disruptions that serve to call this reality into question, and thus by extension to destabilise the perceived homogeneous and hegemonic processes of white and/or patriarchal discourse that may otherwise be perceived as central. García Márquez' *One Hundred Years of Solitude*, first published in 1967, is typically argued to be the key novel in the magic realist mode, not only for its quasi-symbolic account of the history of a Columbian family but also for its frustration of official (or officious) historiography as a means of defining or understanding their lives. This narrative served to cement the detached or canted perspective on historical verisimilitude that often characterises magic realism (rather than postmodernism's much more complete frustration of the same), whilst also canonising a quasi-surreality that would go on to characterise works like Salman Rushdie's novel about post-independence India *Midnight's Children* in 1981 or Ben Okri's novel *The Famished Road* (both Booker prize winners). The tension between ostensibly oppositional forces here – between the naturalistic and the imaginative, the real and the mythical – mirrors a broader distinction between subjectivity and objectivity, the often perilous circumstances of an official phenomenology of history and the personal, if interior, agency that can potentially transcend such events, beliefs or actions.

Neither is the apparent fixity of this definition historically contingent on colonised nations. The art critic Jeffrey Wechsler (1985) has argued that, with regard to painting, the term has a rich tradition that predates even surrealism, and that its diverse manifestations comprise not only individual artists and artworks from both America and Europe (France, Belgium and Germany in particular, and with an influence by the Italian Giorgio de Chirico) but also specific schools and movements such as the German *Neue Sachlichkeit*, the 'New Objectivity' that defined works by Anton Raderscheidt and Otto Dix and that were presented in specific exhibitions as early as 1925. In point of fact it is a German, Franz Roh, who is credited with inventing the term magic realism as part of the title of a 1925 book that detailed the style and approach of this new school of painting. Wechsler's stated project to define the indefinite with regard to magic realism – or the alternative label of 'imaginative realism' that he offers (p. 293) – leads him to offer a reasonably concrete series of salient features of the style. Whilst alluding to the problematic status of magic realist art across several mediums he nonetheless alludes to its specificity and argues that '(m)agic realism does not invent a new order of things; it simply reorders reality to make it seem alien.

Magic realism is an art of the implausible, not the impossible; it is imaginative, not imaginary' (ibid.).

It is, then, the apparently contradictory features contained in the designation 'magic realism' that have been perceived to offer it a certain socio-political valency. The form's attempt to render everyday experiences and sensations strange is one that, like postmodernism, has numerous points of interest given the context in which its representative works were produced. One of the earliest (and still one among only a select few) attempts to analyse the application of magic realism to film was undertaken by Fredric Jameson (1986), who argued that it should be seen as an alternative model to postmodernism, one comprised of and explicable by an attitude towards history and the past. Magic realism, he argues, denies the kind of nostalgic fetishisation of the past that characterises the condition of postmodernism (p. 302), something echoed by more recent commentators. In elucidating the uncanny quality of East Central European filmmaking nations within the wider context of the increasingly unstable and amorphous boundaries of Europe and its constituent members, Agda Skrodzka (2012) uses the term to further amplify the form's engagement with historiographic processes. She uncovers and works to expose 'history as always a mixture of magic and logic', where an avoidance of being alienated from 'lived reality' becomes attendant on decentring or pausing the binary or dualistic oppositions that tend to characterise it (p. 2).

The links between magic realism and postmodernism have generally not been analysed in either literary or cinematic critical discourse. Through consideration of this mode as an adjunct to postmodernism this chapter will highlight the extent to which a series of films in recent Japanese cinema work towards a model that can be defined as specifically Japanese. But rather than proposing or even circumventing a productive cinematic modality or conception of the magic realist, it is precisely the indeterminacy of this mode that opens up a gap or fissure that an increasingly visible feature of recent Japanese cinema may be said to exploit. This is potentially a further line of obfuscation, another muddying of already unclear waters; however it helps to circumvent some of the problems that surround the application of this critical concept to a first world artistic practice, and, ultimately, as Stephen Hart (1983), Fredric Jameson (1986) and Giorgiana M. M. Colvile (2006) have all demonstrated, the mode may best be understood by invoking other categories or wider genres to determine its specificity. However where these commentators contrast magic realism with fantastic literature and surrealism the climate of postmodernism offers a viable potential for cross-pollination in that both are amorphous labels whose precise boundaries and textual characteristics have been contested, divisive, in addition to which they both offer what Jameson defines as narrative 'raw material' (p. 302). And though they may be perceived to stand at opposing ends of a potential spectrum delineating their dialogic relationships to the respective contexts in which they have tended to flower (third and first world forms), nonetheless they both engage with these contexts in similar ways. Moreover the key films to be discussed here narrativise a series of structural antinomies (most overtly urban against rural) that broadly reflect this precept, and it is a tension as much as a harmony between them that characterises the examples from contemporary Japanese cinema, so the concept of a meaningful cross-fertilisation does not necessarily reside in a commonality of style or purpose; it merely uses or even exploits the lack of critical parameters pertaining to both categories to redefine some of the ways that they have been read and applied, and consequently to open a space for developing their use in analysing films.

It is noticeable that postmodernism can be seen as a defining feature of contemporary Japanese cinema. Indeed films such as Nakashima Tetsuya's *Kamikaze Girls* (*Shimotsuma monogatari*, 2004), Satoshi Miki's *Turtles are Surprisingly Fast Swimmers* (*Kami wa igai to hayaku oyogu*, 2005) or Ninagawa Mika's *Sakuran* (2007) may be taken as particularly significant, not only for their prominent markers of the form but also for the extent to which they throw into relief some of the questions and problems surrounding critical discourse on postmodern artistic practices. Specifically one may use a work like *Kamikaze Girls* – an adaptation of a popular manga that details the unlikely route to friendship of two diametrically opposed teenage girls – in order to question what meaning or relevance we may assign to works whose hyperreal stylisation means that they necessarily operate within insular, circumscribed worlds whose depthlessness can feel like a stylistic affectation. This film immediately establishes its (Jamesonian) postmodernism through the protagonist Momoko's lionisation of the past. She is obsessed with the fashion and culture of eighteenth-century France, of Rococo and Versailles, and dreams so much of living at this time in history that she makes costumes to wear in perpetuating her fantasy, thus over-valuing and consuming (as a capitalist subject) an image divorced from any semblance of lived reality or historical verisimilitude. Along with the anime credits that begin the narrative, this period aesthetic bespeaks an artistic and cultural *bricolage*, whilst Momoko's voiceover narration offers a self-reflexivity that stresses artificiality and construction (she literally stops and restarts the narrative), thus positioning Nakashima's film as potentially *about* postmodernity and postmodern artistic practices rather than simply as a postmodern film. That is, it makes audiences so aware of its postmodernity that they are forced to confront it and its socio-cultural implications.

Magic realism, in contrast, has only sporadically been invoked (and even then not fully analysed) as a feature of Japanese cinema. It is significant, then, that the key 1990s' iteration of the form should in fact employ something of its key literary distinction. Miike Takashi's *The Bird People in China* (*Chūgoku no chōjin*, 1998) appropriates a dialogue between postmodernism and magic realism as representative of a wider juxtaposition between urban Japan and rural China, between technological modernity and the vagaries of tradition, and in depicting a middle-class city-based professional encountering a rural peasantry it seems to at least echo some of the perceived postcolonial imperatives of magic realism's raw material. In writing about Miike, Stephen Rawle (2009) describes this film as a 'restrained work of magical realism with little violence' (p.168), and indeed goes on to regard this magic realism as a reaction against a paradigmatic postmodernism found elsewhere in Miike's oeuvre, one pertaining to a 'wild oscillation [. . .] between [. . .] hopeful nostalgia and contemporary anxiety' (p. 177). *The Bird People in China* concerns a journey from Tokyo to a remote village in the mountains of China in Yunnan Province; the central character is a salaryman named Wada who needs to procure some rare gems for his boss, but along with a guide and a yakuza who is owed money by the protagonist's company he finds himself in among a makeshift school wherein people (especially young children) are taught to fly using engineered wings. Whilst there he encounters a young girl whose apparently British grandfather began the school after crashing his plane in the village during a mission in WWII, and he begins to translate from English a folk song that the girl continually sings, which seems important to her and her work.

The proximal relationship of ostensibly diverse nationalities (the folk song is the Scottish ditty 'Annie Laurie') and transnational historical progenitors – it is suggested that an artefact from Yunnan depicting a man with wings was found in Hokkaido and Kyushu in Japan and in fact may be said to have begat Japanese culture and its pre-eminent myths and legends – bespeaks a postmodern frustration of boundaries and of cultural and national homogeneity. In addition the narrative centrality of the character of the yakuza, Ujiie, underlines the transposition and reshaping of Miike's typical concerns and generic landscape in *The Bird People in China*, whilst the fact that the protagonist is a salaryman (another potent urban Japanese stereotype) further highlights the feeling of displacement involved in the narrative, of repeatedly deferred origins and elusive beginnings that provide a diverse global lineage that has forged a localised identity. It also underlines a key magic realist methodology in that familiar elements are presented out of context in order to comment on their fundamental strangeness, to make the known and perceived knowable into unknown, alien entities. That Wada is forced progressively to figuratively divest himself of certain accoutrements of his person (in particular through the loss of all his clothes on the arduous trek through mountainous rural China) seems to bespeak a transformation on his part, a moral as well as a physical journey, but significantly he does not fully embody or espouse such sentimental feelings. Rather it is Ujiie, the increasingly unstable and violent yakuza, who becomes desirous not only of staying in the village in Yunnan but of ensuring that it remains pure, untainted by modernity and civilisation and untouched by outsiders. This is a point of view that highlights the well-rehearsed criticism of magic realism as a postcolonial mode: that it is often the colonised being spoken for rather than themselves speaking, the 'third world' as figured by the first world in its discursive strategies and practices. In response Wada proposes that a middle ground be discovered, noting that they would not be in this location at all if it were not for planes, trains and other features of a contemporary society, and thus that these things should not be hastily sacrificed or easily abandoned.

Concomitantly the film itself uses the intersection of postmodernism and magic realism as a means of highlighting this tension. The rootlessness or homelessness that typically afflicts Miike protagonists is configured as cultural and personal dispersal, whilst the artefact that is exhumed in Yunnan seems to suggest that to have cogent foundations is in itself a practical impossibility. A sudden voiceover by Wada at the end of the film also means that the narrative has, in effect, been recalled by this character and thus can be construed as a flashback, a recollection. The director does not recuperate or reconcile these constituent elements that seem to contradict one another, does not find a clear narrative path or trace a distinct causal trajectory. The apparent motivation for the journey, of finding a precious stone and repaying a debt, is almost summarily abandoned once the destination has been reached. Moreover Wada's statement that he ultimately destroyed the tape recorder used to dictate 'Annie Laurie' and, at the beginning of the film, to record the details of his travels privileges a remembrance of things past and thus a perennial subjective dimension whose implicit fallibility, its inherent unreliability, marks out the pro-filmic as an unstable construct relatable only to the subjectivity of the focalising agent (again reifying a problematic subject position pertaining to magic realist tenets). From this perspective the scopic imperatives of gazing at the ethereal Chinese landscape stressed in several shots throughout the film becomes a means of inscribing a lack in the Japanese subjects, overwhelmed and awed by their environment but inexorably separate and distinct from it, framed as onlookers for whom the act of looking simultaneously encodes subjectivity and lack as determinedly intertwined, the one necessarily entailing the other. These shots in fact echo what Ān Jǐngfū (1994) has said of landscape painting in China, that they 'express distance by the height and vastness of an object [. . .] huge mountains, lakes, and rivers occupy most of the space in a Chinese landscape painting' (p. 120), something that Miike associates with magic realism through the form's aforementioned perceived postcoloniality. In so doing the director stresses its limitations as a cinematic mode, one tied to first world forms and perspectives, and makes it plain that it should be read critically, with circumspection.

The Bird People in China is thus a key magic realist film to the extent that it opens a space for reflecting on the politics of applying magic realism, against which the postmodern bricolage of generic signifiers alludes to a new transnational flow of peoples and cultures, especially in Asia. New Wave director Imamura Shohei's final film, *Warm Water under the Red Bridge* (*Akai hashi no shita nonuruimizu*, 2001), is also predicated on an urban/rural dichotomy, and in fact

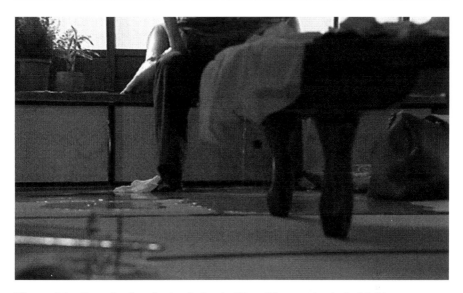

Figure 5.1   Excessive female ejaculation in *Warm Water under the Red Bridge.*

reprises some of the narrative concerns of *The Bird People in China* in that it details a journey undertaken by a professional man into a remote milieu that serves as a journey of self-discovery (albeit one that the director subtly compromises) and of the prevalence of heterogeneity. The protagonist is a middle-aged man named Sasano Yosuke who travels to a small coastal village in search of a golden statue said to be left in that location by a friend. Once there he meets a woman with a strange affliction: water collects and wells up inside her and can only be released through wicked or sinful acts, at which times it tends to erupt from her body in a veritable geyser, an explosion or indeed an ejaculation that becomes both a parodic usurping of masculinity and male agency and a spectacularised marker of the persistence and visibility of female sexual desire (Fig. 5.1).

That Imamura's work is consonant with magic realism should not be a surprise given this director's tendency to use Japanese society and history as a carnivalesque point of departure in excavating peripheral figures or cultures, the sites of Otherness and excess associated with films like *The Profound Desire of the Gods* (*Kamigami no fukaki yokubo*, 1968) or *Eijanaika* (1981) becoming localised acts of resistance to dominant socio-political (and capitalist) norms. Later in his career Imamura's hitherto paradigmatic methodology became somewhat transmogrified as his interest shifted to stories of often isolated, insular communities, and as he had increasing recourse to male protagonists rather than the defiant, earthy, embattled, survivalist women who had populated much of his oeuvre at least until he abandoned feature filmmaking for non-fiction in 1969. *Warm Water under the Red Bridge* follows the director's previous films – the *Palme d'Or*-

winning *The Eel* (*Unagi*, 1997) and the WWII-set comedy-drama *Dr Akagi* (*Kanzo sensei*, 1998) – in that all three works are built around men whose adaptation to and assimilation in a different or altered environment or way of life becomes a means of questioning masculinity as a marker of normalcy or social hegemony. However this is a reframing rather than an obliteration of this director's perennial concerns. The proto-typical Imamurean woman is here more of an adjunct to the male protagonist and his story; however, precisely because of this she becomes an unassimilable symbol, a spectacular sign of the blind spot(s) in the discursive circulation of masculine identities, and to this end circularity is a key motif in the film. Saeko is the magic in the otherwise real. She is linked (as is the female protagonist in *The Eel*, as though these women were the offspring of Immaura's earlier canonical works) to a mother whose fanatical religious beliefs led directly to an accident in which she drowned, and as such to a feminine Otherness that continually disturbs the typically ineffectual patriarchy seen throughout the narrative, most overtly the elderly and infirm residents of the village. Saeko is clearly depicted as central to a strange ecosystem in that her discharges are shown to attract fish to the local lake, which in turn feeds the industry of which Yosuke becomes a part when he begins working on a trawler as a fisherman. She is thus at the organic centre of the village, subtly crucial to its lifeblood and the cyclical flow of its industry, the heart of the local milieu. From this point of view the African man training for an international marathon who is sporadically (and tellingly) seen running round the village offers a contrastive image of circularity and Otherness, one that remains outside and beyond the parameters of this milieu but at the same time one that further disturbs any clear sense of (national or social) homogeneity or hegemonic incorporation. Like Saeko he is a visible anomaly, but surplus where she is central, disruptive (at one point he tries to catch fish illegally) where she is restorative.

These characters are precisely matched mirror images that offer different signifiers of Otherness, different means of questioning the patriarchal normative. This particular aspect of the film also hints at magic realism through reversal – the colonised outsider now a part of the first world – and attendant on this is a subversion of nostalgia, indeed a frustration of any explicit sense of a coherent history, placing the film in a strangely amorphous present that stands at the intersection of past and future and that plays upon very contemporary anxieties (Yosuke has just become unemployed as the film begins) as a means of invoking a postmodernist frustration of historical veracity. Moreover the fact that the protagonist is repeatedly told that he looks just like a man who had previously worked in and around the village as a fisherman stresses the rural milieu as an alternate, mirrored universe of magic realism distinct from the logical temporal flow of the city, the official time of capital, commerce and postmodernity. The past here is a personal, apocryphal, ambiguous entity rather than anything coherent or with any objective veracity (as historiography itself can never have), and at the same time there is a tenuous future tense in the narrative that emerges as an objective correlative. Saeko, during a visit to a research facility in which the science of particles and neutrinos is observed, says that it feels 'so twenty-first century' as she is told about how such study can elucidate the nature of the universe, the place of humanity therein and the lifespan of the sun. Consequently the present of *Warm Water under the Red Bridge* exists as an uneasy confluence of individual pasts and an abstract collective future narrativised in terms of the end of our solar system and of life on Earth. Indeed it is immediately following the visit to this scientific facility that Saeko discusses her past and her mother's death (elaborated upon with a black and white flashback that literally inscribes a cinematic sense of history into the narrative), and the structural proximity of these two moments suggests their Heideggerian prevalence in underlining the uneasiness of the present. It is, in the last instance, particularly telling that the final scene of the film is an argument between Yosuke and Saeko that ends in their having sex in public, which (quite apart from its typically Imamura-esque reverence for animalistic behaviour) also suggests that their own future is perhaps tenuous; that their relationship is founded on uncertain ground, a purely physical connection that defines their union as one of mutual needs and desires that are not always harmonious or compatible. If magic realism is well placed to question or disturb societal norms, its embodiment in Saeko here, placed as it is beside Yosuke's representative postmodernity (the fact that he stands for a displaced city dweller cut adrift from his past), literalises the problematic alliance between the two models as opposing facets of a contemporary condition not reducible to a single social or artistic register.

Imamura's project in *Warm Water under the Red Bridge* is built in part around a desire to question where repositories of identity (personal, national) can be found in modern Japan, and to what extent they offer a cogent image. Two features by Koreeda Hirokazu offer a contrastive model to the extent that their magic realist visions concern groups of disparate people united by extraordinary circumstances. Both *After Life* (*Wandafuru raifu*, 1998) and *Air Doll* (*Kūki ningyō*, 2009) offer very quotidian scenarios against which their magical or surreal elements seem all the more pronounced and meaningful, all the more magical against a reality that seems all the more real. This is particularly true of the former, Koreeda's sophomore feature and the film that established his international reputation, which in fact reverses the typical magic realist polarity in that, rather than the real made strange it is much more about the fantastical made ordinary, real. It concerns the workers and internees at a way station on the way to heaven, a place where the newly deceased spend a week, during which time they must choose a single memory from their lives that will then be physically recreated for them and filmed for posterity by the staff. This memory will then be the sole reminder of their mortal lives, something for the dead to take with them into the afterlife and eternity, a memento of their earthly existence and a marker of life and of selfhood.

Reality for these characters is, then, inextricably bound up in a construction, an artificial reproduction of a real event, as it were a film, which they watch in a theatre and which they take away with them into the afterlife. As such the real and the copy, the original and the fake, merge into one another in a paradigmatic postmodern trope, whilst the problem of history for the postmodern era is also succinctly dramatised by Koreeda in the diverse multitude of deceased and their respective individual histories and memories. On numerous occasions the director draws overt parallels between different people discussing their pasts and their memories. One such juxtaposition directly contrasts an elderly war veteran talking about his desperate attempts to satiate his hunger after becoming a POW with a young girl who didn't have enough money to buy her favourite pancakes at Disneyland, a stark discrepancy in stories of food whose proximal relationship here (Koreeda cuts directly from one to the other) suggests something of the erosion of temporal boundaries within the free-flowing postmodern space, where war and Disneyland become coterminous features of the contemporary psychic landscape, neither more or less 'real' than the other. Indeed the fact that one of the young male workers in the building is ultimately revealed to have died during WWII further bespeaks this apparent disparity between contrastive yet interconnected personal histories.

The naturalistic *mise-en-scène*, which frequently utilises available light to emphasise the dilapidated environment of the central location, as well as the almost perpetually handheld and objective cinematography, both underline the prosaic reality of *After Life*. Moreover the centrality of the workers in the building foregrounds a sense of daily ritual and routine that further enshrines the quotidian at the heart of the narrative. The film begins with two members of staff arriving on a Monday morning and receiving instruction on the upcoming week's schedule, whilst subsequent scenes dramatise the petty tensions and frustrations between colleagues that can accrue within any working environment. The extended and detailed interviews with each of the deceased to ascertain their lives and memories are largely shot in a formal manner, with a frontal camera that recalls a documentary aesthetic. Other aspects of the story also stress the prevalence of quotidian spectacle, something Koreeda mines for comic effect. For example the residual routines of personal appearance, of washing and brushing one's hair that become attendant on the staged and filmed reconstructions of the individual memories, are vociferously upheld and undertaken by the recently dead to the extent that the electricity in the building begins to wane due to everyone using their electrical appliances at the same time.

To offset this variegated realism a contrapuntal thematic thread about subjectivity and perception is developed by Koreeda. The very few instances of a POV shot in the film occur in one particular context and serve to connect two young workers. The first is employed when a young male worker gazes longingly at the moon through a skylight in the ceiling, and it is matched at the end of the film when his similarly young female colleague looks up to the same window and appears to see the same sight. However this latter vision is revealed to be an illusion when a cover with a small aperture (the moon) is lifted to reveal daylight and thus expose the scene as yet another constructed copy of a real phenomenon. Soon after the young male's initial viewing of the moon an older employee looks at the same sight and extols the wonder of something that always remains the same yet is continually perceived differently due to the vagaries of light. It is a crucial line, a quasi-poststructuralist precept underlining the fact that interpretative potential must be allowed for anything seen or perceived: that magic or indeed reality are relative, necessarily subjective terms, and as such that to extol such a dramatic register on film is to engage directly with the specificity of cinema. Attendant on this is the availability of any person's life on a series of videotapes that can be obtained for the deceased to look over. These tapes offer a viewpoint that is apparently entirely objective and as such provide a crystallisation of the discrepancy between, on the one hand, reality, and on the other those perceptions or remembrances thereof that inevitably, inexorably take precedence where selfhood and identity are concerned. From this perspective movies offer a privileged site, a point of negotiation between the subject and the world, the self and the other; they present life perceived through the veil of fantasy where the magic of cinema's realism (or vice versa) underlines the medium's lionisation of the term and this film's extrapolation of its subjective imperatives. That is, *After Life* is about cinema in general and magic realism in particular as a natural register thereof. The deceased have left their earthly bodies behind before entering the site of the school (as cinemagoers figuratively leave their lives behind to enter the escapist space of the film theatre), and thereafter they relate to those lives entirely through a film, a reconstruction whose cheaply practical means of recreating individual memories bespeaks both a reality and a magic, the one necessarily entailed within the other.

These mirrored shots and concomitant thematic weight, then, draw attention to the meta-cinematic subtext of *After Life*. The fact that each individual deceased's memories are filmed – an act that includes rehearsals for performers, set design and decoration, and ultimately a screening in a movie theatre – establishes this precept, whilst the fact that the one-time girlfriend of one character is played in a reconstruction by one of the pre-eminent actresses of the 1950s and 1960s in Kagawa Kyoko further underlines the cinematic import of the film. It reinforces Koreeda's implicit assertion that cinema is an inherently magic realist medium, one in which a pro-filmic facsimile of reality necessarily entails a transformative process of matching a filmic signifier to a phenomenological signified to leave a perennially incomplete sign system wherein the apparent diegetic reality remains unstable, amorphous, elusive. Elements of magic or surreality stress this precept; they underline the real as much as its Other because the latter can be recuperated within the experiential subjectivity of the characters and their 'real' lives: that is, their lives in the (post)modern world. This is, of course, a different conception of magic realism than the ostensibly unassimilable events in the form's literary manifestation – the flying carpets in Marquez, say, or the spirit narrator in Okri – but it is important to recognise a singularly cinematic iteration of magical realism and to reconfigure its boundaries as befits a contrastive medium. *After Life* not only points the way to such a mode but narrativises, allegorises it, and as such remains a key example of the contemporary face of the mode.

In contradistinction to *After Life* the narrative of *Air Doll* eschews any such overtly non-fictive imperative. However it does share its forebear's postmodern emphasis on the real and the copy in that it revolves around the titular sex aid, named Nozumi by her owner, who comes to life one morning when her owner has left for work and who thereafter becomes physically indistinguishable from the 'real' people with whom she comes into contact. She begins leaving the home during the day after her owner has gone to work, and initially becomes human through mimesis, by directly copying those she meets around the city, including an elderly lady going to the police station and a young girl on her way to school. Indeed Koreeda slyly parodies this fact by having Nozumi follow a group of schoolchildren on an excursion who sing a song called 'Mr Echo', which includes the lyrics 'Don't copy me Mr Echo; Mr Copycat', and which seems to be directed at the protagonist when she is invited by a child to join in with them only to then be left behind because she is too cold to hold hands with.

Subsequently she takes a job in a video rental store, a doubly significant event in that it figures as another copy or echo – in this case of the cinema, as Nozumi is told that watching films at home is but a substitute for seeing them on film, a lesser experience – but also because it implies that cinema is a copy or facsimile of reality. In such a landscape of copies, or 'substitutions', Koreeda uses Nozumi to problematise any clear distinction between what is apparently real and what is Other; what is human or otherwise. Moreover with Nozumi there is no particular reason for her transformation from doll to woman, no encounter with any magical agent or fulfilment of a dream or wish on the part of a character. She simply comes to life – as she repeatedly states she 'finds a heart' – and her transformation is not received with any overt disbelief by any of the people who learn of her secret. They are surprised at the development, but neither her owner, her male friend at the video store or her maker whom she pays a visit to late in the film express any real sense of incredulity over what has happened to her. It is not, in context, an entirely anomalous event given that Nozumi becomes a point of departure for a disparate series of sad, lonely characters whose lives are ostensibly no more or less 'real' than hers. What does reality mean in this context? What objective criteria can be brought to bear on lives such as we see in *Air Doll*? Of a young girl living alone perennially eating junk food until she is physically sick, or of a middle-aged woman so desperate to reclaim her youth that she seems to spend all her leisure time covered in oils and unguents. How can one conceive of a common reality that connects these characters and that elucidate their lives?

Like *Warm Water under the Red Bridge*, then, *Air Doll* takes a female character whose magical agency both contrasts and throws light on the reality (or otherwise) of those around her, and it is this using of magic to question reality that marks out Koreeda's vision. It is also what contravenes a purely postmodern aesthetic, to which end it may also be regarded as an exaggerated parable of femininity and of traditional, conservative gender roles. Nozumi is used entirely for sex, is expected to stay at home whilst her 'owner' is away at work and to remain an object throughout. Later in the narrative the fact that she continues to be taken for a doll by her owner even though she does not revert back to the form of a doll when they are together becomes redolent of the extent to which he cannot see past the function she fulfils for him, the clearly circumscribed role that she plays in his life. By contrast, however, Nozumi's owner is in many ways an emasculated male who has taken refuge from the real world and from real women with an entirely functional and subservient inanimate object. An erosion of masculine social agency and the attendant subjugation of women are seen as part of a contemporary post-millennial landscape, which the film invokes in order to transcend the anxious instability of postmodernity and to inscribe a magic realist aesthetic to contravene it.

This change of focus in Koreeda's work is matched by a transformation of stylistic register in *Air Doll*, a departure from *After Life*'s proto-documentary approach that is a consequence of the fact that for only the second time in his feature career thus far the director worked with a different cinematographer than his usual Yamazaki Yutaka. Here he used the Taiwanese Mark Lee Ping Bin, a veteran of films by such esteemed filmmakers as Hou Hsiao-hsien (*Flight of the Red Balloon* (2007)), Tian Zhuangzhuang (*Springtime in a Small Town* (*Xiao cheng zhi chun*, 2002)) and Wong Kar-Wai (*In the Mood for Love* (*Fa yeing nin wa*, 2000)), with which directors he has developed a recognisable style built around long shots and long, fluid, constantly but subtly mobile takes. In these Ping Bin's camera seems almost weightless, appearing to float or drift past the characters as though studying them or explicating their perennially shifting relationship to the world around them. He continually frames and reframes his subjects, glides almost imperceptibly around them (often tracing a semi-circular arc) as much as to express an instability or uncertainty over subjectivity, that the characters have no stable point of view on the world or any clearly demarcated or secure place within it. As such the story deals so fervently with alienation and emotional retardation that it implicitly affirms that there is a reality, a real world, to be alienated from. David Harvey (1990) has argued that it is impossible in an age of postmodernism to be alienated because in a way there is no longer anything from which to be alienated, reality as it is being an essentially empty construct. And it is this that the director employs as a counterweight to paradigmatic postmodernism, the sense of the uncanny that both Jameson (1986, p. 302) and Moylan C. Mills (1989, p. 114) use to describe this form's method of making strange the world around us.

In extending and perhaps refining this paradigm Kitano Takeshi's post-millennial films have adhered to several postmodern and magic realist precepts as a means of distinguishing his new work from his older, more celebrated efforts. Paramount in this regard is *Dolls* (*Dōruzu*, 2002), which has not been recognised for its magic realist and postmodern qualities. The film's portmanteau narrative of three interconnected stories of love, loss and obsession make careful and detailed play with the cultural and artistic lineage of Japan, but few have recognised this facet of the film; indeed one review, contemporaneous with *Dolls'* theatrical release (Romney, 2003), castigated Kitano for the magic realist elements of his scenario, finding fault with scenes such as the one in which two ornate kimonos appear out of nowhere before the protagonists as they trudge along a snowy mountain, as though the film were elsewhere a work of restrained naturalism rather than the stylised appropriation of the Japanese *Bunraku* puppet theatre that it is. These surreal touches may well be out of place in numerous other Kitano works but here seem entirely in keeping with *Dolls'* overall aesthetic and narrative methodology. The film is entirely suffused with a hyperreality that directly engages with the precepts of Japaneseness outlined by Marilyn Ivy (1995) and Alastair Philips (2007) in their respective studies both of Japan and its cinema. The introduction to this book has already outlined how *Hana-Bi* subverted Kitano's hitherto prevalent, indeed defining, topographical anonymity by situating its protagonist's journey as a specifically Japanese undertaking, one that presents (though arguably does not fully unpick the contradictions in presenting) the country as at once a commodity and at the same time a potential space of growth and personal regeneration. From this point of view numerous (predominantly Anglophone) critics and reviewers greeted *Hana-Bi* as a spiritual, even meditative work, with one review in a (now-defunct) popular magazine concluding its review of the film – which ends with a scene that features the protagonist Nishi shooting both himself and his wife on a beach – by referring to this desolate dénouement as an uplifting example of this director's transcendental style and worldview (Grundy, 1998, p. 102).

In contradistinction *Dolls* concerns itself with a pointed critique of such fetishised gazing, and in so doing regards Japan as a haunting and uncanny space, with its uncanniness inseparable from, indeed a defining aspect of, its nominal touristic spectacle. Like *Hana-Bi* it similarly presents a vision of 'Japan' as an imaginary, commodified space, but its exaggerated *mise-en-scène* of Japaneseness is not only a hollow and performative site of empty excess but also, significantly, an eminently finite construction given the expanded play (replete with stage) that frames the narrative. Kitano anchors the narrative of this film in a story that literally seems to traverse the length and breadth of Japan; or at least that traverses the imaginary spaces of perceptions of the country as it details the story of a young man, Matsumoto, who abandons his lifelong partner, Sawako, in order to marry his boss's daughter and thus cement his position in the company. When said partner attempts suicide and becomes catatonic he removes her from the hospital and proceeds to take her with him on what becomes a protracted journey, on foot, through Japan, with her physically bound to him by a length of red rope. This journey literally entails a trek through four distinct seasons (from the lush greens of spring and summer to the deep burnished red of autumn and the cold white of winter) as they slowly reconnect with one another and tentatively revisit their former relationship.

Further to this spinal narrative Kitano branches out to consider two subsidiary stories whose thematic connection to the thread of the so-called bound beggars is made explicit through the precept of looking and being looking at, seeing and being seen. These concern, on the one hand, an ageing yakuza who recalls the girlfriend he deserted decades before only to encounter her exactly where they parted, following which he learns that she has been waiting for him patiently ever since. On the other hand is a pop star named Harue and two obsessed male fans, one of whom, Nukui, blinds himself in an attempt to meet his idol following her premature retirement after being involved in a car accident that has scarred her face and ruined her career. The stories overlap and intersect in several ways, both narratively and visually (the couple walk past all the other characters at different points in the story), but it is the thematic connection that predominates throughout. Kitano in fact establishes the theme of looking from the very beginning of the narrative of *Dolls*. The film begins on a literal stage with a *Bunraku* performance of the 1711 *Shinjū* (Love Suicide or Double Suicide) play *The Courier of Hell*, by the form's most acclaimed exponent Monzaemon Chikamatsu. The opening shots of static dolls and their handlers (*kurogo*) as they prepare to take the stage before the performance appear to reinforce the typical anti-illusory properties of the classical Japanese theatre. However a subsequent shot taken from the optical POV of one of the dolls as it looks straight out into the faces of the diegetic theatre audience – much as the opening tableau presented the dolls as implicitly the objects of an extra-diegetic spectator's gaze – begins to disturb this notion by conceiving of a cinematic découpage whilst remaining within the form of the theatrical. Thus theatre and cinema are figured from the outset as competing sites of watching and visual consumption, something that both underlines the theatricality of the film's narrative and, more significantly, infers a connotative space of performance and spectatorship as a central feature of the film's magic realist vision. This not only underlines the extent to which this form remains an entirely subjective mode – a means of circumventing dominant, realistic aesthtics and the ideological thrusts therein – but it also problematises such subjectivity, queations its veracity. Again the film may be taken as one about rather than merely representative of a magic realist modality.

Following this prologue the film opens out into the aforementioned story of the young couple and their apparently cathartic and therapeutic journey through 'Japan'. The actual stage is replaced by a figurative stage as the couple appear to walk through different landscapes and seasons. The introduction to these characters sees them figured as the object of a series of scornful and mocking gazes cast onto them by those people who they pass on their journey, and thereafter they are commented upon (indeed physically ejected from one environment) as their travels progress. To this end the story of the yakuza offers a clear parallel in that his one-time girlfriend is, like the bound beggars, subject to the voyeuristic gazes and passing comments of those around her as she sits alone in the park awaiting her lost boyfriend. Moreover the perennial spectacle of the pop star Harue, the constant public consumption of her image (she is seen at one key moment signing copies of a photo book), becomes a further fixed object of a series of gazes, and indeed this reinforces a postmodern precept in that it is a facsimile of a real person, a constructed persona, that is viewed and consumed, a person reduced to a likeness that then becomes a commodity, the real and the reproduction aligned with the two becoming indistinguishable.

Concomitantly there is an attendant focus on blindness throughout *Dolls*. The fact that Nukui takes his own sight to get near to his idol, who has herself shunned the gaze of the world, throws into relief the figurative blindness of both Sawako and the old yakuza's girlfriend, neither of whom recognise their one-time partners when they are reunited with them. The vision associated with the dolls in the aforementioned early shot contrasts their subjectivity with a lack thereof in the characters, and from this point of view the nominally extravagant *mise-en-scène* becomes a performative site of Japanese culture and tradition that stands for the repressed or disavowed desire to be seen on the part of the characters, the self-conscious desire to have writ large in public their feelings of guilt (Matsumoto) or of love (the yakuza's girlfriend) or of devotion (Nukui). In other words their need is not simply to feel or to do but to be seen in the process of such, and the tension between magic realism and postmodernism from this point of view bespeaks a tension between the surface and the suppressed, the façade and what is buried or dormant beneath. The empty excess of postmodern design is transfigured into the tangible uncanny quality of magic realism through its overall subjectivity of style; we look at characters who cannot see but who nonetheless perform, who refashion the world around their extremes of action and emotion. This style then legitimates the tangible cultural lineage that is inscribed in the very fabric of the film as an oppressively performative site of national spectacle that the dolls variously represent and revolt against. It is, in other words, magic realism employed as a critique of, and counterweight to, the exaggerated surfaces of postmodernity.

Reinforcing this textual dichotomy is the narrative of *Dolls*' journey. Marilyn Ivy, in her work on the ghosts of Japanese modernity, has discussed the concept of the journey as itself a potential site of performance. Drawing on the well-known tourist campaign by Japan National Railways in the 1970s that urged women in particular to discover Japan, she discusses how discovery in this particular context relates more readily to the subject than to the external world around them, something she goes on to relate to *Bunraku* conventions (pp. 29–65). Alastair Phillips (2007) has already drawn on this national campaign in his study of Imamura Shohei's *Vengeance is Mine* (*Fukushu suru wa ware ni ari*, 1979), stressing how Japanese geography – a 'cognitive map of Japan' (p. 235) – becomes a means to question and disturb official constructions of Japanese national identity. And so it is for Kitano that the perceived specificity of the Japanese sense of seasonal change and transience evoked through the bound beggars narrative (Davies and Ikeno, 2002, pp. 153–8) becomes an oppressive force, especially as experienced by Sawako, who has to traverse an interior landscape of strange dreams and hallucinations as much as the geographical trek that is fostered upon her.

In *Dolls* magic realist elements such the ornate kimonos that appear before the protagonists on a mountain stand uneasily beside postmodern precepts of surface excess to open up a textual space for questioning identity and selfhood. Where the latter is concerned the notion of a touristic experience gained through cinema is one with significant currency within postmodern studies, with Ellen Strain (1998) in particular using E. M. Forster and the critical discourse of Dean MacCannell in order to equate the practices of tourism with those of cinema. She notes that 'mass tourism has only grown through the expansion of the environmental bubble or the physical boundaries between tourists and the foreign environment' (p. 150), such that the perception of this environment from the insulated point of view of, say, the 'framing mechanism' (ibid.) of a train or bus window becomes akin to the experience of watching images in a film (that is, on a screen). Again, this de-realising of the world so that originals and copies or reproductions become indistinguishable from their referent in 'reality' echoes the construction of the hyperreal as posited by Jean Baudrillard (1994). In *Dolls* all the world is indeed a stage, its men and women merely players, but this stage becomes identical to the world depicted in the narrative: or at least the stages of the classical Japanese theatres (from the stylised excesses of *Kabuki* used in the explosive colours of the summer and autumnal scenes to the spare blankness of the dramatic space of a *Noh* play that characterises winter) begin to look like ostensibly real spaces. They are what Umberto Eco (1998) would define as '(a) bsolute unreality [. . .] offered as real presence' (p. 7): the materiality of the world de-materialised, and to the characters who pass through it these immaterial images confer upon them a transitory nature in a way that corrupts the over-valuation of Zen and *mono no aware* to stress a contrastive materiality – that of the body, the corporeal form. Unlike the privileged visions that entrance and entrap the characters in Kurosawa Akira's comparable *Dreams* (*Yume*, 1990) – a privilege that ultimately entails access to a definable tradition – the stylised world here coldly circumscribes the fates of the blind beggars. As with the criminal family in Oshima Nagisa's *Boy* (*Shōnen*, 1969) they eventually reach the end of Japan when the melodramatic excess of the seasons turns to a monochromatic winter and the pair literally fall from a cliff, as though 'Japan' encompassed the whole world and they have tumbled from its final stretch of land. It is a postmodern sense of space that is informed by magic realist logic, with the resulting fracturing of the narrative representing a divided or split identity. Where the excess of the object meets a lack in the subject(s), and where the world demands to be seen but the people cannot see, the slippage between these poles enshrines indeterminacy and liminality as narrative touchstones, and the import therein for a journey whose end point seems to be a personal and national abyss is to foreground not only a touristic sense of space but also the alienating precepts therein (the logical position within its scopic imperative).

With regard to Japan this is a subtly subversive concept. The concept of travelling through this country has animated a number of non-fiction books, many that work to reconcile the modern face of the country with the history and tradition that has variously defined and delimited it. Alan Booth's *Looking for the Lost* (1996) and its forebear *The Roads to Sata* (1986) are also about vision, about seeing the unseen in their explicit attempts to unearth and to map out the disparities between competing dichotomies (contemporary and traditional, perception and apparent reality) that have accrued around Japan, whilst the more irreverent *Hokkaido Highway Blues* considers the apparent prevalence of discursive social and cultural practices to be found off the beaten track in the country (as it were, the repressed of Booth). These books – along with the numerous recent Gaijin in Japan studies such as Dew (1999), Carey (2005), Stevens (2009) and Garcia (2010) – variously explore a sense of nationhood in which coherence lies in imaginary incoherence (and in the mind and perception of the foreign observer) that the compromised eye (or 'I') of the fragmented, decentred individual subject can only imagine. In the final, tellingly titled chapter of *Looking for the Lost* ('Ghost Roads'), Booth notes that:

> [T]he past is a generously amorphous fog. What is old is old; there is no need to bother oneself overmuch about causes and results. [. . .] All history, even – or rather especially – the recent history of the 1930s and 1940s, is a tangle best left for the senseis to unravel. (p. 386)

In other words there is a vicious circle in which the past is a distant entity, a fiction, an incomplete narrative lacking a narrator or a narratee, and glimpsed through the haze of a present that stresses fragmentation and by extension a concomitant desire to idealise a lost past. And so it is in *Dolls* that the accumulated weight of a cultural tradition becomes an autonomous, over-valued entity such that it haunts and taunts the present through its suddenly life-given dolls – its *dramatis personae* and erstwhile arbiters of a historical lineage – who become puppet masters dictating the fates of the film's protagonists. That these protagonists almost throughout remain both blind and performative, desirous of being seen yet unable themselves to see, suggests the extent of Kitano's critical, excorporative stance towards the canonisation of 'Japan'.

If Kitano maps out a magic realist vision filtered through genre cinema and an authorial brand then the younger Toyoda Toshiaki has remade this paradigm in his own image. The work of this director has typically remained within the *seishun eiga*, or youth film, genre; however for his fourth picture, after *Tokyo Rampage* AKA *Porno Star* (*Poruno sutā*, 1998), the boxing documentary *Unchain* (2000) and *Blue Spring* (*Aoi haru*, 2001), he moved defiantly beyond these horizons to make a film whose relationship to magic realism is less pronounced than a majority of the others in its field but which nonetheless employs this mode in its vision of Japan as seen from the margins, the periphery, of its society. The film *9 Souls* (*Nain sōruzu*, 2003) is a prison break narrative, one that traces the exploits of the titular ensemble, once free, as they go about trying to reconnect with the outside world and their former lives and relationships whilst travelling together in a ramshackle camper van. Its tone develops steadily from broad comedy to portentous tragedy, from light, playful scenes following the gang's exploits together to a sombre darkness that increasingly takes hold as they disband and attempt to follow their individual lives. This change then offers a correlative of their progression from rural Japan to urban, downtown Tokyo, and from a single unit to an increasingly fragmented collection of dispersing individuals.

It is the treatment of these characters in *9 Souls* that facilitates much of the film's magic realism. After a brief scene that fills in some details surrounding one young character's crime via a depiction of the animosity between him and his father, the narrative of *9 Souls* starts immediately in prison. It opens with the beginning of his incarceration, which positions this character (named Michiru) as a primary focaliser as he is introduced to the titular nine characters who are already locked up together and who are thus already well acquainted with each other. Following this concise introduction the film cuts abruptly to their escape, the precise details of which are left entirely vague as one is simply shown them emerging from a hole in the ground seemingly in the middle of nowhere. The fact that this condensed single scene acts as a prologue to the film – the title follows after separate onscreen introductions to the characters as they run for their lives – underlines the fact that literal imprisonment is not a concern of the narrative. Rather it is a sense of figurative, internalised entrapment and lack of freedom that begins to predominate, and it is how the protagonists variously come to terms with this – or, more properly, fail to come to terms with it – that Toyoda traces.

This begins to highlight *9 Souls'* particular sensibility, its subjective perspectives and manifestations, and it is from this that Toyoda's magic realist tenets are born. Strange moments begin to permeate the story, most overtly when the gang stumble across a gentleman's club in a remote rural location. They are outside their van following a physical altercation between two of their number when they suddenly see a sign advertising this club, which establishment's anomalous appearance figures as a marker of the distinction between urban and rural, as well as an ironic signifier of estranged 'normalcy' in that visiting such a club would be a typical act for such men. From this point of view the physical anomalousness of the establishment in this setting reflects something not only of these characters' skewered experience of the world beyond the confines of their jail cell but also of their divorcement from normality and the 'real' world. It is a perceptual schema, one wherein an effacement of discrete spatial boundaries correlates to a comparable postmodern frustration (already noted in Kitano's *Dolls*) of that between image and phenomenological referent, and thus between the typical simulacral (over-representational) import of film as a medium. Such a conception has frequently figured in discourse on the city and the cinema as complementary sites of both experiential modernity and postmodernity – see Baudrillard (1988) and Clarke (1997) – and Toyoda's methodology here extrapolates from this urban-centrism in order to disturb clear demarcations of topography and space. In point of fact there is a further sense of self-reflexivity in the film at this point; as the characters enter the club the first interior shot has the camera track up to (and through) a door with a circular window, the effect of which is to replicate an iris out and thus to markedly refract physical space through the cinematic apparatus. And the fact that this is a technical device associated with silent filmmaking, the cinema of the past, further offers a cinematisation of real space (or spatialisation of cinema) that obfuscates distinctions pertaining to spatial and temporal spheres that are ostensibly clearly differentiated, and thus to the characters' dislocated experiences of the world around them.

Entering this building is, then, a journey through a portal into the past and into the cinema for the characters; it is a realm where distinctions are eroded and the real is displaced by representation: where the consumption of images highlights a lack of reality. It is a figurative space of destruction that calls to mind David Harvey's argument for the centrality of 'creative destruction' to the project(s) of modernism, an essential means of starting anew by building on the ashes of an old order (1990, pp. 10–38). For these characters, who are seen to be birthed when they escape from prison (symbolically, existentially emerging from a hole in the ground), the act of creation is writ large. However personal destruction is extrapolated as spatial destruction, through which Toyoda raises the spectre of an anxious modern/postmodern ambiguity. The very first shot of the film is a sweeping, long camera take over urban Tokyo during which buildings and landmarks incrementally disappear until all that can be seen is the Tokyo Tower. It is a vision that is implicitly associated with the young Michiru, and relates to his subjectivity (or proto-subjectivity) as defined and constructed by urban experiences, reflecting something of the Lacanian cooption of urban space that Rob Lapsley (1997) identifies as a key facet of how cities feature as mirrored others in both the dramatic and experiential imagination (Toyoda follows the aforementioned shot with a scene in which Michiru's problems with his father are expounded, dramatising his difficulty ascending to the Lacanian Name of the Father. He has, in effect, been imprisoned both literally and figuratively, and his inability to enter society bespeaks the extent of his pre-subjectivity amidst the Mirror stage marker that is the vertiginous city space). Here the so-called 'no-place space' of the postmodern city (Featherstone, 2007, p. 98) is twisted to mark out Tokyo, localising a topographical specificity as a means of reiterating the tension between modernity and postmodernity and of arresting a clear temporal trajectory that complicates this city's status as clearly located in the latter. If, as Edward Dimendberg (2004) in particular has argued, there is an intertwining of the cinematic and the urban, then it is one that Toyoda plays upon directly, rewriting as he does the historical trauma of the Pacific War and the firebombing of the Japanese capital as a fantasy of personal estrangement and frustrated subjectivity, an individual view of the city as a historically transformative space that implicitly refers back to the modern narrative of Japan's post-war urban reconstruction and economic prosperity at the same time as it frustrates this national story in aid of a trajectory that encompasses a personal sense of alienation and exile. The connection is, of course, that of money, of capitalism as the context of the postmodern, which is here taken to an extreme of greed and personal depravity in the person of Michiru's brother, whose job as a loan shark makes him a literal arbiter of consumption. The Tokyo of 9 Souls is still contingent upon capital, on transactions as a marker of social intercourse, and it is this that Michiru seems to want to explode, to destroy. Yet in so doing he ultimately destroys himself, taking his sibling hostage as he does before ultimately plunging to his death from the top of a skyscraper. Wechsler (1985) has described the strangeness of city life as a key focus in magic realism and, not unlike Koreeda, Toyoda complicates the affectless vision of postmodernity in order to stress a magic realist sense of alienation and isolation. As already noted the catalyst for tragedy in 9 Souls is the breaking apart of the gang, with its constituent members unable to face life alone. Without each other they are all in one way or another vulnerable, open to attack, and in lieu of any viable alternative tend to casually drift back into crime, into patterns of behaviour that have always dominated their lives. This is underlined in particular by the medical condition that afflicts one character who succumbs to violent fits and needs to be nursed back to health, a task that is always undertaken by one fellow prisoner, a dwarf. However in a final scene, when this character is being harassed by schoolgirls who have recognised his face from a wanted poster, the dwarf has already departed the gang and he is shown as a result to be entirely weak and unable to take care of himself when alone in the world. In point of fact the dwarf, named Shiratori, is the most pragmatic of the nine escapees; he is the first to depart the gang (he finds a girl whom he had previously been close to in the aforementioned strip club) and views all the travails that he encounters with a casual practicality rather than the desperation and recourse to violence that afflicts the others. His leaving seems to destabilise the group, as it is after this visit, when they all proceed without him, that things begin to go wrong for them. It is noticeable that this character of all the nine most easily deals with freedom, and concomitantly it is apparent that he alone retains something of his life in jail as a significant facet of his 'freedom', as though he can cope best with being free from prison because he was best able to cope with being in prison. On more than one occasion he is shown diligently going through the routine of the morning exercises that were expected of him whilst in jail, a practice that, when challenged by a colleague, he defends by noting that his nerves 'don't feel right' until he has completed them. It is also notable that Toyoda uses a dwarf as ostensibly the most normal and well-adjusted character in the film. The actor Yamada Mame, had already appeared in a minor role in *Blue Spring* (as a school gardener whose nominal difference to those around him and whose friendship with the protagonist throws light on said lead character's estrangement), and Toyoda's recourse to him in *9 Souls* serves a similar purpose. As in Werner Herzog *Even Dwarfs Started Small* (*Auch Zwerge haben klein angefangen*, 1970), which dramatises a revolt by a group of dwarfs in the institution in which they are being held, Shiratori's ostensible physical disparity from those around him underlines not estrangement from normalcy but rather the normalcy of estrangement or difference. That is, the relationship of the dwarf to the objects and the people around him, looming over him as they do, represents not an abnormality on his part but rather a distorted view of that world, its characters and objects. This exaggerated, uncanny depiction of Japanese society reflects perhaps the clearest magical realist impulse of Toyoda's vision in *9 Souls*, which emerges in the space left by the tension between modernity and postmodernity. It engages with the concept of *Shūdan ishiki*, the group consciousness that is often regarded as a touchstone of Japanese nationhood – as 'the foundation of Japanese society' (Davies and Ikeno, 2002, p. 195) – and uses it to allegorise a contemporary Japan where imprisonment and estrangement are factors of everyday life, and where uncanniness is a feature of reality in the country.

Although magic realism remains an under-explored facet of cinema, and the boundaries or specific delineations of postmodernism have always been divisive and contested – and indeed now appear to be eroding altogether – there is nonetheless a use value associated with their employment as critical terms in describing specific films' engagement with their cultural and socio-political context. From this point of view the interbreeding or cross-pollination of these ostensibly contrastive categories may be a productive means of reinvigorating their emphases and specific arenas of distinction, redefining their parameters as a means of defining new works that increasingly frustrate older or more established modes. The fact that critics such as Jeffrey Nealon (2012), following Raul Eshelman (2008), have argued there has been a decisive paradigm shift into an age beyond the postmodern – with the latter identifying what he terms 'performatism' as a direct cultural form of rebuttal to postmodernism's over-determined yet under-developed episteme; the fact that 'there are simply too many narrative strategies and motifs that go unexplained, too many artistic devices that diverge from the expected postmodern patterns' (p. 10) – speaks of the ongoing anxiety over the appropriation and application of these terms. However, as this chapter has attempted to argue, it is precisely this indeterminacy that can in fact be productively applied in order to reconfigure and potentially reanimate their critical impetus. Contemporary Japanese cinema has worked to open up this liminal space and exploit the fissures and gaps to productively situate key films within a reconstituted discourse that need not slavishly adhere to successive eras and sites of linear contextuality. If, as Donald Richie (2001) has claimed, the fantastic and the realistic offer the two overarching narrative registers in contemporary Japanese cinema (p. 217), then the films covered above offer a counter-example of convergence where the parameters, the stylistic and narrative contours, of both are challenged and reconfigured, and where a cyclical imperative is implied in postmodernism's frequent frustration of historical verisimilitude. In this at least they are key films in modern Japanese cinema.

6. JAPANESE DOCUMENTARY CINEMA: REALITY AND ITS DISCONTENTS

I personally can't define the difference between a documentary and a narrative film [. . .] one day when I was wondering, What exactly *is* a documentary, as opposed to the other kinds of movies that we make? I finally decided that if you just attach the camera to the top of a bull's horns and let him loose in a field for a whole day, at the end of the day you might have a documentary. But there's still a catch here, because we've selected the location and the type of lens that we want.

Abbas Kiarostami (Saeed-Vafa and Rosenbaum, 2003, p. 117)

Every film is a documentary. Even the most whimsical of fictions gives evidence of the culture that produced it and reproduces the likenesses of the people who perform within it [. . .] we could say that there are two kinds of film: (1) documentaries of wish-fulfillment and (2) documentaries of social representation.

(Nichols, 2001, p. 1)

With the proliferation of films in documentary form over the course of the past two decades, no one is quite sure what the term *documentary* means anymore. The popular sense of the word in Japan has degenerated so that it is used to refer to television gossip shows and the *dokyumento* shelves at video stores.

(Nornes, 2003, p. 1)

The attitude of inquiry provided by a poetics is particularly apropos for the documentary insofar as poetics has [. . .] occupied an unstable position at the juncture of science and aesthetics, structure and value, truth and beauty. Documentary film is itself the site of much equivocation around similar axes given nonfiction's too-frequently presumed debt to the signified at the expense of the signifier's play. It is 'film of fact', 'nonfiction', the realm of information and exposition rather than diegetic employment or imagination – in short, at a remove from the creative core of the cinematic art.

(Renov, 1993, p. 13)

There is no such thing as a documentary, yet everything is a documentary; 'reality' can only be created, not recorded, yet the real, the non-fictive, is an absolute, a guarantee that an audience can learn about the world around them, and thus perhaps learn something about themselves. This apparent paradox of documentary filmmaking – or at least on discourse about the form – is one that has incrementally come to define its horizons and procedural methodology; it has shaped ways in which non-fiction has been produced, received and explored, and has further gone hand-in-hand with an increasing popularisation of its boundaries and stylistic contours. A relatively recent proliferation of critical work on the documentary after decades of uneven, at times almost non-existent academic discourse, has steadily explored, defined, redefined, reconceptualised and challenged the boundaries of its objective validity (or otherwise) as well as its openness to wider currents and critical frameworks of reference and representation. Abbas Kiarostami (in Saeed-Vafa and Rosenbaum, 2003) has reflected upon the essential impossibility of the documentary, on the extent to which an objective, unmediated view of the 'real' is a practical as well as an aesthetic impossibility and should not necessarily be held to be at the forefront of non-fictive filmmaking. Other practitioners have remained in thrall to a view of non-fiction that stresses a tangible reality that can be captured and explored. Albert Maysles' recent assertion that 'as a documentarian, I happily place my fate and faith in reality. It is my caretaker, the provider of subjects, themes, experiences – all endowed with the power of truth and the romance of discovery' (2013, p. 10) can perhaps be regarded as something less than the totalising project it has sometimes been taken to be (if only implicitly) but is nonetheless a view that still has some currency. Concomitantly, if it is true, as James Quinn has noted, that people are 'more and more sceptical about documentaries' (2013, p. 14), then perhaps this relates more than anything else to the destabilisation of the centrality of reality as a transparent, tangible, unambiguous presence, as well as to the attendant frustration of the phenomenological referent as paramount, its possibility or desirability as a goal in non-fiction.

If there is a more widespread or pervasive scepticism about documentaries it is interesting to note that this has been attendant on a dramatic increase in their visibility and popularity: when documentaries and individual directors like Michael Moore, Werner Herzog, Errol Morris and Morgan Spurlock have become increasingly successful in cinemas and have created what Dave Saunders calls a 'new wave of big-screen non-fiction' (2007, p. 12). Despite the fact that the mode is as old as cinema itself – is in a sense inseparable from the perceived, albeit embryonic mimesis of the medium's beginnings in actuality films – it is only in these comparatively recent years that it is has, in Nick Fraser's words, 'emerged from a cave of unknowing into something like sunlight' (2013, p. 10). However critical focus has attended conceptual and formal ambiguity, such that, as Nornes suggests, the very designation 'documentary' has become ever more ambiguous and uncertain, ever more open to problems of interpretation (2003). Nichols and Nornes' respective recognition of the slippery distinction between feature and non-fiction films has become a central feature of discourse on the subject, being echoed and/or raised by commentators such as Mark Cousins, (2004) Patricia Aufderheide (2007) and Mitsuyo Wada-Marciano (2012) among others. Nichols subdivides the documentary into six distinct subsets that broadly work like generic frameworks in that they 'set up conventions that a given film may adopt; and they provide specific expectations viewers anticipate having fulfilled' (2001, p. 99), which in itself already employs a feature narrative framework and presupposes an engagement with non-fiction in which spectatorship, even suture and interpellation, become salient questions. And if Nichols' binary classification and stylistic/methodological modes of and approaches to non-fiction filmmaking suggest the extent to which observable parameters of documentaries can be problematic or problematised, then this is by no means a new concept. Neither is this a nationally specific feature or one that is localised within individual figures who have exemplified a particularly idiosyncratic approach or stylistic methodology. Rather it is a broad trend that can be argued to reflect or encompass larger (stylistic and industrial) paradigm shifts, especially the relationship of cinema to television, wherein the increasing mainstream of documentary filmmaking outlined by Michael Chanan (2007a) lays bare and helps make visible an increasing number of alternatives or genres. The belief, or even the comfortable assumption, of commentators like Geoffrey Nowell-Smith (2008, p. 85) and Julia Hallam and Margret Marshment (2000) that there is a conventional form of non-fiction against which creative or experimental works can be judged is increasingly a problematic, if not an erroneous, point of view. Indeed it is inviting to consider this breaching of ostensibly discrete boundaries to be a feature that metonymically encapsulates a much wider artistic trend inherent in both transnational and now trans-medial cinema, of digital forms of shooting and editing that have permeated so much filmmaking in recent years and have specifically impacted upon works of non-fiction through a greater availability of technological means in addition to what has been frequently thought of as digital immediacy or even authenticity.

This latter notion offers a useful and productive introduction to, as well as a foundation for, a specifically Japanese canon of documentary filmmaking. Mitsuyo Wada-Marciano (2012) has explored in detail the thoroughgoing appropriation of non-fiction modalities by directors like Koreeda Hirokazu and Kawase Naomi, who have typically alternated between features and documentaries as a defining aspect of their careers, with the one impacting upon the other. The hybridisation of some of their key films attests to the prominence of this paradigm not only within documentary filmmaking and studies thereof in general but with regard to those from Japan in particular, and it is with this conception in mind that this chapter will seek to outline and delineate the textual properties and historical lineage of some of the most significant non-fiction films and their directors.

Wada-Marciano's account of new Japanese non-fiction is a lucid and enlightening example of the kind of reframing that is currently reanimating documentary studies, and a pertinent example of how such a project can enhance debates on the specificity of Japanese additions to the form. One vital aspect of her study concerns what she describes as a 'post-studio' filmmaking environment (2012, pp. 51–5), which is a key aspect of any analysis of modern Japanese documentary cinema as it begins to infer the ways in which non-fiction filmmakers can be placed within the context of the country's cinema in general. She also echoes Nornes (2013) in discussing a specificity of Japanese documentary filmmaking that, whilst not homogeneous in and of itself, nonetheless defines it against particularly Western norms and practices (Wada-Marciano, 2012, p. 54). Nonetheless despite this connection a detailed account of the modern Japanese documentary film has yet to be undertaken, a study to match Nornes' two mammoth studies *Japanese Documentary Film: The Meiji Era through Hiroshima* and *Forest of Pressure: Ogawa Shinsuke and Postwar Japanese Documentary*. The useful *Imagining Reality* (Cousins and McDonald, 1996) contains a section entitled 'Aspects of Asia', with some insightful reviews of individual films and filmmakers, whilst Eric Barnouw (1993) has examined the prevalent trends of Japanese documentary filmmaking. But these are exceptions rather than the rule. On the one hand this is particularly surprising when one considers that since 1989 Japan has played host to one of the world's foremost documentary festivals in the Yamagata International Documentary Film Festival, held once every two years in the city of Yamagata. However on the other a notably small number of Japanese films have managed to succeed in competition in Yamagata (Chinese and South Korean documentaries in particular have tended to prosper in recent years). Indeed, contrary to the aforementioned aesthetic and practical considerations, several notable figures in the field have remarked on the extent to which the viability of the documentary in Japan, its success as a distinct form, has begun to erode, as an adjunct to which it is noteworthy that almost every major name in Japanese non-fiction cinema since (and including) Hara Kazuo in the 1970s and 1980s has migrated to feature filmmaking and at most oscillated between the two media. As Imamura Shohei hinted in *A Man Vanishes* (*Ningen johatsu*, 1967), it is almost as though any truth(s) of modern Japan have no objective or independent veracity: that is, they remain inaccessible to those who attempt to document them in a more or less straightforward manner, who simply point their cameras and ask questions and in so doing overtly attempt to capture something real. The truth, a truth, in Imamura's film – which concerns an investigation into the prolonged disappearance of a man, a quest that involves his fiancée as well as the increasingly hapless director himself – continually eludes Imamura, as enquiries beget more enquiries and a centrifugal structure becomes prevalent wherein the form continues to expand, to emanate outward as answers are continually interrupted and deferred and the focus drifts from the ostensible subject to those around him.

However the theme of the present study – that most modern, post-1997 Japanese cinema recapitulates earlier modes and models – is as true of documentaries as it is of feature films. Wada-Marciano is largely correct to assert that Japan's new, younger documentary directors have eschewed the methodological rigours and painstaking personal and political commitment of arguably Japan's most famous and acclaimed director of non-fiction, Ogawa Shinsuke. She does, however, elide other key filmmakers, especially Tsuchimoto Noriaki, and thus offers a partial picture of the lineage of contemporary Japanese documentaries. It is true that she seems to draw from Nornes for some of her points regarding the disturbance of a notable history in recent Japanese non-fiction, but there is much more to say than that Ogawa and his filmmaking collective (Ogawa Pro) represents the single face of this lineage, its accepted paradigm (2012, p. 52). As such it is not entirely accurate to suggest of the new canon of Japanese non-fiction that 'the sense of novelty [. . .] distinguishes it from the postwar Japanese documentary tradition' (ibid.), as there is a viable sense in which this tradition was itself posited against, for instance, the work of a director such as Kamei Fumio in the post-war period. This director – who has been called 'the most important director in the history of Japanese documentary' (Nornes, 2003, p. 12) – made a series of three films collectively entitled *The People of Sunagawa* (*Sunagawa no hitobito*, 1955–6) about the increasingly violent struggle that ensued when the government requisitioned land in order to expand on an airport runway to accommodate US forces still in Japan. This example of documentary as direct action prefigured Ogawa's monumental *Sanrizuka* series that made the name of his collective in the 1960s: films that were similarly concerned with the construction of an airport (Narita), and which when placed beside Kamei's work bespeak an ongoing sense of political struggle shaping individuals and communities. Moreover the neglect of names like Tsuchimoto or a more recent but no less vital director like Sato Makoto denotes both a limited vision of the scope and breadth of Japanese documentary cinema and a limiting conception of the variegated methods and meanings of contemporary figures whose relationship to their progenitors is at times complex and overtly dialogic. If there is a 'novelty' to such works – and this is an eminently contentious point as the anti-standardisation that is signified by the term tends to imply (erroneously) a uniformity of style and/or subject in the films and filmmakers of earlier generations – then it is not necessarily to distinguish them from the past so much as to imbricate them in a dialogue between said past and the present (their particular present) as it stands in discursive relation to it.

In other words the private spaces that Wada-Marciano regards as endemic within modern Japanese documentaries, along with the discrete 'personal documentary' mode that is perceived to contrast with the expansive and often forcefully political works of Ogawa Shinsuke and his filmmaking collective in particular (pp. 52–3), are defined as such in relation to their forebears rather than directly against them. Dialogism is already implied in this author's terminology. But it is important to note that many modern works of non-fiction from Japan are subtly intertextual constructs whose relationship to the past (even if only as a point of departure or contestation) remains an integral feature of their stylistic and methodological practice. This then alludes to an interrogation of whether or not our relationship to or perception of any apparent reality has changed over the course of several decades; and, concomitantly, whether the relationship of individuals to the state has remained concordant over time. This is not to suggest that modern Japanese documentaries grow clearly or organically from their progenitors: there are, of course, key distinctions to be made and boundaries to be observed. What should be stressed is a prevalence of theme and variation, a textual and methodological tension rather than a direct opposition between past and present that helps to cast light on the latter and further elucidate the Japaneseness that Nornes (2013, pp. 209–16) and Wada-Marciano (2012, pp. 51–73) in particular have read into them. The concept of a personal documentary and a *Riaruna eiga* (realistic film) does indeed contrast with the canonised Japanese non-fiction of the 1960s, addressing as it does 'the relative subjectivity of the viewer' by momentarily rupturing the representational transparency of the pro-filmic event and thereby recalling 'any person's experience of viewing the imperfect image on the small display screen of a digital camera' (ibid., p. 53). However the point here regarding the mediation and representation of the real is but one manifestation of what has been shown to be a pervasive feature of discourse on non-fiction, albeit one pertaining to the particular ways and means of digital photography.

The aforementioned sense of fiction in reality and vice versa is useful here, and is reinforced by the co-presence in both forms of particular themes and narrative subjects, to the extent that a sense of cross-fertilisation should be a significant, even a central, feature in discourse on either medium. Chief in this regard is the representation of illness, disease or physical impairment. It animates the yakuza and samurai genres, with their frequent emphasis on ritualised physical punishment – on decapitation and disembowelling, respectively – and informs a number of other individual films: from dramatic works like Kurosawa Akira's *Ikiru* [*Living*] (1953), Imamura Shohei's *Black Rain* (*Kuroi ame*, 1986) or Ichikawa Jun's *Dying at a Hospital* (*Byōin de shinu to iu koto*, 1993) to genre films like Honda Ishiro's *Attack of the Mushroom People* (*Matango*, 1960), Tsukamoto Shinya's *Tetsuo: The Iron Man* (*Tetsuo*, 1989), Fujiwara Kei's extreme body horror *Organ* (1996) or Aoyama Shinji's *EM Embalming* (*EM enbāmingu*, 1999) and including modern filmmakers like Kitano Takeshi and Miike Takashi, who echo many of the films cited above by locating selfhood and identity purely in the corporeal. Numerous documentary directors have taken illness and disease as a point of departure in their work, offering explorations of disease, of physical or mental illness, that variously articulate both collectivity and individuality and as such explore some of the key themes not only within Japanese culture but with regard to its socio-political landscape. In many cases it is not illness *per se* that animates the films but a figurative sense of people at the mercy of something much larger than themselves over which they have no control. This is certainly the case with Tsuchimoto Noriaki, whose exalted career was built around a series of films that documented the onset of Minamata disease in a series of detailed, moving, angry, political films he made about the methyl mercury poisoning that affected the citizens of this town and surrounding areas in western Japan in the 1950s and 1960s. For him the status of his subjects as victims of the capitalist state rather than of a specific illness is made paramount in the screen time given to the protests and political demonstrations by the victims in perhaps the most famous film of the series, *Minamata: The Victims and Their World* (*Minamata: kanja-san to sono sekai*, 1971). This documentary enshrines a commonality of experience, but Joan Mellen has argued that it (and like films) do 'not deal with the central dilemma at the heart of the culture: how democratic social institutions are to be freely chosen [. . .] if the concepts of the individual [. . .] have not yet been made fundamental elements of one's experience as a Japanese' (1979, p. 428).

Conversely, the concept of a *Shiteki dokumentari*, or personal mode of documentary cinema – one that has 'shifted the framing of reality to the now ubiquitous digital image [. . .] [whose] cheap, democratic utility links it to the banality manifest in home videos, video diaries, and surveillance cameras' (Wada-Marciano, 2012, p. 54) – effectively individualises the landscape of Japanese non-fiction, both before and behind the camera. This is not, as De Michiel and Zimmerman imply (2013, p. 365), a specifically Japanese phenomenon; nonetheless there is a sense that it defines the contours of a majority of this country's documentary output in recent years. There is in fact a strong tradition in Japanese non-fiction of an auteur brand: of directors whose films offer a readily identifiable signature, chief in which regard is arguably Hara Kazuo, a director who occupies a pivotal place within Japanese non-fiction for his place in a perceived era of transition and development from the political to the personal. This director's first feature documentary, *Goodbye CP* (*Sayonara CP*, 1972), is a confrontational and challenging portrait of disability, particularly of the perceived Otherness of the mentally infirm. This stark film follows a cerebral palsy sufferer and his girlfriend (among several others), and it stresses the director's presence through the force of his apparently invasive methodology, the fact that he ultimately seems to intrude and negatively affect the lives of his subjects. By this means Hara also asks for a response from his audience, demands that they take a position on what they are seeing and thus become active in thinking for themselves about how they feel regarding the victims, their illness and perhaps more pointedly about its representation on film. Brian Winston in particular has written about what he terms 'the repressed in documentary studies' (1995, pp. 230–41): that is, the extent to which non-fiction films have significant consequences for those involved before the camera, those who are filmed and whose lives and experiences are opened up to public consumption, even perhaps exploited. From this point of view Hara's film is as much about its director as it is about its nominal subjects.

If Hara offers something of a nodal point in the development of Japanese non-fiction it is a paradigm that has proved influential. Key in this regard, as Wada-Marciano argues, is the work of both Koreeda and Kawase, whose documentaries best represent the kind of small, intimate, ostensibly depoliticised mode that is seen as particular to many modern non-fiction films from Japan. The latter's film *Tarachime* (2006) – which like several earlier Kawase films plays almost as a home video, in this case of the director's own pregnancy from conception through gestation and birth – is examined by Wada-Marciano as representative of this director's form of so-called *Riaruna eiga*, in which the director's camera is located within 'her filming events', in an echo of reality television wherein its perennial presence naturalises its observatory role and confers apparent 'reality' on the pro-filmic event only through its ability to capture and represent it (2012, p. 62). However there are several Kawase films that complicate this form, films of which it could be said that the camera's ubiquitous diegetic presence is narativised as much as naturalised. In other words she often frames her own present absence (or vice versa) as a defining feature of her work, and perhaps a more cogent film from this point of view is the earlier *Letter from a Yellow Cherry Blossom* (*Tsuioku no dansu*, 2003), as it begins to demonstrate the limitations of clearly distinguishing her work as an oeuvre from that of her predecessors. It is also the key film to consider when thinking of Kawase's place in the pantheon of Japanese non-fiction. Kawase is a director who has always eschewed any sense that she has drawn inspiration from or can be productively placed in a lineage with any specific forebears. However this particular film serves to frustrate such an easy demarcation or separation. It also demonstrates that the personal film paradigm and conceptions thereof can amount to more than a simple consideration of how subjects especially close to the filmmaker's heart are framed and elucidated.

Letter from a Yellow Cherry Blossom is centred upon a terminally ill man in his final days (the film critic and notable photographer Nishii Kazuo), and over the course of the film he is questioned by Kawase about his life and work. As such it not only calls to mind those numerous Japanese documentaries that patiently and painstakingly depict often serious illness and physical debilitation but also helps to foreground some of the problems surrounding the demarcation of the personal documentary form, what precisely this may be said to mean, to whom is it personal and why. Nishii himself asked that Kawase document his last few days alive, and she responds with an almost unflinching focus and single-minded purpose. However this is not a purposeful focus on his illness or the specific details of his suffering. Kawase begins the film with silent 8 mm footage from Nishii's funeral, establishing death, the fact of his passing, immediately as an abstract, anterior state, and thereby defining the subsequent film as one concerned with life, with being alive. Nishii is suffering from a tragic illness, so the political import of particularly Tsuchimoto's studies of disease is of course absent, but it is nonetheless striking how the film forgoes any direct engagement with his physical debilitation. Indeed it is never even stated precisely what Nishii is suffering from, with no elucidation at all as to the nature of his ailment or the status of his deteriorating health beyond the fact that he is increasingly close to death. On such occasions as his physical suffering obstructs or prevents his continued participation in filming – such as when a trip around the hospital grounds brings about a violent fit of uncontrollable coughing – Kawase tempers any prolonged public exposure to his discomfort by removing the sound of his clearly desperate situation so that all that can be heard is the ambient sounds of birds chirping, aurally redolent as they are of a bright summer day and as such a counterpoint to the hitherto distressing sounds and a means of seeing beyond the immediate, cold fact of his impending death to the world he will leave behind.

The subject of *Letter from a Yellow Cherry Blossom* is, then, avowedly not Nishii's illness or his physical suffering *per se*; Kawase is concerned not to negate or marginalise his suffering but to see beyond it, to disavow any sense that he is or should be defined by it. Instead the director is concerned with what this terminal illness facilitates: the perspective on life that exposure to death brings about. The dialogue between (ostensible) director and subject is entirely concerned with topics that are not directly related to his ailments, with Kawase a perennial presence in the film, constantly engaging the bedridden Nishi in a discourse on topics such as documentary filmmaking, memory, life and death and poetry. However she remains invisible, always behind the camera, a disembodied and probing voice that inveigles Nishii even when her camera moves away from him to consider other images, such as the view immediately outside his hospital room window (a means related to the aforementioned aural juxtaposition that serves to frame him within a context of life rather than death). Late in the film there is a discussion between the director and her subject in which it is stated that the former will inevitably take centre stage given the latter's death; that this event will inexorably frame her as the film's focal point, its locus of meaning, and by extension the figure for whom it is most personal and relevant. As if to offset this potentiality Kawase includes a scene in which some friends and students of Nishii's spend time by his bedside, talking with and taking photographs of the protagonist and his surroundings, and she incorporates a selection of their snapshots into the film as part of its general methodology and reflective critique. This multiplicity of images – a circuitous way of de-centring but also arguably of re-inscribing an authorial aesthetic (in that Kawase has chosen to include them) – is important to her ruminative inquiry as it frustrates or problematises the possibility of a singly authored text. One scene in particular features Kawase decrying the term documentary, stating that it suggests something staid or petrified: something that will 'eventually end up in storage [. . .] on the other side of what we call "the present"'. However the film begins with the director asserting that she 'make[s] films to leave something behind. Something to prove that I lived': in other words a record of a life, and it is the liminal space between these apparent poles of reality – between (Kawase's) life and (Nishi's) death, and between documentary and memory – that animates *Letter from a Yellow Cherry Blossom*. It is a film about the process of trying to record a memory that will negate or evade any perceived status as documentary. If, as Tony Dowmunt (2013) has suggested, the practical aesthetics of non-fiction (especially in the digital age) facilitate a more comfortable sense of authorial agency than feature filmmaking, then Kawase here further reinforces the precept in order to problematise her presence as a director and, arguably, an auteur. It is about her choices (as seen in the photographs) and decisions in shaping a response to Nishii's life, something that she amplifies in order to make her point. As such the concept of the personal documentary becomes predicated on an individual response that confronts its audience with said individuality – makes it available for critique or even rejection – so that the term in this context means as much for each viewer as for the director.

Koreeda has similarly made documentaries about illness and physical affliction, both terminal and otherwise, ones that are lauded by Wada-Marciano (ibid., p. 57) as neutral and objective studies but that, unlike *Letter from a Yellow Cherry Blossom*, narrativise a space for the personal form. Indeed it may be argued that the television projects *August Without Him* (*Kare no inai hachigatsu ga*, 1994) and *Without Memory* (*Kioku ga usinawareta toki*, 1996) are important works as they each serve to subtly question their own different projects. These works look at, respectively, an AIDS patient in the final two years of his life (Japan's first gay male to openly admit to contracting the disease through sexual intercourse) and a man who suffers from a condition that has left him unable to form new memories. The objectivity perceived as central to these films is at times something of a smoke-screen as Koreeda uses the appearance of such a mode only in order to question and problematise it. Both films feature voice of God narration, and at least initially they each feature a narrative transparency wherein the diegetic presence of the director and his crew is not made overtly manifest. In the former, however, those behind the camera are inveigled or manipulated by the protagonist into becoming part of his network of carers and companions. *August without Him* in particular presents a discourse on the limits of objectivity as either a practical possibility or a standard of value in documentary filmmaking. What begins as a record of a vivacious, hedonistic personality gradually succumbing to an illness that robs him of the means of engaging (if not the will to engage) in a majority of personal pursuits transforms into an examination of and reflection on the fundamental impossibility of non-fictive filmmaking to remain detached and simply record a subject from a position of impartiality. It is, in effect, the same problem that Imamura explores in *A Man Vanishes* but with the opposite trajectory; it traces the protracted awaiting of a known and expected disappearance rather than the aftermath of one so sudden and surprising, but nonetheless both works demonstrate how the filmmaker and his crew become embroiled in the subject's life, indeed seem unable to extricate themselves from it. Koreeda increasingly seems to reflect on this man, Hirata-San, as a person, making judgements about the ways in which he appears to manipulate or alienate his friends and implying resentment at the extent to which he takes the film crew around him and his status as their subject for granted. Moreover the carefully structured non-linear approach of this film – the fact that it juxtaposes extended scenes following and talking to the subject with brief, ruminative reflections from the director during the month following his passing (hence the title of the film) – is further testament to its interest in looking beyond its immediate (ostensible) subject. These directorial interjections frequently, ironically, come in the form of still life shots that mark Hirata's absence, his death, and it is the ramifications of this disappearance that mark out *August without Him* as a film about its director as much as its subject, about his reaction to Hirata and the point and purpose of his film about him.

Though peripheral to the present study, the significance of Koreeda lies as much in the production and exhibition of his work as its narrativity or style. The significance of television to Japanese documentary filmmaking in the 1990s and shortly thereafter has been discussed by Wada-Marciano (2012, p. 5) as an important means by which non-fiction films began to be produced and viewed. The availability of funding has, in addition to the increasing availability of democratising digital equipment, led to a veritable explosion of new films and filmmakers that according to some directors has resulted in a perceived laziness on the part of filmmakers. This digital revolution has been implicitly criticised by Sato Makoto, who has seen a lack of professionalism in its ease of technical means (2006, pp. 14–40), a criticism by an important director whose own work demonstrated a painstaking production process and a commitment to conceptualising the parameters of documentary filmmaking. Sato very broadly followed, and in Japan was perceived to be a disciple of, both Tsuchimoto and Ogawa Pro in that he combined the detailed personal involvement with his subjects that characterised the latter with the examination of environmental pollution and its devastating effect on humanity of the former. His canon is best exemplified by *Living on the River Agano* (*Aga ni ikiru*, 1993), which focuses, like Tsuchimoto's *Minamata* series, on the victims of Minamata disease, in this case the elderly residents of a relatively small but close-knit rural village on the banks of the Agano River in Niigata in Chubu, in the west of Honshu (the largest of Japan's four chief mainland islands) who suffered due to the Showa Electrical Company's pollution of the titular river. Conversely Sato spent an extended period of time doing exactly as the title of his film denotes; he lived along with his subjects on the Agano River, helped out with their various laborious activities (especially their harvesting of the land) and along with his small crew of seven became deeply embroiled in their lives, community and fight for recognition as victims of Minamata disease.

However Sato should not be perceived as a mere facsimile of these forbears; one should in fact use their ostensible similarity as a means of distinguishing his work and its attitudes. He had studied with Ogawa Pro and embarked upon *Living on the River Agano* as a means of continuing its project and practical methodology. He had planned not to repeat some of the limitations he had perceived in his forebear, an ideal he unfortunately felt he did not accomplish (Nornes, 2007a, p. 256). The focus on illness in *Living on the River Agano*, and especially in the follow-up he made twelve years later entitled *Memories of Agano* (*Aga no kioku*, 2005), is not unlike Kawase's in *Letter from a Yellow Cherry Blossom*; the director clearly desires that his subjects not be defined or characterised entirely by their illness, entirely as victims. It is true that the largely elderly people in Sato's films are not as seriously ill as many of their counterparts in Tsuchimoto's work, suffering as they do from a different strain of the disease known as Niigata Minamata disease after the town in which they live (and which was discovered only in 1965 after the original outbreak in 1956). Nonetheless their direct connection to and reliance on the land in the remote location in which they live (which facilitated the disease in the first place) means that their lives have been inexorably affected by their increasing disabilities and physical deterioration. However, with the exception of a small number of scenes in which the residents discuss their physical problems, or one in which they visit a court in a nearby town to have their case officially heard (although the hearing is never depicted), there is comparatively little focus on this aspect of their lives. Indeed through the form of the film Sato ultimately seems increasingly anxious about the focus and structure of his documentary, and to this end it has been speculated that the follow-up *Memories of Agano* was made as a means of rewriting the project of *Living on the River Agano*. If the first film is increasingly fraught with the sense that the objective perspective of his camera was in a sense overriding his own (Sato at one point states in voiceover that he only noticed the sadness of one man's reaction to the subject of a particular scene when he looked over his footage), then the latter becomes precisely predicated on the liminal spaces between perception and presupposition, between the human eye and that of the camera. This short film is in fact prefaced by a note stating that the director did not want his film to be subtitled (in Japanese as much as any other language – something required in *Living on the River Agano* due to the thick regional accents of its subjects) because he wanted his audience to concentrate not on what the people before the camera were saying but on other details of their lives: on the way they spoke and behaved, the ways that they engaged with one another and the way they lived, ultimately to concentrate on what is termed in the film the 'spaces they lived and died'.

Sato became increasingly concerned with exploring both the potentiality and the limits of documentary filmmaking. Indeed he remains significant in that, like several post-millennial documentaries from Japan, his work contains a discourse on itself, on its processes, methodology and attitudes, reflecting the so-called second level of meaning proposed by Michael Chanan pertaining to 'the drama of the film-maker in the process of making the film' (2007b, p. 235). However for this director it was the opposite consideration to that which has tended to define Japanese documentary filmmakers. It was the sense of authorial selfhood or subjectivity as an *a priori* 'fact' – a known and knowable entity distinct from any processes of cinematic signification – that had contaminated non-fiction and as it were muddied the waters of its ideal incarnation. Before his death in 2007 (he committed suicide), Sato was highly critical of those filmmakers that extol artistic subjectivity as a structural or an organising principle, whose individual use of and engagement with non-fiction made it as much (if not more) about those behind the camera as those before it. More specifically it was the details and practices of the personal documentary form as it came to be developed in Japan by directors such as Tsuchiya Yutaka, Mori Tatsuya, Kobayashi Takahiro, Shigeno Yoshihisa or Matsue Tetsuaki that disturbed Sato. And indeed he is not alone in this pronouncement; Hara Kazuo has echoed its 'centrality' to Japanese non-fiction (Hara and Bingham 2010, p. 220), as has Kawase (McDonald, 2006, p. 246), whilst Iizuka Toshio, sometime assistant to Ogawa at Ogawa Pro and more recently an acclaimed documentary director in his own right, has said:

> [T]he Ogawa tradition is dying. Directors like Ogawa-san and Tsuchimoto-san were social artists [. . .] Subsequent directors, beginning with Hara-san [Kazuo] [. . .] have been far more interested in personal visions and stories. I think this is typical of a situation today in which community spirit [. . .] has become increasingly rare. (2009, p. 173)

To Sato, who wrote several studies of non-fiction, the very term 'documentary' became highly problematic as it seemed increasingly to denote any subjective intervention in reality or the real as opposed to allowing a subject or subjects to fundamentally conceive of themselves. His conceptualisation of the term concerns a practical methodology wherein the director must remain open to what may happen beyond the perceived scope of his or her project. Again *Memories of Agano* is a particularly rich film from this point of view as it is replete with an increasing sense that the lives of its subjects are evading Sato's gaze but that there is a cinematic process of simply allowing a camera to follow and record its own film. It begins with the director and his cameraman attempting to find some of the specific locations at which they filmed *Living on the River Agano* in the early 1990s. Subsequently hardly any communication made by the citizens of Niigata is framed as central to the narrative; the camera tends to drift away from them as though literally in search of the film's subject elsewhere, as though the truth or reality of their lives were not to be found in their own to-camera reflections on their suffering or their hardships. It feels ultimately as if the camera and director are looking at or responding to different things, as if there is a fundamental discrepancy between a human and a mechanical perspective (which of course there is), and that for him it is the almost affectless objectivity of the latter that should be privileged. One shot remains focused on a kettle as it boils, a shot that plays out whilst a recording of an interview can be heard but crucially not seen. However unlike, say, the shot of the vase in Ozu's *Late Spring* (*Banshun*, 1949), which has been almost endlessly debated (Nornes, 2007b), this object has only denotative value. As well as stressing the quotidian as the horizons of the film it also reflects the disjunction of sound and image that is central to Sato's project, the fact that what people say is not ultimately the most revealing aspect of their lives, especially with a camera present. Extended scenes of one old man singing reinforce this precept, a performance for an audience and an admission that reality is to be found elsewhere.

Ultimately the fact that Sato has sporadic recourse to scenes from *Living on the River Agano* in his follow-up – and more significantly that they are projected onto a makeshift screen suspended between two trees out in the open in Niigata – demonstrates the extent to which *Memories of Agano* is intended as a mirror held up to its predecessor, a film about a film as much as it is about its nominal subjects. Away from his most famous and acclaimed films Sato similarly made films that centre on illness, disability and indeed art. However, once again, there is a desire to see beyond victimhood in the films *Artists in Wonderland* (*Mahiru no hoshi*, 1998), *Self and Others* (*Serefu ando azazu*, 2000) and *Hanako* (2001) such that the capacity to create art becomes paramount, even over biography and personality. Onscreen information about Gocho Shigeo, the disabled photographer portrayed in *Self and Others*, twice states his name and profession, along with his family history, before offering details of the spinal tuberculosis that led to his physical disability (he died in 1983 – the film is comprised of his photographs, personal correspondence and images of his house and hometown), whilst his absence within the film means that his photographs in effect stand in for him, represent his life. These films' focus on handicapped artists – on Gocho, a mentally handicapped artist named Shige (who obsessively writes letters), and the autistic food artist Imamura Hanako – bespeaks a desire to reconceptualise how art is defined, its function and indeed its lasting effect. The subject of *Hanako*, who makes images (largely of animals) from food, produces art that is by its very nature transient, impermanent, born from the organic. Her father notes that what his daughter makes was initially dismissed by him as trash, as literal garbage, whilst her mother immediately saw its value and began taking the photographs that have become the lasting record of her daughter's endeavours. It is an art form that, for most, can only be seen at one remove, something that remains second hand. As such it disturbs conventional conceptions and considerations of art, as well as introducing a tension between permanence and impermanence, the ephemeral and the immortal – between what is practical, quotidian, and what has artistic merit (indeed what such merit may be said to comprise) – that resonates much more than Hanako's disability, which the discussions between the members of her family do not dwell on. Of *Artists in Wonderland* Sato said that he wanted to 'make a film that isn't about showcasing the talented artworks of a handful of disabled people and saying, "Oh look at the great art they are creating despite their handicaps"' (2005), and it is this ideal that nominally connects Sato's work here to Kawase's and to Tsuchimoto's, and to perhaps the most visible point of connection between disparate Japanese non-fiction filmmakers.

Of the post-millennial directors to have appeared outside the personal documentary phenomenon – indeed who have variously employed microcosmic subjects as markers of a much wider interest in Japan and its twentieth-century history and transformation – perhaps the most interesting is Fujiwara Toshi. That such a distinction rests almost wholly on two films – the two-part *Fence* (*Fensu*, 2008) and a study of the devastation around Fukushima entitled *No Man's Zone* (*Mujin chitai*, 2012) – is testament to the particular vision of these interrelated and thematically connected works. The former, commissioned by a local city as part of a lawsuit it was bringing against the Japanese government, builds on its titular spatial demarcation in order to incrementally construct a vision of Japan at a crucial juncture in its 'development' and to unpick the extent to which the country has in a sense reneged on itself, its own tradition and history, in the years since WWII. The film is about this city (Zushi) in Kanagawa Prefecture in the Kanto area of Greater Tokyo, at the heart of which stands a US military base whose anomalous presence as a forbidden, almost sovereign space, has cast a forbidding shadow over the town. In particular the numerous elderly residents of the city have long been affected by this site, as the grounds – constructed by the Japanese as an ammunition preserve during the war but ceded to America as a naval base following their defeat – have resulted in perennial disruption and displacement in their lives. As a consequence, *Fence*, though ostensibly concerned with a small section of modern Japan, in fact becomes a microcosm of the country and its post-war 'development' and reconstruction. The US presence at the literal, topographical heart of the town is a perennial marker of the loss of the Pacific War and by extension the nationwide transformations that characterised the decades from the 1950s onward: when, as historian W. G. Beasley notes, a defence agreement 'gave Japan the protection of a nuclear umbrella [. . .] [in return for which] she provided air and naval bases [. . .] [and was provided with] access to American capital and technology [. . .] a rich market for hi-tech consumer goods' (1995, p. 279).

The film is thus nothing less than a microcosmic study of post-war Japan and its ongoing and problematic relations with the US. It is, as noted, a two-part documentary. Its constituent sections – entitled *Lost Paradise* and *Fragmented Stratum* – are divided in such a way as to reflect or mirror each other, and thus to highlight a sense of dialogue at the film's core. The lost or desecrated paradise of Part One is ostensibly a small village, Ikego, in the city of Zushi. Yet Fujiwara's film is notable for the centrifugal quality of its structure, the way it emanates outward from its single location and begins to find connections that adumbrate a symbiotic and almost discursive practice of identity formation in relation to both environment and socio-political era. An early shot is taken from a car travelling through the city, and from this Fujiwara sporadically dissolves to individual interviews before dissolving back to the travelling shot (which is tellingly left unfinished, incomplete) as a marker that the film itself will be about time and space, an ongoing process wherein projections from numerous different pasts into the present speak of a matrix of different, competing subjectivities bound up in the film's own point of view as a detached presence. This is echoed in several similarly mobile shots that travel the perimeter of the US grounds looking at and through the fence, and further in a series of almost pillow shots that return to the natural world surrounding the city to bracket the various interviews that comprise the majority of the narrative.

This travelling shot is also a signifier of the film's enforced ground-level perspective. The director states soon after said shot that an aerial view of the city was a practical impossibility owing to post-9/11 suspicion of aircraft over US airspace. He is keen to map out the geography of the base and its surrounding environs, detailing precisely where the subjects live in relation to the base and where the elderly residents used to live, in some cases the land they owned. However this topographical certainty and precision, its visibility, contrasts with the aforementioned diversity of views and responses to the US that it contains. As part of the lengthy interviews conducted on camera for the film Fujiwara follows two elderly gentlemen around Zushi as they discuss their enforced removal from their homes. Included in these scenes are three schoolgirls who follow their social elders and listen to their stories, at times asking questions and at one point themselves being questioned by Fujiwara, who asks them whether they are aware of the turbulent history of the location that is now the school at which they study.

To this they respond that they had no idea, highlighting both the gulf between generations and the largely hidden past of the city.

Fujiwara closely parallels these people's connection to the rural land around Zushi. Where the men speak fondly of fishing and, later, of the obstructions caused by an inaccessible tunnel the girls (to one man's evident displeasure) throw rocks and splash in the river: a practical reliance on the natural resources of the land juxtaposed with a playful appropriation of it. Similarly there is a recurrent pair of interviewees – an elderly man and his mother – whose house is constructed in large part from cedar wood from local trees; Fujiwara returns several times to work being undertaken on this building by a specialist craftsman intent on preserving its physical heritage with more modern supplementation. However there is no explicit judgement entailed here, no sense that the traditional is being valorised; nor in fact is there a complete condemnation of the US presence in Zushi. In Part Two Fujiwara twice cuts from subjects discussing the harmful effects of foreign species and parasites within Japan to shots of American women with prams in the base, but in a voiceover he admits to the mischievous impulse here, and proceeds to relay figures stressing the Japanese government's culpability in themselves using taxpayers' money for the continuance of the base. Moreover it is also made clear that their base and the fence around it has contributed to the preservation of the natural landscape in the immediate vicinity of the city, and one elderly interviewee expresses surprise that the US tenants who rented her house treated it with great respect and preserved its traditional design and construction.

Such ambivalence has been perceived by several commentators to be a specifically Japanese characteristic. However, one might postulate that *Fence* is in fact about this very custom (in Japanese *Aimai*) and its socio-cultural canonisation. One of the recurrent interviewees in the film is a specialist in the natural world who discusses the wildlife around Zushi; he states at one point that the cedar trees that used to be grown purely for use as lumber are now left in the wild, and that this has had a marked effect on the surrounding wildlife and eco system as more birds have taken root there whilst animals less inclined to the increased darkness and shade have been seen much less. His point is that 'whether something is good or bad depends on the conditions of each place': that the environment as it is at present (indeed at any given time) is not inherently positive or negative; it is beneficial to some and less so for others depending entirely on personal circumstances. And so it is with the city – a place with a troubled history, with scars, but that also appears to offer a good standard of living for its residents, a place where the aforementioned elderly man and his mother live in reasonable comfort in their old, very large house and where the natural landscape is retained and protected.

Part One of *Fence* is ultimately concerned with the war and its immediate aftermath; two separate yet intertwined scenes take the director to family plots to look over individual graves and shrines and to consider quite ruefully the lineage of loss that they articulate and that the contemporary country is in part built upon (some tombstones have information that is now difficult to read, connoting the erosion or increasing invisibility of this history). Part Two, by contrast, has a wider focus concerning history both more distant and more recent. It immediately makes clear its concern with Japan's post-war history by including as an onscreen text some of the controversial ANPO security pact with the US (signed originally in 1952 and amended in 1960), as well as the reminiscences of the elderly citizens who lived through the devastation. This section of the film expands on its forebear by investigating further the stratified and strictly demarcated spaces in Zushi as representing the country at large. It also looks at numerous ancient artefacts that were found in the Ikego district of the city, significant tools dating back to the *Yayoi* period over two thousand years ago, all of which makes *Fragmented Stratum*'s focus on the past as a determining factor on its present a more complicated question that it may appear, certainly beside the corrosive impact of the war as detailed in *Lost Paradise*. The research into and subsequent unearthing of these objects proffers a city dating back almost through recorded history, something specifically Japanese to contrast with the perceived despoiled national heritage in the post-war eras.

In addition to engaging with *Aimai* as a perceived national custom (Desser, 1988, p. 63 and Davies and Ikeno, 2002, pp. 9–16), Fujiwara is almost perennially concerned with disturbing or decentring narrative transparency in *Fence*. The film begins with a series of shots taken in the hills around Ikego, but included amidst these is a shot in which several cyclists' way along a path is disturbed. Here the crew find themselves in the way of others and thus their presence is immediately underlined, as it is subsequently when Fujiwara includes a shot (closed off and bracketed from the ostensibly identical preceding and following shots by fades to and from black) in which the sound man is visible shuffling across the frame before an interview with the subjects begins. Indeed Fujiwara's own on-camera presence (something he credits his cinematographer, Otsu Koshiro, with developing, as he had done likewise whilst working with Tsuchimoto Noriaki) is another facet of this methodology, as is the sporadic recourse to oblique cinematography and a contemplative visual aesthetic. One scene in particular – an interview with a bedridden local historian in Part Two of the film – is filmed from outside the window of his room and framed so that a tree in the garden on the first plane of the image occupies a much more prominent place in the composition than the ostensible subject (Fig. 6.1). It was in fact a practical decision (the man in question spoke much more readily off-camera) (Fujiwara, 2009, p. 161), but it becomes redolent of the film reaching beyond its nominal boundaries and facilitating an awareness of form and function that helps to frame the documentary as a construction and its narrative not as a transparent window onto history but a record of how that history has been processed, how Ikego's residents

Figure 6.1   Distance and self-reflexivity in *Fence.*

define themselves *vis-à-vis* both the memory of the past and the camera in the present.

Fence, like *Living on the River Agano*, is ultimately about the people that populate its patient, generous narrative. Both films are, of course, about their respective subjects' personal stories and experiences of the events or problems that are the nominal focus of the narratives. But the often protracted interviews with people by both directors are allowed to run on beyond such discussions so that the way they behave on camera, they way they interact with the director or with other people they meet, become as significant as their experiences and life histories. This is especially true of both films' elderly subjects in general, but it has more specific ramifications. Part Two of *Fence* closes with a scene in which a woman not previously interviewed or even identified discusses her gardening as she works. It is a moment almost entirely unconnected to the thematic exegesis of the film as it has hitherto developed, one both peripheral and yet central in that it extols a simple sense of the quotidian, of the pleasure of home and of work as the backbone of what has been variously lived and lost in Zushi and Ikego.

Other than television documentaries on Tsuchimoto and Hara Kazuo and a film about the making of Amos Gitai's *Kedma* (2002) the only major non-fiction film that Fujiwara had made prior to *Fence* was a documentary about the aforementioned Tsuchimoto Noriaki, director of the Minamata series. *Cinema is About Documenting Lives* (*Eiga wa ikimono no kiroku de aru: Tsuchimoto Noriaki no shigoto*, 2007) follows Noriaki as he talks about his work and discusses his methodology, his attitude to non-fiction and in particular the practical travails of his landmark films. Significantly, as if to update and re-inscribe the corrosive histori-cal lineage of both this film and *Fence*, *No Man's Zone* centres on a comparable subject – the fallout of the Fukushima disaster of 2011 – and is a narrative that is similarly divided: between interviews with those directly affected by the Tsunami and resulting nuclear pollution, and documenting the devastation in and around Fukushima. These latter scenes are frequently accompanied by a pensive voice-over (written by Fujiwara but spoken in English by the Armenian actress and fre-quent Atom Egoyan collaborator Arsinée Khanjian) that asks us to reflect on the political nature of representing disasters onscreen: on what these images mean to an audience consuming them at a remove from the disaster itself (whether they be like a drug or a stimulant), something that makes *No Man's Zone*, along with Sato's *Memories of Agano*, arguably the pre-eminent contemporary example of the documentary that becomes about itself. It is the key means of clearly distinguish-ing these films from the plethora of personal documentaries in Japan. Indeed it offers a riposte to such films, and in so doing denotes the multi-faceted face of contemporary Japanese non-fiction, the discrepency between the insularity of the latter and the open, questioning, historical visions of the former.

Vision is in fact a key to the film. Premiered in competition at the sixty-second Berlinnale in 2012, *No Man's Zone*, like the work of Tsuchimoto (and to a degree Ogawa and Sato) engages in a discourse on dichotomies of vision and blindness, visibility and invisibility, what is seen and what is hidden. The political impetus of Tsuchimoto's Minamata series was to bring to light, to make publicly visible, the scandal and personal trauma associated with the titular disease and the attempts of its victims to fight not only for financial recompense but for recogni-tion of their hardships. This director's *Shiranui Sea* (*Shiranui-kai*, 1975) in fact elaborates on this struggle, in that the director talks to several people who have struggled with admitting to their affliction; he considers the social stigma of the disease, of people too frightened to, as one person says, 'come out of the closet', and in so doing he decries the policy of officially categorising and recognising victims that has left many in a state of liminality, in limbo: neither able to deal with their illness nor in a position to be able to put it behind them or forget about it – in other words officially invisible. As *Living on the River Agano* makes clear, in the early 1990s there were over three times the number of officially unrecognised victims of Minamata Disease as of those whose symptoms had been recognised (around 2,000 of the latter), and it is this tension that in large part characterises the political and indeed emotional trajectory of the narratives.

Visibility or otherwise in these films also relates to the pollution and its toxins that cannot be detected but are consumed and ingested, and this is as central to *No Man's Zone* as to its forebears. However Fujiwara extrapolates from this not only in the 'ghosts' he encounters around the disaster sites (workers who desire not to be recorded), but also in a consideration of the almost completely hidden second nuclear reactor at Fukushima, which is likened to the Imperial Palace in

Tokyo in that it cannot be seen from even a short distance owing to the wooded area in the immediate vicinity. There is another connection here in that the materialist or classical Marxist rhetoric in evidence particularly in Sato's *Living on the River Agano* – in the images of elderly workers connected directly to their work and the practical fruits of their labours (harvesting and boat making in particular: one artisan is circumspect about allowing the latter skill set to become a commodity, about handing it down or passing it on to others) – is countered and in a sense complemented in Fujiwara's film by an implicit consideration of the capitalist paradigm that, as in Tsuchimoto's and Sato's Minamata work, has resulted in the devastation that is depicted. Towards the end of the film there is a section detailing how Japan has always been an agricultural nation (as opposed to a nation of samurai, of warriors), and how its modernisation has corrupted such a practice. It is a further engagement with image and perception, with the samurai as metonymy, and it details both the extent to which this image has been officially canonised and, crucially, the cost of such canonisation.

No Man's Zone is a ruminative and atmospheric documentary that Fujiwara has described as, potentially, a science fiction film. Indeed echoes of a film like Werner Herzog's *Fata Morgana* (1969) or even Jia Zhangke's *Still Life* (*Sanxia haoren*, 2006) abound in footage of the wreckage around the stricken nuclear reactor that seems to be taken from another planet. As noted the few people Fujiwara encounters amidst this devastation are prefectural police officers patrolling the quarantine zone, but they are referred to as 'ghosts' (echoes of Sono's *The Land of Hope* (*Kibō no kuni*, 2012) here) and their proximal distance from the camera becomes a present absence in the film as they refuse to be filmed lest they be seen by the families of those who have died. This paradoxical impetus becomes a central referent for the narrative, as *No Man's Zone* is less an example of the kind of postmodern documentary postulated in particular by Linda Williams (2002) than it is a film about postmodernity, about the condition theorised by Jean Baudrillard (1995) in relation to the Gulf War wherein images of the conflict circulated alongside, and in effect became indistinguishable from, the other shows or even the advertisements that surrounded them on air. Fujiwara's film examines the import and ramifications of this, as it were, real unreality. It seems to point towards a pervasive sense that the images it contains offer an inexorably hyperreal vision wherein the distinction between original and copy, signifier and signified, is disturbed. However the import of the voiceover is to ask whether such images of devastation do not in fact rewrite reality and erase history to the extent that they override the world as it existed prior to the disaster, leaving only that disaster and its after-effects in the imagination. This is the perennial image whose reality becomes inextricable from its image-ness, but at what cost? As the voiceover asks in the film, 'what is the point in seeing it'? Susan Sontag (1965) has discussed images of disaster in science fiction cinema, images she terms 'sensual elaboration' (p. 212) for the way in which they offer a cathartic vision of 'living through one's own death and more, the death of cities' (ibid.). In so doing they distract us from actual or anticipated horrors and 'normalize what is psychologically unbearable' (p. 225), whereas *No Man's Zone* and its litany of the already-destroyed and the once-extant deny such an imperative. They presuppose the hyperreality of the news images that have saturated the world, images of the Tsunami itself, and contend that this world is dead because there are no images of it left to circulate and consume: it is deceased because it is no longer representable, wherein the film facilitates not an eschewal but a reflection on the 'psychologically unbearable' and thus the limits of postmodern practices. If, as William Tsutsui (2004) has argued, films like *Godzilla* (*Gōjira*, 1954) 'relieve us of the tedium of modern life' (p. 108), then *No Man's Zone* in effect highlights the indulgence behind such tedium, the distance from such disasters. As Khanjian notes on the soundtrack: 'in the end, everything we have seen seems to have lost meaning when facing images of disasters that we cannot see', a line that summarises the particular tension of postmodern affectivity, where the aforementioned invisibility becomes a key means of destabilising the circuitous logic of image and consumption, the seen and seers. Werner Herzog has spoken of this connection between the world we inhabit and representations thereof; he has often discussed the need to renew said world by capturing new images of it, a visual imperative he terms the 'ecstatic truth' (2002, p. 301). Fujiwara, in approaching the problem from a different direction, broadly re-inscribes this need through lamenting its lack, and perhaps the impossibility of its ever being fully recovered.

This aspect of *No Man's Zone* is also significant in that it separates image from soundtrack, the visual from the aural, which becomes an intrinsic norm throughout much of the film. Khanjian's voice is initially heard over a black screen before fading out as the image fades in, and thereafter aural snippets of interviews with those affected by the disaster are heard over images of the devastated areas around the nuclear reactor. This technique effectively inscribes a universality into the reflections, as though the voices of all those affected were being heard at once, simultaneously, and moreover being heard from an indeterminate textual time and space that reflects something of their literal homelessness within their country. The subtext is such that appearing on camera would imbricate them in the discursive practices of a conventional aesthetic of documentary filmmaking and thereby fundamentally change both their relationship to the film and by extension the audience's. The few people who do appear on camera in this way represent different generations – young, middle-aged and elderly – and thus the various reactions owing to different circumstances are explicitly detailed to avoid any sense that the film negates a human element. Erik Knudsen has talked about moving beyond conventional patterns of non-fiction that 'reinforce the role which the documentary genre is expected to play' (2008, p. 108), and Fujiwara here demonstrates how such an aesthetic can be realised. On two separate occasions the subjects of brief interviews (with people Fujiwara happened across whilst out filming) walk off and disappear as the camera remains behind to watch and record this disappearance. They seem to evade the film's grasp, fall through its fingers, highlighting the fact that *No Man's Zone* exists in a dialogue with perceived conventional non-fictive practices of découpage, something that is crystallised around its soundtrack and narration.

The measured voiceover by Khanjian is significant as much for the voice involved as for what she says. Returning to Bill Nichols' classification of documentary filmmaking, *No Man's Zone* fits in part into his conception of the 'expository mode' of non-fiction wherein the filmmaker aims to provide a polemical or rhetorical work that stresses 'the impression of objectivity and well-supported argument' (Nichols, 2001, p. 107). Nichols notes that this particular model employs a voice of God to inform, to convey to and to convince an audience of a particular position, state of affairs or way of thinking, and that this omniscient extra-diegetic narration is typically that of a 'professionally trained, richly toned male voice of commentary' (ibid., p. 105). By employing a soft, humane female voice (and moreover one speaking in English) Fujiwara disturbs and comments upon this facet of expository documentaries, drawing attention to their hegemonic patriarchal normativity and, by extension, to these features as they define Japan. Moreover Khanjian's detached voice is not, as is typical of the expository mode, 'distinct from the images of the historical world that accompany it' (ibid., p. 107). Rather the voiceover adds a different dimension to the images, sound and vision together forming something like a montage in that a meaning arises from the collision of these constituent elements of the film's style. Fujiwara had a range of figures in mind when conceiving of this aspect of *No Man's Zone*, and worked in vain through numerous scenarios that included Juliette Binoche, Bulle Ogier and Jeanne Moreau (even Chris Marker was a possible contributor at one stage of its evolution) before finding Khanjian through a chance encounter. Her own story of witnessing the damage and destruction in Beirut reinforces her relevance as a performer and offers another prominent, if implicit, tragedy, whilst her gendered Otherness, already connotative of an implicit anxiety over a male, patriarchal normalcy, is exaggerated both with regard to Nichols' model of documentary film and with Fujiwara's own conception of the Other. The director relates this to a disparity pertaining to the Animist religious traditions and practices of Japan. There is a notion (relayed at the very end of the film) that a plurality of Gods exist, with 'everything being a different God' (Fujiwara, 2014), something that has been compromised, subjugated and sublimated in the twentieth-century history of the country. These images thus stand in contrast to Japanese modernity, so that *No Man's Zone* (again like *Fence*) offers 'a re-examination of the history of modern Japan' (ibid.) and as such consolidates Fujiwara's position among the pre-eminent documentary filmmakers of the new millennium.

No Man's Zone also follows *Fence* in that it is a film about contested space, focusing most overtly on elderly residents of those villages close to the Fukushima nuclear reactor who are being forced to leave their homes and relocate. In point of fact, if Fujiwara's cinema may be said to be built around narrative and thematic explorations of breached or ruptured boundaries (Bingham, 2009b), then *No Man's Zone* is a particularly apt, representative text. Its subject explicitly concerns the demarcations of space that define zones of safety or otherwise in those populated areas in close proximity to Fukushima. This salient aspect of the aftermath of the 2011 tragedy – again also a central narrative problem in *The Land of Hope* – is traced in detail by Fujiwara, and these nominally simple spatial demarcations are then mapped onto the amorphous subjective boundaries that separate them from the official responses to the disaster in terms of demarcating topographical space with the quarantine zone of 20 km around the disaster zone, connoting the disjuncture between official and individual responses to the tragedy.

In contrast to Fujiwara, the New York-based Soda Kazuhiro began his career in documentary filmmaking for television with the Japanese broadcaster NHK before moving to cinema with studies of specific social institutions and services. Like his contemporaries in Japan he has also worked in feature films, although in contradistinction to Fujiwara, Kawase, Koreeda *et al.* this was at the beginning of his career, and at present he appears to have left this phase of his oeuvre behind. Indeed his work is in other ways anomalous when seen in the context of his peers in modern Japanese non-fiction. The fact that he is based in New York points not only to a geographical distance from his contemporaries but also reflects a methodological and stylistic discreteness, that his work is to a large extent beholden to a model of documentary cinema that is anathema to a majority of Japanese forms as they have typically been comprehended and conceptualised. Indeed his adoptive home underlines the fact that one of his most significant influences has been the direct cinema that developed in that country (alongside its cousin *cinéma vérité* in France) by filmmakers such as Richard Leacock, The Maysles Brothers, D. A. Pennebaker, Robert Drew and later Frederick Wiseman. Soda more or less explicitly echoes the non-interventionist practices of these filmmakers, never appearing onscreen and following subjects in the course of their lives without overt recourse to intervention or interruption. He does not always follow the contours or ideals of direct cinema – for instance his work is built in part around interviews with his subjects which is a feature that Pennebaker and Wiseman in particular have tended to rigidly eschew – but for the most part he has remained within the parameters of its ideas and ideals.

However, as is perhaps suggested by his anxiety over using the term 'direct cinema' in relation to his work (each is subtitled 'an observational film by Soda Kazuhiro) (Soda and Grey, 2007), Soda's films have at the same time remained entrenched within Japanese stories, and this has led in some films to a productive tension between nominally opposing forces or practices: in other words to a specifically Japanese appropriation or variant of direct cinema rather than a mere facsimile of it. He has covered markedly different subject matter: from a study of the political campaign of an inexperienced candidate for the Japanese Liberal

Democratic Party in *Campaign* (*Senkyo*, 2007), to a consideration of depression and mental illness in *Mental* (*Seishin*, 2008) and a film following those who care for people with a physical disability in *Peace* (2010). These films are concerned with daily rituals and routines, with how the subjects interact with the public and indeed with the perceptions and presuppositions therein. *Mental* is a portrait of the patients of a small town outpatient mental clinic in Okayama Prefecture in the west of Japan. Recipient of the Best Documentary Award following its premiere at the 2008 Pusan International Film Festival, it is a patient and protracted film that follows a small number of subjects over an extended period of time, detailing their day-to-day lives and allowing them to reflect on their condition, to talk about their lives as a therapeutic, at times performative act. Soda begins as a detached observer (albeit one who directly interviews his subjects) but increasingly these subjects begin to turn the focus onto their director. One patient in particular frequently addresses him, talking with others about him and even singing a song about him, at which times the point of Soda's work becomes a means of reflecting on both the practical limits and by extension the use value of objectivity as a stylistic and methodological practice. It becomes an ideal that is increasingly frustrated, albeit without the personality of the director intruding into and becoming a part of the narrative landscape of the film, leaving *Mental* suspended between the objectivity of the director and the subjectivity of his cast, and suspended furthermore between Japan and the West.

As an adjunct, arguably even a corrective, to the imperatives of the aforementioned personal films *Mental* is thus a valuable documentary. It is also worth noting that, despite his pervasive recourse to direct cinema, Soda himself has identified Sato Makoto as a key influence on and progenitor for his work. The painstaking way in which he spent years becoming familiar with the patients in *Mental* bespeaks something of his debt to Sato, and reinforces the sense of a Japanisation of a foreign model, one that, as a correlative to the aforementioned breakdown of objectivity, increasingly views its subjects with both compassion and discretion as regards their social stigma. To this end Soda's typical methodology of juxtaposing his observational passages with apparently arbitrary shots taken in and around the environments in which he is working (not unlike Koreeda in *Without Memory*) serves to underline a disconnection from 'normal' everyday life as well as to interject a contradistinctive model to that of Koreeda. The film then becomes a test case for the validity of a Japanese non-fictive aesthetic, something hinted at in *Campaign* with that film's fly-on-the-wall observation of a political campaign that echoes arguably direct cinema's most significant early work, *Primary* (1960), which followed the presidential primary in Wisconsin between JFK and Hubert Humphrey in 1960. From this point of view at least it is a crucial film.

Many of the most popular non-fiction films made in and about Japan in recent years have been made by (and largely for) non-Japanese, and have tended to implicitly reaffirm quasi-Orientalist structures by virtue of their desire to speak for their subjects, even if only by virtue of making their insular worlds visible. In other words these films and filmmakers work to open up and make public hidden or marginalised spaces, and this they do as largely impartial observers. Wim Wenders' *Tokyo-Ga* (1985), Kim Longinotto and Jano Williams' numerous documentaries made in Japan – *Eat the Kimono* (1989), *Dream Girls* (1994), *Shinjuku Boys* (1995) and *Gaea Girls* (2000) – in addition to works like David Gelb's acclaimed *Jiro Dreams of Sushi* (2011) and Jean-Pierre Limosin's *Young Yakuza* (2007) are excavations of subcultures or of otherwise hermetically sealed, largely unseen milieus that the filmmakers' tend to observe from a neutral standpoint, admitting neither to valorisation nor denigration but purporting to allow their audience to make up their own minds about what they see. Indeed Longinotto and Williams in particular remain almost entirely invisible in most of their films (these are quite strictly observational documentaries), and as such they retain a faith in the reality that they represent. By contrast those films about Japan made by Japanese (Fujiwara being the most overt example) tend to develop a discursive space in which there is less presupposed faith in any kind of unified and unitary reality, and in which the medium of film becomes inextricably a part of the narrative. If, as is characteristic of a postmodern age, we cannot easily separate the 'real' from the artificial, and cannot any longer pretend to any semblance of a clear overview or grand narrative of our times, the documentary as it has continued to develop in recent Japanese cinema offers by turns a particularly relevant paradigm and a significant qualification of the same. Many of the works of Kawase, Fujiwara and others reject rigid demarcations almost as a matter of course, variously eschew or at least complicate the form itself, but do so in a way that anchors, even historicises their films within an identifiable lineage, even if this is only as a point of departure. Indeed this stylistic and methodological practice of theme and variation has been the pre-eminent paradigm across the much of the history of Japanese documentaries. Soda offers an obvious point of contrast here given his adoption of a foreign and largely alien model, but the very fact of this difference as allied to an identifiably Japanese practical paradigm strengthens the arguably recondite presence of the latter as a national model.

Fujiwara Toshi has claimed that modern Japanese cinema is by no means a vibrant era of non-fiction – indeed he all but dismisses digital technology and heralds Sato Makoto as perhaps the last Japanese documentary director to have made a significant impact on the form (2014) – but it is noticeable that there has been a group of filmmakers who have sought to engage with the medium, to challenge and redefine it, and this at least in part allows one to posit the post-millennial era of Japanese documentary as an important one. Like the contemporaneous movement in post-millennial independent Chinese documentaries examined by Chris Berry and others (2010), it works to foreground socio-historical commitment and commentary and to delineate a space for a multi-layered engagement with Japanese society and history. On the other hand the private and personal film model, along with the emphasis on illness, has continued in films like Sunada Mami's *Ending Note: Death of a Japanese Salaryman* (*Endengu nōto*, 2011), which was co-produced by Koreeda and which, in its study by a daughter of her father succumbing to abdominal cancer, may in fact be connected to international works such as Jonathan Caouette's *Tarnation* (2003) or Andrew Jarecki's *Capturing the Friedmans* (2004), which similarly find directors (both diegetic and otherwise) ruminating on their own lives and insular family problems. As such it suggests, as does Soda's work, that the multi-faceted face of the Japanese documentary means that it is not an entirely hermetic artform, that it can be productively juxtaposed with other films from around the world and conceived of as part of wider currents that have animated the post-millennial popularity and visibility of non-fiction.

7. MODERN JAPANESE FEMALE DIRECTORS

Across the history of the cinema in Japan images and stories of women have remained salient, if not central, to numerous films, filmmakers and genres. The prevalence of female-centred narratives can be traced back to the country's earliest films; this was even the case when women were officially prohibited from acting on the screen (as they had similarly been prohibited from appearing on stage), when the theatrical figure of the *onnagata*, or female impersonator, predominated in lieu of any actual female performers. However, this pervasive interest in and recourse to onscreen narratives anchored by women has traditionally not found a correlative in women behind the camera. There have traditionally been few opportunities for female filmmakers to work within Japan's studio system, and prior to the 1990s there had been only a small number of women working as directors. This despite the fact that women writers have for centuries held a pre-eminent position as authors, with some of the most celebrated titles in the Japanese canon – including *Genji monogatari/The Tale of Genji* and *Makura no sōshi/The Pillow Book* – being written by female writers (Murasaki Shikibu and Shonagon Sei, respectively).

Japan is, and always has been, a markedly patriarchal society. In the immediate post-war years (following a 1946 decree), there was an enforced move to guarantee gender equality and women's rights constitutionally, and thereafter the rapid development of Japan's bubble economy helped to bring into focus ongoing issues and problems surrounding what Vera Mackie has termed 'the politics of everyday life and everyday relationships' (2003. p. 1). It has been a protracted and difficult process; women's liberation only began as a visible movement in the

1970s, whilst statistics even in the 1990s and later suggested that gender inequality in the workplace was still a problem, with Japan ranking fifty-fourth in a 2009 United Nation's poll on this very subject. Furthermore, as Kumiko Fujimura-Fanselow has discussed in detail, whilst the early 1990s in particular had been seen by some as an era of and for women – *Onna no jidai* – such thinking did not remain viable or its results a practical reality beyond this decade (2011, p. 17). Indeed Sugimoto Yoshio has considered the ways in which Japan's system of family registration (*koseki*) has continued to reinforce normative patriarchy and to regulate and naturalise the disenfranchisement of women (2003, pp. 146–82), whilst facts such as that the legalisation of the contraceptive pill only occurred in Japan in 1999 has meant that even women's bodies have until very recently continued to be controlled and regimented.

As a cultural correlative, Laura Mulvey's 'Visual Pleasure and Narrative Cinema' (1975) was not translated into Japanese until 1997, over twenty years after its publication in *Screen*. It has been noted that 'self-consciously feminist film and video artists [. . .] always faced severe criticism in their struggle for legitimacy' (Nornes, 2007a, p. 140), although Nornes (ibid.) and others (Hori, 2007, p. 89) have discussed the apparent, albeit qualified, refuge from this sexism and subjugation offered by documentary filmmaking for such pioneers as Sakane Tazuko and Atsugi Taka in the 1930s and 1940s. Moreover, as argued in particular by Ian Buruma (1984), Anne Allison (2000) and Leith Morton (2003), the variegated worlds of erotic manga or Shojo manga (comics primarily concerned with young women) had for several years enabled female writers and artists to subvert dominant gender tropes and become 'empowering and liberating in their portrayal of female sexuality' (Morton, 2003, p. 248).

However feature filmmaking has traditionally remained a world inaccessible to women, at least, that is, until recently. As Keiko I. McDonald has noted, the situation has begun to change dramatically for the better (2006, p. 244). In a recent essay that explores sexual difference and alternative gender positions and subjectivities, Alejandra Armendariz (2011) looks at two nominally representative texts and argues for the presence of transgressive female characters. She outlines the ways in which the protagonists of two particular Japanese films enact a discourse of sexual difference through their agency in the narrative, and how these films construct their stories around 'the sexual and symbolic act of the encounter with the Other' (p. 22). It is an intriguing study, one that yields numerous insights into the position of these films and their directors with regard to several of the most prominent conceptions of film theory pertaining to gender, sexuality, suture and psychoanalysis. It must be noted, though, that the perceived explicitness of Armendariz' key texts has not typically animated all the myriad films by female directors that have begun to predominate in Japanese cinema in the last fifteen years. In point of fact it is interesting from the point of view that some of the directors in question have expressed a desire not to be classified as female directors or storytellers (Bingham, 2014, p. 198–9). This chapter will be concerned with exploring and expanding upon some of the salient tenets of this discussion in order to fully contextualise and adumbrate how several films by young female directors offer pictures of specifically modern femininity in their work. In analysing films whose feminist perspectives and/or textual strategies are often less than overt it will explore the extent to which such a thematic may be regarded as specifically Japanese, or whether there are more universal structures and models of discourse that can be applied to help elucidate studies of Japanese texts. The filmmakers to be discussed herein – Nishikawa Miwa, Kawase Naomi, Iguchi Nami, Ogigami Naoko, Ninagawa Mika, Kitagawa Eriko and Tanada Yuki – are all successful figures in Japanese cinema, and all have made films about women. They have also negotiated a textual space for themselves that is often neither fully mainstream nor its opposite: neither populist nor art cinema. In this way they can be seen to inhabit an indeterminate space, something that is in fact often mirrored in their neither fully feminist nor masculine stories. The chapter will explore this aspect of their work, and will also reflect on the intertextual imperatives of several key films and filmmakers, something that underlines the broader project of modern Japanese cinema and its recapitulation of earlier modes and genres.

The cinema of Japan, throughout much of its history (at least since the 1920s), has generally been perceived to have been replete with numerous male directors who, if arguably not feminist, then at least have been concerned in their work to depict and explore problems relating to women in Japanese society. Attendant on this is the fact that women have long made up the majority of the film-going audience in Japan. A 2009 symposium specifically devoted to the topic of women in Japanese cinema (at the high-profile Nippon Connection festival) led producer Kito Yukie to estimate that as much as 70 per cent of regular cinemagoers in the country are female (Bingham, 2010, p. 58). Indeed a film festival named 'Peaches' has in recent years been designed specifically to exhibit the work of female graduates, and on the international stage the Japan Foundation in the United Kingdom has begun to reflect this audience composition with lectures by prominent filmmakers like Yokohama Satoko and a touring programme of notable works (entitled 'Girls on Film') covering a spectrum of titles and attesting to the continued predominance of images of femininity in Japanese cinema. Concomitantly there is a marked prevalence within critical and academic work of explorations of women before the camera, notably Joan Mellen's *The Waves at Genji's Door* (1976), Sato Tadao's *Currents in Japanese Cinema* (1987) and David Desser's study of the Japanese new wave *Eros plus Massacre* (1988). Desser in particular has recourse to a quote from the prominent actress Hidari Sachiko, who noted that 'if you want to say something about Japan you have to focus on women' (p. 108), an assertion that would appear to have gained no small measure of currency in Japanese cinema, with filmmakers like Naruse, Ozu, Mizoguchi,

Yoshida Yoshishige, Imamura Shohei and Itami Juzo all contributing to a prevalent mode of melodrama that used female protagonists in order to engage with the socio-political specificity of Japan. For instance both Imamura and Yoshida within the space of a year directed contrastive films that traced a tenable history of twentieth-century Japan through the fortunes of a single female protagonist who lives and struggles through decades of change and upheaval. The dramatic crux of both films is the historic radio address by the Emperor Hirohito detailing Japan's surrender to the US and the end of the Pacific War, something that Yoshida's protagonist in *Akitsu Springs (Akitsu onsen*, 1964) receives with shock, subsequently collapsing, whilst for Imamura's protagonist in *The Insect Woman (Nippon konchuki*, 1963) the news of the surrender is not only immaterial but in fact a direct hindrance to her as the crowds on the street halt the progress of her car and directly obstruct her passage.

These diametrically opposed reactions – both in a way excessive, both in public spaces – find through overt female focalisation an explicit renewal of socio-political history; in other words the point of these narratives in this particular context is to review and to re-view the past. Experiencing this seismic event through these contrastive female perspectives facilitates a sense of seeing it anew, and by extension revisiting its seismic ramifications, something especially marked at the time of the films' production when Japan was beginning the era of economic prosperity and globalisation that grew out of wartime defeat. The fact that both women, despite their polarised reactions, soldier ever onward further offers a rewriting, or at least a reappraisal, of Japanese history and Japanese his-story, a disavowal of the catastrophic climax of a (masculine) drive for war and colonial expansionism. It is a project that rhymes with the aims of numerous perceived women's directors, whose work has frequently sought what Hidari boldly claimed to be the preserve of women on film, to comment on and offer opposition to Japanese social hegemony. This opposition or tension is particularly productive with regard to the work of many female filmmakers in Japanese cinema. It reflects the work of Laura Mulvey, which refracts classical Hollywood through a psychoanalytical lens in order to explicate its fundamental masculine bias, the way it subjectifies men and objectifies women through the gaze, the look that freezes the female as desired object, as a spectacle, at the same time as the narrative revolves around an exploration or demystification of her perennial enigma.

The prevalence of female directors in Japanese cinema is a relatively recent development. In the history of Japanese cinema from its birth until the 1960s there were only two names of significance for their features. One of these, the actress Tanaka Kinuyo (a frequent member of Mizoguchi's repertory of performers and a major star from the 1930s through to the 1970s), had to overcome significant obstacles to her career as a director, not least from Mizoguchi himself. The other key figure at this time, a director of arguably more significance as she was Japan's very first female feature filmmaker, was Sakane Tazuko. Sakane had also worked with Mizoguchi (as a script girl and assistant director in the 1930s), whilst at the same time struggling to direct her own films. Her feature debut, *New Clothing* (*Hatsu sugata*, 1936), which is unfortunately no longer extant, was Japan's first feature to be directed by a woman, and her subsequent body of work includes several significant documentaries. *New Clothing*, whose Mizoguchi-like story concerns a tentative, ultimately abortive relationship between a prospective Geisha and a young man destined to become a Buddhist priest, was a commercial failure, and Sakane was not able to complete any more features. She retired in 1962 after more than ten years of being able to work only in continuity and as an assistant editor at Shochiku studios (McDonald, 2007, 128–46).

Beyond these isolated figures there were throughout the 1950s and 1960s significantly more female documentary filmmakers than feature directors. Tazuko Sakane had only been able to find work as a non-fiction filmmaker at various stages of her career, and then only in Manchuria at the Manchuria Film Association during the Pacific War (at which time she made no less than ten documentaries, largely about the turbulent wartime conditions in that part of occupied China). In the 1980s, a decade marked by a decline in studio productions and traditional genre material, one particular female director emerged, Kazama Shiori, whose work reflected the new means available to independent filmmakers as well as the trangressive sensibilities that frequently went hand-in-hand with their status on the periphery of the industry.

From the 1990s onwards one of the most important young female directors has been Kawase Naomi. A documentarian as well as a feature filmmaker, Kawase began her career making short, intimate, 8 mm non-fiction films that frequently centred on her elderly grandmother. Her first feature, *The God Suzaku* (*Moe no Suzaku*, 1997), builds in several ways on these documentary films, most noticeably in that it is a loose, observational portrait of a family and of a community living in the mountains, one that is concerned with the rigours of living in such a remote location. It eschews nothing of the practical considerations of everyday life, of such quotidian details as the journeys to and from school and work and the reliance on travelling salesmen for basic amenities such as food, all of which Kawase dwells on at significant, narratively disproportionate, length and which become significant micro-narratives. There is a story of sorts that follows an extended family comprised of a father (Kozo), his wife (Yasuyo) and elderly mother (Sachiko), and both their young daughter (Michiru) and Yasuyo's nephew (Eisuke). This family live in a remote village in the mountains of Nara Prefecture – where Kawase herself was born – and the narrative looks at the impact on the household of Kozo losing his job due to the official abandonment of a proposed railway through the hills. Yasuyo has to take a job in order to help out with the family finances, but this takes its toll on her already frail health and leads to a tough decision to move away and return to the city. The perceived idyll of the mountain locale, coupled with the timeframe of the film (moving from a prologue set in 1971 to the main body of the narrative fifteen years later at the height of the miracle economy), has led Keiko I. McDonald (2006) to assert that the film is about a vanishing traditional way of life in the face of encroaching modernity and capitalist expansion: about 'a world continually ravaged by its "civilizations"' (p. 257). However it is in fact more complex than this outline suggests. The railway, the typical, portentous symbol of the impending, impinging modern world, is in fact crucial to the lifeblood of the village. A scene at a local meeting makes clear its necessity for the community's as much as for Kozo's own well-being when everyone votes in favour of it, whilst a neighbouring family having to take their elderly to a nursing home in the city bespeaks the potential rigours of living in so isolated a place and thus the practical need for such transportation.

Mirrored moments abound throughout the film. These include Eisuke looking around a tunnel through the mountains built for the railway (replete with closely matched, dramatically low camera angles as he enters), a children's song that opens and closes the film (again with identical cinematography, this time pans from characters out to the mountains beyond), whilst the break-up of the family, seen when the elderly neighbours move away, finds a correlation in Yasuyo and Michiru moving away to the city at the very end of the narrative. These rhyming scenes are employed to map out the development of the film, tracing different and divergent responses to similar events. Most overtly the aforementioned song concerns the game of hide and seek and is initially sung by a group of children whilst playing. At the end of the film it is recapitulated when Sachiko sings it, and the fact that Kawase repeats the earlier camera move, sweeping up and away from the elderly woman after she has mournfully intoned the song and (ambiguously) closed her eyes, becomes a marker of loss – of the vibrancy of children, the community and attendant notions of life and growth giving way to the isolation of this single old lady, to loneliness and possibly death.

This structural care and detail creates a veritable tension as otherwise in the film Kawase has almost no recourse to conventional causality or mainstream principles of construction or découpage – a tension that reflects the pull between rural and urban, the personal and the familial. From this perspective the open, digressive structure also serves to highlight the interconnected nature of the lives and events that are depicted. This is not simply an intertwining of the human lives that populate the village but also refers to the characters' connection to their surroundings, to the world in which they live and whose isolation inexorably shapes their lives and relationships. It is perhaps most evident in Kozo's reliance on work in the mountains for employment; however it is also present in Michiru and the increasingly close bond she has with her older cousin. Of practical necessity they ride together on his motorbike to the school bus stop every morning and home every afternoon, but Kawase uses this repeated travel not to simply fetishise a narrative *temps morts* or a sense of quotidian detail for its own sake. Rather these journeys become, for Michiru, a treasured time away from the strictures of family on the one hand and school on the other, a literal in-between space where being alone with Eisuke reinforces their lifelong closeness and indeed helps to foster further feelings such that they seem to be on the point of developing an unnatural union. It is a marker of the unhealthy potentiality of too insular a familial bond and that blood relationships can only offer family members so much, and as such facilitates an enquiry about the limits of family life in a location where personal and individual horizons are more strongly defined by this traditional institution.

Shara (2003), Kawase's belated second feature, is similarly concerned with movement and stasis. It is another portrait of a family and a community, not as remote as in *The God Suzaku* but a comparably small and seemingly hermetic location in which there is a close bond between residents and an implicit sense of insularity. The family at the heart of the narrative is not an extended unit like that of Kawase's debut but is similarly comprised of a mother and father (Reiko and Taku respectively) and a teenage child, in this case a boy named Shun. This film also echoes Kawase's feature debut in that the narrative begins with a scene that establishes people and place before jumping forwards to pick up the lives of the characters several years hence. In this case the young Shun is playing with his brother when the latter suddenly disappears, and when the film jumps forwards in time this unresolved incident is still hanging over the protagonists.

A family coping with the sudden, unexplained loss of one of its members offers another connection to *The God Suzaku*, but here the disappearance of a child rather than a family head is a more tragic occurrence. The fact that it happens at the beginning of the film reveals this import, and establishes an attended temporal antinomy, one between past and present, as a correlative to the dichotomy between movement and stasis. These are inscribed directly into the style of the film as its restless camera is perennially moving, either towards, away from or around the characters, locating them precisely within an immediate spatial context and elucidating their physical proximity to one another. Even when observing static subjects Kawase tends to keep her camera subtly mobile, her compositions in flux, which imparts a sense of impermanence to the film that, along with the narrative, stresses the inexorable, impersonal flow of time and thus a poetic dimension to contrast with the otherwise quotidian detail emphasised elsewhere. Moreover the camera seems always to be exploring the spaces of the diegesis, to be searching out the protagonists as though they were lost. On several occasions it moves protractedly through different locations, seemingly penetrating the space before coming to rest on a character or characters (as though the town itself were a protagonist), which crystallises the centrality of loss and disappearance, the absence (of Shun's brother) at the heart of the film.

Time is also a major aspect of *Shara* in that Kawase throughout the narrative respects the temporal duration of the events that she depicts. This encompasses a procession and performance involved in a street festival, a final scene in which

Reiko (played by Kawase herself) gives birth and the journey home from school of Shun and Yu, which is significantly shown on two separate occasions in structurally rhyming scenes early and late in the narrative. The first time sees them both on a bicycle, riding carefree through the streets, whilst later they have to run desperately when they are called from school in an apparent emergency relating to Shun's mother. This detailed emphasis on, as it were, real time not only reinforces a nominal documentary aesthetic – as though the camera had happened upon this village and can but react to what transpires before it – but it further allows Kawase to subtly thematise time as a central aspect of the story. This redoubles the theme of transience, a sense of a life cycle – life, death and ultimately rebirth (given the film's final scene of Reiko's labour and a new brother for Shun) – and further it stresses not interconnection in the way that *The God Suzaku* does but rather the opposite, a sense of separation. This is not to suggest that the lives of the family members are divorced from one another, nor indeed that the community is not united or bound by its constituent citizens (there is here another echo of *The God Suzaku* in that both films contain scenes that depict in detail an official meeting of a group of senior village men). The point in this case, at least until the very end of the narrative, is that everyone lives their own lives, responds in their own way to pain, loss and grief. In the former film the family seem to work through it as one. In this film however the protagonists each internalise their pain and react to tragedy in different ways. It is true that the horizons of the small village are dominated by a group mentality – for instance the festival of Basara, whose preparations and undertaking are depicted in detail, bespeaks a sense of communal spirit and endeavour – but this is not necessarily a positive feature of the domestic landscape. A key scene early in the film sees the family informed that a body has been found that is likely that of the missing child. Shun's immediate response to this news is to disbelieve what he has heard and run away; however his father holds him in place and refuses to relinquish his grasp whilst his mother crowds around him, in effect negating his personal response in a symbolic gesture of cocooning him within an enforced collective grieving that demonstrates the potential strictures of family and of tradition.

The final moments of the film make this precept, this tension between individual and communal points of view, diagrammatically clear. The camera leaves the home of Shun's family almost immediately following the birth of his baby brother and backs out of their house, across the street and right through a neighbouring house before craning up above the rooftops and dissolving to a helicopter shot that lifts us high above and away from the village in order to regard it from on high in a perspective unavailable to any character within the world below. There is a complex process of signification here. The film closes on a birth, the appearance of a young brother, and this both echoes and in a sense disavows the disappearance of an older brother at the very beginning of the narrative. Moreover the camera leaving this scene – itself both a disappearance and an appearance (the camera disappearing from this significant narrative event in order to facilitate another appearance, to make visible a different, much larger space) – marks out both its objective veracity and its singular perspective. In so doing it presents a contemplative aesthetic that affirms the representational imperative of the film, of the family as a repository of meaning in Japan and Japanese cinema, and of the need to move beyond it, as the camera literally does in its audacious final shot.

One of the ramifications of this subject is the picture of gender that is entailed within the respective communities and families, which in both films relates to ostensibly traditional models and the divisions between men and women therein. In *The God Suzaku*, Yasuyo has to find a job to help make ends following her husband's enforced unemployment, a similar situation to that of her mother-in-law who, it is implied, entered the workplace whilst her husband was away fighting (she talks of wartime difficulties and that she only has a comfortable life in her old age because of her son's family). There is thus an inscription of history pertaining to women at work, to the need for a female workforce because of problems with regard to men and the male population. Conversely the stratification of gender within the gravitational pull of the family is more marked in *Shara*, where the heavily pregnant Reiko remains at home whilst the job of organising Basara (a traditional event) is undertaken entirely by her husband; we see him chairing a committee composed entirely of men, and there is even a scene in which Reiko is rather severely berated by her husband for not serving him and a colleague with Sake when they are talking at his house.

This stratification of gender is mirrored by other young female directors in Japan. A contrastive voice to Kawase's can be found in the work of Iguchi Nami. This young director's feature debut *Dogs and Cats* (*Inuneko*, 2004) concerns the tentative relationship between two young women: old school friends who begin to live together when one, Suzu, leaves her lazy, inattentive fiancé and moves out of her home. She moves in with Yoko, who is looking after the home of a mutual friend whilst she is studying in China, and the pair who seem on the surface to be like the titular pets (i.e. polar opposites) are gradually revealed to be in many ways almost identical. Indeed, in a distant echo of Bergman's *Persona* (1966), they even seem to exchange lives and identities, or at least their individual selves become indistinguishable. After work Yoko buys yellow flowers for the house and arrives home to find an identical bunch already arranged by Suzu, and this, in addition to rhyming scenes in which Suzu tries on Yoko's spectacles and, subsequently Yoko borrows Suzu's contact lenses and helps out by undertaking her housemate's job as a dog-walker, cements a sense in which their lives and personalities merge. Iguchi even underlines the similarity visually when she shoots Yoko struggling to find the right home and dog in precisely the same way as she had earlier shot Suzu, with the same camera set-up and same jump cut to comically denote her having taken the wrong road.

The sense of an almost communal identity here becomes satirical, almost parodic, connoting as it does that the film is nominally about woman rather than women. In other words it mischievously suggests that there is, or may be, a commonality of female experience, a point that concomitantly implies that a single, unilateral feminist approach or perhaps critical framework may be insufficient to elucidate the myriad subjectivities of contemporary womanhood or female selfhood. This is crystallised when it transpires that the two young women have always shared the same taste in men. Suzu, whilst out walking a dog, falls down and is helped by the man whom Yoko secretly desires. Conversely, when she invites him back to their house, Yoko becomes perturbed and immediately leaves to spend the night with Suzu's ex-fiancé, her ex-boyfriend from their school days. There are even precisely matched lateral tracking shots (two of only a very limited number of mobile shots in the whole film) of Yoko and Suzu running after leaving their house in consternation following a confrontation with their housemate, and the picture of gender that accrues from this is one of the limits of and limitations on female selfhood and subjectivity, of the tenets of a post-feminist milieu that, as Angela McRobbie notes, entails an 'active process by which feminist gains of the 1970s and 1980s come to be undermined' (2004, p. 255). It is also a milieu where apparently contradictory demands become imperative: of desiring equality at the same time as desiring both desire and the need to be desired. From this point of view the film seems on the surface to point to a confusing landscape of young womanhood where the protagonists are fundamentally torn and uncertain. In so doing it asks precisely what the undermining of earlier feminist ideals amounts to, what comes in their stead.

To this end there is a sense in which the characters in *Dogs and Cats* are presented as children, or at most as adolescents. Their behaviour throughout the film is not always commensurate with adulthood (their aforementioned attitudes to men are highly immature), and their respective jobs are both what one would associate with teenagers (Suzu's employment as a dog-walker and Yoko's job in a convenience store). Moreover the closing credits contain childlike drawings of animals that move around the frame in a manner that recalls crude flipbook animation. These credits, coming as they do after an abrupt open ending that resolves nothing – that leaves the girls' lives with their problems and interpersonal tensions entirely intact – cements this youthful perspective and suggests that these 'children' of feminism extol an age wherein femininity and female selfhood can infantilise women. Moreover the lack of psychological insight or ostensible depth of characterisation that is attendant on this narrative methodology goes hand-in-hand with Iguchi's observational aesthetic. She looks at rather than with her protagonists, eschewing POV shots and largely any shot size closer than a medium shot (usually taking long and extreme long shots), and in so doing stresses the primacy of the camera's point of view, the lack of a gendered or biased perspective on the characters and narrative. This coupled with the fact that female desire and female gazing animates the structure of looks within the film (hence the motif of eyesight and glasses) – and that men remain almost exclusively the desired objects rather than the desiring subjects – provides an ostensibly fractured perspective. It is as though the camera's detached presence looks on in wry amusement at these girls groping towards a subjectivity that continually eludes them, that they are unable to attain.

Iguchi also uses these precepts to animate a narrative opposition between similarity and difference that is in fact made manifest from the very beginning of the film through a prominent cinematic intertext. She immediately signals such a relationship through the credits in *Dogs and Cats*, which unfold over a burlap background of the type that became a trademark of the films of Ozu Yasujiro. Indeed the beige colour of this cloth in *Dogs and Cats* directly echoes Ozu's late colour films, which all (except one) invariably employed this tone as a contrast to the often bright red and white characters of the credits. The point of having the ghost of Ozu so prominent throughout the film is to draw a distinction between the Japan that Ozu's work described and documented and the country in the new millennium, the key distinction being the erosion of the family unit that was a staple of the director of *Late Spring* (*Banshun*, 1949), *Tokyo Story* (*Tōkyō monogatari*, 1953) and *The End of Summer* (*Kohayagawa-ke no aki*, 1961) among many others. The landscape of *Dogs and Cats* is dominated by individuals rather than families, by young characters who to all intents and purposes are estranged from any viable familial relationships. It is a measure of the lengths to which Japan has transformed that the family unit no longer seems to be at the heart or the centre of the country, and as a result Iguchi's protagonists appear cast adrift, not so much aimless or in overt need of a family around them as they are in want of a way to define themselves against something tenable or tangible (another reason for the marked similarities between the two protagonists). This intertextuality, representative as it is of a postmodern cultural landscape of pastiche and self-reflexivity, of the director implicitly measuring her work against a notable forebear, offers a textual counterpoint to a narrative landscape marked by a complete absence of earlier generations, of parents either literal or figurative. It is a contrapuntal concept that further reinforces the divorcement from second-wave feminist ideals noted above, and it is a question that Iguchi poses but notably does not answer.

Iguchi's de-dramatised narrative sensibility in her debut was immediately carried over into her second feature, the much longer *Don't Laugh at my Romance* (*Hito no sekkusu o warau na*, 2007). This film concerns another tentative relationship, this time between a young male university student named Mirume and a middle-aged lecturer called Yuri, and the physical intimacy between them that means something different to them both. To the former it is a meaningful emotional connection whilst the latter (who is married to an older man) regards it much more as a repeated sexual tryst to compensate for the lack of physical intimacy in her marriage, and Iguchi traces this story alongside two other characters

– the young student's friends (a boy and a girl, the latter of whom, En-chan, is secretly in love with Mirume). Employing and refining the long shot/long take methodology and chilly, autumnal *mise-en-scène* of *Dogs and Cats*, *Don't Laugh at my Romance* can be read explicitly as a treatise on looking and not looking, hiding and being seen, invisibility and visibility. It both engages with and critiques some of the precepts outlined by Laura Mulvey, particularly the binary opposition of active male and passive female as encoded in the former's power to look at and demystify the latter. Within the film the protagonists are often desirous of looking but not being looked at, seeing without being seen, perennial voyeurs. Several early comedic moments see various characters hiding from others, some-thing both Mirume and En do when they are confronted with those on whom they have cast their gaze. The former in particular attempts to spy on Yuri but is almost immediately rebuffed, which confers power on the desired object rather than the desiring subject, a subversive notion that strips the gaze of its controlling imperative and subjectivity. When Mirume spies on Yuri through the door of her college workshop he ducks below the window when his object appears to catch him and return his gaze. This is shot from inside the room, so that we are looking at Mirume looking; however following his desperate attempt to evade being seen Iguchi cuts to a shot taken outside the door and behind Mirume as he hides. As he then slowly rises to peer again through the window he (and we) are taken by sur-prise as Yuri pops up on the other side of the window, pulling a silly face and effec-tively parodying and negating her objectified status, whilst Iguchi's editing serves to implicate the audience and by extension the conventional masculine subject position in this negation (Fig. 7.1). Mirume goes on to model for Yuri, involv-ing his being coaxed into getting undressed for her, which further underlines his transformation into object, following which their almost purely sexual liaisons mean that the relationship is undertaken on her terms. Moreover the fact that En works at a cinema, which becomes a recurrent location throughout the narra-tive, is also significant here as it offers an implied site of convention and codified looking that Iguchi slyly subverts by setting two key scenes in the quotidian spaces of the foyer directly outside the theatre itself, especially one of the aforementioned scenes of hiding when En drops behind the counter to avoid being seen by Yuri.

The very title of the film – *Don't Laugh at my Romance* (the Japanese title translates directly as *Sex is not a Laughing Matter*) – further implies this sense of looking, more properly of being looked at, with an added dimension of judge-ment and condemnation. It is one of the two key films discussed by Armendariz in her exploration of textual transgression marked by a female's encounter with the Other. She notes that Iguchi positions Yuri as a 'symbolic mother' whose relationship to Mirume transgresses and facilitates Oedipal desire in that she instigates the relationship (2011, p. 30). However the director also complicates this precept; Yuri is married to a much older man, one whom Mirume mistakes for her father, and typically for Iguchi the time with the young student is for her a

Figure 7.1   Parodying the male gaze in *Don't Laugh at my Romance*.

regression into being almost infantile. One scene in particular shows Yuri finding and attempting to set up a tent in her studio after sleeping with Mirume, thus establishing their relationship as a site of escape from the tribulations of being an adult. At the same time Yuri's marriage is in a sense a negation of adult agency and responsibility on her part; a scene late in the narrative, again following sex between Yuri and Mirume, sees the former plead with her young lover to fill her portable heater with gasoline as she can't do it. Her husband, she notes (whom she perennially refers to as 'Inokuma-san' – Mr Inokuma, as though he were a professional superior), always does it for her, and this has left her somewhat help-less with regard to undertaking menial domestic chores for herself.

This is then extended into a scenario in which 'the authoritative "no" to the son's desire for the mother is not pronounced by Yuri's husband' (the symbolic father) (ibid.) as he is a father figure to both lovers. Instead Yuri simply leaves, travelling unannounced to India; Mirume is stranded as a pre-Oedipal subject-in-waiting, whilst Yuri undertakes an encounter with a different, a racial, Other that points to a reconfiguration of the film's concerns with this concept. Again Iguchi leaves the narrative open and unresolved, its tensions and conflicts ongoing. She does, however, offer a quote that is significant following the film's final shot – '[j]ust because you can't see each other doesn't mean it's over' – which transfig-ures the matrix of looks and gazes of *Don't Laugh at my Romance* and offers some-thing of a route beyond looking and being looked at that has hitherto defined this film's relationships between self and Other, suggesting as it does that desire may supersede the look.

The vagaries of (problematic) female selfhood are in various ways addressed by both Kawase and Iguchi. Of note for her lack of interest in overt recourse to such stories is Nishikawa Miwa. A former assistant director to Koreeda Hirokazu, Nishikawa has produced a body of work that, of all her female contemporaries, most explicitly eschews any engagement with feminine stories. However this does not necessarily preclude any sense of dealing with or reflecting on female identity. This is especially so in that she has often been taken to be a director who is concerned with the social psyche of modern Japan (Mes, 2006), and the gender divisions that frequently animate her work, even though they frequently seem to privilege the male, nonetheless reflect contemporary perceptions thereof. *Dear Doctor* (*Dia dokutā*, 2009), Nishikawa's fourth feature, is an apt case in point. It concerns an ageing doctor in a rural village whose lack of detailed expertise in treating complex cases is brought to light following his treatment of an elderly female patient. Unfolding in flashback from a framing story in which two detectives investigating the doctor's criminal negligence interview villagers about their relationship with him following his disappearance, the narrative posits this patriarchal figure as, in Laura Mulvey's terminology, an enigma to be resolved. He is thus broadly, implicitly, positioned in the narrative as a mystery to be investigated and, perhaps more tellingly, as a physical threat to be neutralised.

Elsewhere the film offers a more subtle and penetrating vision of gender in modern Japan than one simply based around a man and his various personal problems and professional shortcomings. Nishikawa in fact echoes Iguchi and implicitly positions her film in a dialogic intertextual relationship with a notable forebear, in her case Kurosawa Akira's *Red Beard* (*Akahige*, 1965), which is used to throw into dramatic relief the picture of contrastive men and women in Nishikawa's film. *Dear Doctor*, like *Red Beard*, begins with a brash and idealistic young intern, Soma Keisuke, arriving at a remote clinic in order to study under an older mentor figure, someone whom he eventually comes to respect and to emulate. The scenario of Kurosawa's period drama by and large overcomes a potentially problematic representation of women (largely the mainstay of the clinic's patients who are variously psychologically scarred and as a result either predatory or pathetic) by dint of its period setting, the fact that it may be argued to reflect a time when women were overtly second-class citizens. This is then positioned by Nishikawa as a marker of the past, which serves to establish the film's antinomy between past (social and cinematic) and present as central to the narrative. On the one hand the village where Dr Osamu practices is depicted as an antiquated space, a site of the past given that it is populated almost entirely by elderly people and further that is presided over (as one of the detectives says, 'held together') by this patriarchal figure, one who is celebrated, even literally worshipped, by his patients for what they erroneously believe to be his miraculous medical abilities. On the other hand there is Osamu's main victim's daughter, a relatively young woman from Tokyo who is herself a successful doctor, and she represents a contrastive paradigm of an urban milieu in which woman are accepted into positions of power and responsibility (indeed whilst visiting her mother she is teased by her sisters for being just like a man).

Nishikawa's sensibility in *Dear Doctor* is not aggressive or forceful regarding its gender politics, befitting of a director who has been seen as comparable to 'the pre-straight-to-video salad days of Japanese cinema [. . .] reminiscent of art-house films of prior generations' (Laird, 2012, p. 98). However Nishikawa's feature debut, *Wild Berries* (*Hebi ichigo*, 2003), had earlier complicated the picture. This offbeat *shomin-geki* is defined even more than *Dear Doctor* against works from previous eras in Japanese cinema. It concerns the travails of an extended family that result from the father's secret unemployment and the loans he has taken to obtain money and hide his lack of a job, something that necessitates the intervention of his estranged son (himself a criminal) in order to offset losing his house and his family. The cinematic forebears that carry the intertextual imperative of *Wild Berries* are the excessive, satirical family films of the 1980s. In this decade the generic model of the *shomin-geki* became a point of departure for a new generation of independent directors who capitalised on its popular visibility and familiarity in order to subvert its intrinsic norms and thus define themselves against previous cinematic figures. Films such as Ishii Sogo's *Crazy Family* (*Gyakufunsha kazoku*, 1984), Morita Yoshimitsu's *The Family Game* (*Kazoku gēmu*, 1983), Suo Masayuki's *Abnormal Family: Older Brother's Bride* (*Hentai kazoku: Aniki no yomesan*, 1984) or Itami Juzo's feature debut *The Funeral* (*Osōshiki*, 1983) show Japanese families in a state of crisis and implicitly juxtapose these crises against those in earlier canonical iterations of the genre by Ozu Yasujiro, Gosho Heinosuke and others. The latter film here is an explicit intertext given that *Wild Berries* also has a central scene at a funeral, and moreover one in which this paragon of a spiritual tradition – of mourning the deceased through recourse to Buddhist doctrines – is shockingly interrupted and parodied. Itami shows this through the inability of several characters to sit formally throughout the ceremony (connoting their estrangement from tradition), whilst Nishikawa uses the wake as a setting for a fight between the husband and a debtor looking for money, a fight that leads to the coffin falling to the ground and to the corpse almost falling out onto the floor.

Patriarchal lineage and succession is central to *Wild Berries*. There is a deeply problematic line of men in the film that reflect the aforementioned psychoanalytical precepts and the oft-discussed connection to feminism that animates particularly Freudian and Lacanian application within film studies (Humm, 1997, pp. 16–26). Nishikawa's picture of Japanese family life seems on the surface to be not only conventional but deeply traditional in that the practice of the female remaining at home with her family until she marries and enters her husband's family is observed. The daughter, Tomono, is around thirty years of age and still lives at home pending her imminent engagement to a colleague at work, whilst her mother has done precisely the same, adopted her husband's family, her chief duty in which involves caring for her senile father-in-law. After a visit Tomono's partner remarks how close and how polite her family is, but this façade is immediately shattered when they leave and Tomono's father berates his daughter's boyfriend for his softness and laziness, whilst her mother (whose hair is beginning to fall out due to stress) tells her frankly that the family is collapsing. The opening shot of the film is telling from this point of view; it begins on a long shot of the breakfast table as the members of the household each appear to take their meal, before slowly tracking in to frame them all in a tighter shot, bespeaking the film's desire to peer beyond the surface, to look into this family beneath the harmonious image that is presented to the world and which, given Tomono's assertion that her mother enjoys caring for her father-in-law, even some members of the family itself seem to believe. Nishikawa's sequence shot for this scene further establishes the long take as a central feature of the film, as well as inscribing the discrete distance and power of the camera to be able to assert its own subjectivity over the variously corrupted and inhibited identities of the protagonists.

The senile father/grandfather, who still lives in the past (he verbally attacks his daughter-in-law for feeding an imperial soldier poor food), represents the untenability of said past, and by extension its traditions. The corrosiveness of past generations – those since the Pacific War (the war that is sporadically relived by the grandfather) – continues with Tomono's father. He has failed along with Japan's economy (he complains about the economic state of the country), whilst his criminal son Shuji, whose crimes consist of stealing bereavement money from funerals, perpetuates a negation of and disdain for tradition. Indeed towards the end of the film he berates his mother for spending money on a plaque for his grandfather. Beside these problematic men, Tomono and her mother are victims who suffer at their hands: the mother through being entirely left to care for her father-in-law as though it were no concern of anyone else and the daughter through the fact that her boyfriend ends their relationship after the aforementioned exploits at the grandfather's funeral. However these women are not simplistic paragons of morality or virtue; Tomono's mother in effect kills her father-in-law when she ignores a seizure, whilst she tells her daughter that her good nature is boring and uninteresting compared to the wayward Shuji: that life is dull with her around. Family life here, especially as tradition and social custom has dictated it, is an untenable and alienating institution – a patriarchal and oppressive entity that corrupts and oppresses men as much as women in that it demands an exalted social status, a hierarchy of the Symbolic at whose apex they are expected to sit. It is the enshrinement of a familial model that seems unrealisable in the contemporary world that is at issue in *Wild Berries*, and its gender politics are based forcefully around this concept.

The emphasis in the work of Iguchi Nami and Nishikawa Miwa on problematic relationships is shared by several other female directors. *Kakera: A Piece of*

Our Life (*Kakera*, 2009), the debut feature by Ando Momoko, echoes *Dogs and Cats* in that it concerns a young girl who leaves her inattentive and casually indifferent boyfriend, and as in Iguchi's film her life thereafter is defined by a tortuous relationship with another woman. However in this case the relationship is a sexual one, as the woman, Haru, meets and becomes intimately involved with a prosthetic surgeon named Riko. Ando flirts with a forceful, if simplistic, picture of gender relations here, especially as Haru's boyfriend is depicted as a selfish and obnoxious partner who is only interested in Haru for sex. In one scene the camera creeps over Haru and her boyfriend as he makes love to her prostrate body (after she has banged her head and fallen) and comes to rest on a television on which is playing wartime newsreel footage of conflict and fighting, suggesting in no uncertain terms that a war of the sexes lies at the heart of the narrative, albeit one that is complicated elsewhere in the story. The lesbian relationship with Riko is in fact far from an ideal union. She is possessive, suspicious and denies Haru a life and identity of her own, the point being, ultimately, that one must define oneself as an individual rather than through relationships with others; that any group or collective mindset is a fundamentally untenable proposition.

Such a concern with women and abusive or indifferent men has animated other films, like Tsuki Inoue's short *The Woman Who is Beating the Earth* (*Daichi o tataku onna*, 2008) and Kazama Shiori's earlier *The Mars Canon* (*Kasei no kanon*, 2002). Narratives of romance and problematic courtship have also been explored by another key female director in modern Japanese cinema: Tanada Yuki. In contrast to many of her female peers in modern Japanese cinema Tanada does at least aim towards an exploration of the difficulty of women in defining a space for themselves as distinct from the men around them. The young female protagonists of her films *Moon and Cherry* (*Tsuki to Cherī*, 2004) and *One Million Yen Girl* (*Hyakuman-en to nigamushi onna*, 2008) retain narrative agency and manage ultimately to live their lives on their own terms, to find an apparently personally fulfilling route to an autonomous female selfhood, even though this is frequently problematic. *Moon and Cherry*, her feature debut, concerns a young university student, Tadokoro, who after joining an erotic writing club becomes involved with a young woman named Mayumi, for whose serialised novel she has taken to practical research that involves sleeping with anyone who can help her story. Tadokoro, being a virgin, is quickly enlisted by Mayumi to sleep with her, and further to engage in a series of increasingly outré sexual encounters that, as Armendariz notes, turn him into a 'passive object' even as he becomes ever more sexually active (2011, p. 32). However he falls in love with Mayumi, thus complicating a relationship that she needs purely for her story and her career, and is distressed when, at the end of the narrative, she almost summarily dismisses him when her professional use for him has elapsed.

Perhaps Tanada's most commercially successful film, *One Million Yen Girl* is a female variation on both the *seishun eiga* and the family drama. It is about a

21-year-old girl named Suzuko who, after a criminal case leads to a short spell in prison, finds that her family life and social notoriety are such that she wishes to move away and live in anonymity. This plan involves saving up one million Yen before embarking on a journey that sees her travelling around Japan and living hand to mouth, taking menial jobs in a variety of both rural and urban locations and stubbornly resisting forming any relationships or emotional ties with the people with whom she comes into contact. The film is a clear attempt to negotiate a space for reflecting on a girl's coming of age, a journey to adulthood (literally, in that she is leaving home) and more significantly to womanhood. Her life even before her migration away from home is beset by problems with men; her criminality, indeed her imprisonment, comes after she reacts angrily to the insensitive behaviour of a potential male housemate whose depression following a relationship break-up leads him to throw out on the street a little kitten that Suzuko subsequently finds dead. Her throwing away all his possessions then lands her in jail, and she refuses to pose as the housemate's girlfriend even when told by the police that this would result in a less severe penalty, her problems thus beginning with her determination to remain independent, to not be tied to a man.

Tanada thus insists quite forcefully on her female protagonists' autonomy and self-sufficiency. The romantic partners that both Suzuko and Mayumi become involved with all figure as subservient and indeed sentimental characters, occupying the roles typically ascribed to female characters in such films. Tadokoro falls in love with Mayumi, whilst the prospective partner to Suzuko in *One Million Yen Girl* rushes after the protagonist at the end of the film to declare his feelings, and it is Suzuko who explicitly denies him this opportunity by walking away when she sees him. It is problematic, however, that these girls seem apparently so comfortably able to assert themselves in such a manner; it feels like a self-conscious mission statement rather than an organic aspect of the narrative. In *Moon and Cherry* the assertion is that Mayumi has to deny any emotional life and connections in order to succeed as a professional writer. In other words this character's success in her job comes at the cost of other, personal avenues of her life. There is no prospect as far as the narrative is concerned of combining a career with a relationship, at least in this male-dominated profession (to which end Mayumi complains of having to write under a pseudonym in order to be able to publish her work), but there is no sense on the protagonist's part that this is a problem for her and especially none as to why she is so happy being on her own.

One Million Yen Girl subtly carries a similar, and similarly problematic, message. Suzuko finds in the first two places that she visits – the places in which she explicitly denies any contact with the local people – that she has a natural talent and ability to do the jobs that she undertakes, and as such she manages very smoothly and successfully. Conversely it is in the third place, which in contrast to the previous two locations is an urban space, that she becomes romantically involved with a co-worker, and here she struggles to adapt to the work and finds herself constantly making careless mistakes even though it is only a menial job. The subtextual meaning herein reinforces the idea of a mutual exclusivity between female personal and professional success and happiness, that to progress in the latter requires a concomitant sacrifice of the former, but this feels like an antiquated feminist impulse. In addition the point-making feels strained, as the narrative events that it facilitates, indeed requires, are not always convincing, especially given the fact that Suzuko seems to be very close to the boy she subsequently abandons.

Tanada's subsequent film, the manga adaptation *Ain't no Tomorrows* (*Oretachi ni asu wa naissu*, 2008), features an ensemble of high school students on the cusp of graduation (one marker of a tentative entry into adulthood) whose respective relationships and attitudes to sex are detailed and juxtaposed. The vagaries of physical and emotional maturation are paramount in the film, and this is broadly refracted through one particular character, a lustful boy called Hiruma, beside whom are three key female characters: Tomono, a reserved girl engaged in an affair with a teacher; Chizu, a naïve teenager who is confused by the onset of menstruation after having lived a sheltered home life and who thereafter becomes preoccupied by having sex; and Akie, one of the more popular and pretty girls in school, who pursues a relationship with an overweight classmate named Ando. These trajectories intersect with those of a group of male friends including Hiruma (who comes to blackmail Tomono into having sex with him when he learns of her relationship with her teacher), Ando and their friend Mine. The latter becomes involved with Chizu when he finds her unconscious on the school grounds following the beginning of her period, whilst Ando's relationship with Akie becomes untenable for him when he learns that she desires him primarily for his overweight physique.

It is the contrast between these characters and stories that structures Tanada's film and animates its central themes. Chief in this regard is the discrepancy between the physical and the emotional. Hiruma is obsessed with sex at all costs; he is perennially talking about sex, reading erotic literature, even paying Ando so that he can feel his breasts in lieu of having a girlfriend whom he can grope. Conversely Mine turns down an offer of sex from Chizu as he does not feel enough for her; he desires a relationship and wants intercourse only with someone that he loves. Moreover both Hiruma and Mine are seen to be inexperienced and ineffectual when they do have sex. The former is unable to achieve an erection after having brought Tomono to a remote hut on the beach to fulfil his deal with her, whilst the latter is awkward and ejaculates almost immediately when he begins intercourse. Ando by contrast is used by both boys and girls, Hiruma and Akie, because of his body. He represents an ironic inversion of the objectified female (something Tanada parodies in a scene with Chizu and Mine in a porn cinema watching a film where the woman is completely naked and the man only has his trousers off), and Akie is herself used to this given her preter-naturally well-developed breasts.

Against these male attitudes the girls in the film represent different poles of innocence and experience. Chizu's lack of awareness of her body (she initially believes that menstruation follows sex) and her subsequently almost voracious interest in intercourse is contrasted with the indifferent attitude of Tomono, who has a sexual relationship with her teacher. The connection between these characters is underlined by the fact that both Chizu and Tomono pass out at certain moments of the film; the former, as already noted, is found unconscious by Mine following her discovery of menstrual bleeding, whilst the latter col-lapses in school during an assembly before later almost fainting during sex with Hiruma. Akie can be juxtaposed with these girls by virtue of her body and desires. As noted she initiates a relationship with Ando because of a personal predilec-tion for overweight men, something that her fellow pupils regard as a perversion on her part when she is seen to secretly hoard Sumo Wrestling magazines, and which comes to pass when she appears to lose interest in Ando following his weight loss, completely ignoring him at school when their paths cross. Akie contrasts with the films' other young female protagonists in that she throws into relief the ostensibly unnatural relationship between Tomono and her teacher on the one hand (facilitating a question as to what is a natural, healthy relationship), whilst on the other she provides a point of contradistinction to Chizu's lack of bodily awareness and experience in her own (implied) sexual maturity. The sum total of these girls' personalities and experiences contrasts with those of the boys in that we see an obsession with sex on the part of Hiruma and Chizu, a desire for emotional connection on the part of Tomono (who shows no interest in sex whatever) and Mine, and a pair of characters in Ando and Akie for whom physi-cal problems define and delimit the horizons of their lives and respective identi-ties. Together these various micro-narratives add up to a picture of the specific problems and pressures of youth, whilst the fact that the story is viewed to a large extent from a male perspective – and moreover from the point of view of a male who remains obsessed by sex – bespeaks something of the film's ostensible con-cordance with generic norms pertaining to the teen comedy and thus its subtly subversive potentiality.

Similarly both a part of and a commentary on the *seishun eiga* is Kitagawa Eriko's feature debut *Halfway* (*Harufuwei*, 2009), a film that was conceived and co-edited by the popular director Iwai Shunji, with whose unusual teen romance film *Hana and Alice* (*Hana to Arisu*, 2004) this forms a diptych. *Halfway* is a film whose narrative horizons are built exclusively around the fluctuating emo-tions of its protagonists – with a young teenage boy and girl whose relationship defines the parameters of their lives to the extent that they are almost always either together, talking on the phone or otherwise thinking about each other. Kitagawa and Iwai's conceit is to construct a narrative and cinematographic style that directly reflects this scenario. It is built entirely around this fledgling, embry-onic relationship and the threat that is posed when the boy, Shinozaki, decides that he is going to leave his home town in the northernmost Japanese island of Hokkiado to attend university in Tokyo upon graduating from high school. Like Toyoda Toshiaki's *Blue Spring* (*Aoi haru*, 2001) the film takes place almost entirely within and around the school grounds, and even those scenes that depict Haru and Shinozaki at home eschew any elucidation of their family life. The narrative is given over entirely to their relationship, an apt comment on the insularity of their youthful obsession, and Kitagawa elsewhere subverts the ostensibly clichéd material. Haru is initially depicted as a girl obsessed in a way that is common in so-called teen idol films. She faints when she shakes hands with Shinozaki at a school basketball match, and thereafter she speaks to her friend in the nurse's office about her dreams of approaching him and asking him on a date. The fact that soon after this he himself also repairs to the nurse with an impact injury from said basketball game suggests a nominally generic narrative, and subse-quently the fact that he asks her out only reinforces this conceit of a literal dream come true. However once her wish is granted and she begins seeing Shinozaki there are immediate complications to their union, not simply the impending end of their high school years but also Haru's jealousy and irrational, possessive need to remain with Shinozaki at all times. This is a mirror image of the excit-able, dreamy side of her nature that is made manifest in the opening scenes, the proximal dramatisations of which become redolent of the film's desire to take its generic foundation to its less-than-idyllic logical conclusion, to engage with the problematic ramifications of such adolescent behaviour and emotions. Haru is almost perennially immature and childish with Shinozaki – both in her initial obsession with him and the tantrums she repeatedly throws when things don't go her way when they are dating, such as when he stops to help a female school worker with a flat tyre on her car. As such *Halfway* is preoccupied with disil-lusionment and the erosion of youthful ideals in the face of reality, so that the title of the film becomes reflective of these characters' liminal position between adolescence and adulthood. But just as Kitagawa does not eschew the less posi-tive aspects of her protagonists' behaviour, she is similarly attentive to the less-than-eventful moments that they spend together. There are numerous scenes in *Halfway* that depict the ostensibly dead time that Haru and Shinozaki spend in each other's company, scenes that do little if anything to contribute to a transpar-ently causal narrative structure but that depict the simple pleasure they take in each other's company, alongside which are several extended montage scenes that condense and compact the couple's time together, especially as their separation looms on the horizon.

The effect of these scenes, as well as providing a contrast with the protracted quotidian moments elsewhere in the film, is to mirror another aspect of the narrative. Haru is throughout the film herself preoccupied with photography, with capturing memories of her time in high school, and the film itself acts as an extended or elongated correlative of this feature of the story. It summarises the couple's time together, holding such moments for a short, reflective moment before they vanish and pass into memory, and as such has both an immediacy and intimacy as it communicates distance and reflection, moments at once happening and retrospectively being recalled and remembered: youth as a physical, biological reality and as a state of mind. Concomitantly, the style of *Halfway* reinforces a similar sense of transitory time. Shot on DV with a brightly autumnal *mise-en-scène* reminiscent of the work of Iguchi Nami, the frequently handheld cinematography is perennially moving in a visual approximation of the wayward, unstable, shifting emotions of the characters. Moreover, again like Iguchi (and Nishikawa), Kitagawa offers a forceful negation of a gendered camera and by extension subject position. Her camera at times leaves the protagonists entirely (at one point to pan 360 degrees before finding them again) to stress its detachment from either of their perspectives, the better ultimately to encourage an observation of rather than a complete emotional attachment to their dilemma and to make the film's themes more diagrammatically clear, to which end the prevalence of autumn, of the seasonal colours and tones that predominate in the several extended exterior scenes in the film, reinforces the aforementioned sense of change and transience. Davies and Ikeno have argued that this perceived singularly Japanese sense of the seasons (*Kisetsu*) is today a much more symbolic or metaphorical concept than a reality (2002, p. 157), and this aspect of Halfway, again like *Ain't no Tomorrows* (which is specifically set during summer), is an apposite means of stressing the fact that the film is about youth in general rather than about specific characters in a particular story. From this perspective it becomes a reflection on a country in Japan that is itself experiencing a period of adolescence following a symbolic rebirth in the wake of the death of its era of economic excess. This is a point further facilitated by the emphasis on the difficulties of growth and maturation for much of the narrative, of the very literal need to grow up and develop, as Haru must by letting Shinozaki leave Hokkaido to further his education.

Kitagawa followed up *Halfway* with an adaptation of her own novel *I Have to Buy New Shoes* (*Atarashī kutsu wo kawanakucha*, 2012), a comparable narrative in that it is another ostensible love story whose portrait of a relationship is embedded within an extended, at times protracted, narrative methodology that destabilises conventional generic exegeses. However unlike Kitagawa's *seishun eiga* debut this feature traces the growing crescendo of a relationship rather than the fallout from one: the tentative development of a close friendship rather than the immediate gratification of a youthful obsession. It is, moreover, a relationship that never fully flowers, and as such offers a further contrast to *Halfway* and this film's immediate formation of a romantic couple that, despite pressing problems, is seen to endure and at least potentially to continue despite the postscript of the couple's separation. *I Have to Buy New Shoes* – once again produced and co-edited by Iwai Shunji (and this time photographed by the director) – also concerns a relationship that would have to endure physical estrangement. It concerns a Japanese woman named Aoi, a journalist who lives and works in Paris and who becomes involved with a younger Japanese photographer, Sen, after he has travelled to the French capital for a brief stay with his sister. Thereafter, over the course of three days together, they become increasingly close, eventually confiding in one another about their lives and particularly their sadness and regret over aspects of their careers, relationships and families (Aoi in particular lost a child at five years of age who was born congenitally unhealthy).

The location of the film is, of course, a romantic cliché, and Aoi says as much during a boat ride down the Seine. It is the city of light and love that offers a resplendent backdrop to a developing romance, and Kitagawa and Iwai seem to conspire in this presentation. Many of the most iconic sites in the French capital are employed, and Kitagawa narrativises the canonisation and consumption of these sites as iconic, culturally encoded spaces. Indeed like Eric Rohmer's short *The Bakery Girl of Monceau* (*La boulangère de Monceau*, 1963) or Richard Linklater's more directly comparable *Before Sunset* (2004), the sense of mapping a distinct and knowable topography is offset by an attendant and discordant subjectivity: that is, the certainty of physical space is juxtaposed with the awkward indeterminacy of human social intercourse. There is a protracted scene early in *I Have to Buy New Shoes* in which Aoi, over the phone, guides Sen from the Japanese Embassy past the Arc de Triomphe, down the Champs-Élysées and to his hotel near the Place de la Concorde close to the Louvre. This is followed by extended scenes of the pair getting to know each other, in particular of Aoi getting increasingly drunk to cover her shyness, to the extent that she cannot make it home by herself. Physical and as it were emotional space are contrasted, and this particular tension then serves to highlight other productive contrasts that animate this film. A dichotomy between seeing something apparently real and something embellished is central to *I Have to Buy New Shoes*. Sen talks at length about his work as a photographer-for-hire who became a specialist in retouching photographic portraits of actors and musicians. As such he has struggled with the impositions made on his photographs by those for whom he has worked. Digital photography, he notes, is an impure or problematic example of the medium because of its plasticity, the fact that work can be manipulated, distorted, in the name of perfection or idealisation. It distorts reality, and it is this that tempers Kitagawa's apparently rose-tinted depiction of Paris, its glamour and touristic spectacle. The subtext is that the world, always ostensibly the same, can in fact look different to different people for different reasons, or can change over time for any individual. Sen tells Aoi that after he became a professional photographer he took up mountain climbing because the view changed wherever he happened to be, something he further substantiates by noting that when he slept in Aoi's bath her bringing her home after their first day together he was able to see the whole room differently from that particular vantage point. Perspective, like identity, remains potentially in flux, at the behest of innumerable forces, and the organic processes, the uncertainties and imperfections therein, are offset by the plasticity of Sen's work and his art.

Art and creation are in fact narrative and thematic touchstones throughout *I Have to Buy New Shoes*. In addition to Sen's work as a photographer there is his sister's boyfriend, a painter, and a close friend of Aoi, who is a fashion designer and who uses Aoi's basement for her clothes and costumes. There is even an emphasis on two separate occasions on cooking and food preparation as a creative endeavour as Aoi is responsible for a meal for an Easter party with friends, whilst at the beginning of the film her work as a journalist takes her to a shop full of intricately painted Easter eggs. The contrast between these respective artistic practices throws further light on Kitagawa's own project, as it underlines this film's almost meta-fictive engagement with Paris as a cinematic city, a space perennially seen and re-seen, created and recreated, but that can still offer up fresh, subjective images when seen through particular eyes. As in *Halfway* there is a distinct lack of a sexual dimension to the central burgeoning relationship; however the tentative union between Aoi and Sen becomes another kind of creation (as opposed to the rather superficial relationship between Sen's sister and the painter), something that, like a precious artwork, will remain all the more important to those involved for its not being completed (i.e. petrified), for being mysterious, not becoming known. Like great art their relationship seems a process, a journey without a destination, unfinished and therefore alive. Indeed Sen and his sister's relationships are contrasted throughout; where the former is not physically intimate the latter almost immediately is, and where the latter illogically proposes to her boyfriend before leaving in a desperate attempt to stay close to him and overcome the physical distance between them, the former parts from Aoi with a tacit understanding (on both sides) that the two will most likely never meet again. Sen and Aoi's final moments together involve the former taking pictures of the latter with the Eiffel Tower positioned behind her. Crucially this Parisian metonym is out of focus in the film's images, as indeed is the space around both protagonists (for the first time in the film), connoting the extent to which Aoi has replaced and simultaneously renewed the spectacle of the city, both frustrated and facilitated a touristic consumption of its image (Figs 7.2a/7.2b). Sen even says that Aoi and the Tower are now Paris for him, that they represent the city, Kitagawa in effect overwriting a postmodern impetus that defines and delimits nationhood through perceived representative symbols, a surface of meaning, and thereby connoting the contrastive depth of the central relationship.

If the films of Tanada Yuki offer reasonably superficial pictures of female selfhood and identity then they at least do so with an eye to challenging traditional gender roles and boundaries. Comparable is the work of Ogigami Naoko, who after studying film in America went on to direct several successful short films

Figure 7.2   Envisioning touristic spectacle at the beginning and end of *I Have to Buy New Shoes*. Note the deep (upper picture) and shallow (lower picture) focus that connotes a regression from landscape as touristic spectacle to landscape as mere backdrop.

and features and to develop an aesthetic based on minimalist, wryly humorous, languorous, naturalistic, ostensibly undramatic scenarios built around small and insular groups. Like Kawase and Tanada, Ogigami has also made a film about Japanese women abroad, in her case in Helsinki, Finland. *Kamome Diner* (*Kamome shokudō*, 2006) concerns two Japanese women: one, Sachie, who has opened a diner on a quiet street, and the other, Midori, a Japanese traveller who is invited to stay with Sachie following a chance encounter. *Kamome Diner* provides an interesting point of contrast with *I Have to Buy New Shoes* not only in its gently comedic tone but also in that it engages with questions of nation-hood and perception. It is interesting that these modern female directors should make films about Japanese abroad – and about women in particular. Films about Japanese in foreign countries, especially Japanese films, have not been as forthcoming as those works about foreigners (*gaijin*) in Japan, which have proliferated particularly in Hollywood: from *The Teahouse of the August Moon* (1956) and Samuel Fuller's *The Crimson Kimono* (1959) through *The Yakuza* (1974) and *Black Rain* (1989) and on to *The Last Samurai* (2003), Quentin Tarantino's *Kill Bill Volume 1* (2003) and Sofia Coppola's *Lost in Translation* (2003) to name only the obvious few. However films about Japanese abroad, especially by Japanese directors, are much less common. Ogigami, like Kawase and Kitagawa, stresses a certain sense of alienation on the part of her visiting women, especially as Sachie's diner is initially unsuccessful and is viewed quaintly, as a curiosity, by a number of local residents. Moreover she also broadly echoes Kawase and Kitagawa in critiquing canonical constructions of nationhood and identity. In *Kamome Diner* there is a protracted discussion about nationality and food – about what dishes represent particular countries – with Sachie noting that she does not want to cater for homesick Japanese by serving Sushi, etc. but hopes to transcend specific tastes and boundaries. Furthermore during a talk with Midori, who randomly opted to come to Finland from Japan by blindly pointing to a spot on a globe, Sachie asks whether she would have travelled to Alaska or Tahiti had she pointed to those places. Midori says that she would have, and accompanying their dialogue Ogigami cuts to brief shots of Midori standing in a tableau composition (as though for a photograph) in these places: in the snow beside a model of a seal and in the sunshine dancing in a hula skirt, respectively. She employs these clichéd pictures in order to comically suggest the limitations on perceptions of national identity that seem to represent or even become the nation, that override the multitude of diverse and ever-changing constituents on this (amorphous) precept with a stereotypical shorthand that summarises a national character or selfhood. This theme is also present in the young Finnish man who frequents Sachie's diner, a Japanophile with a rudimentary grasp of the Japanese language and a selection of T-shirts featuring samurai and other canonical national symbols and metonyms. Again the picture is of consumption of nationhood (hence the central location of the diner, a site of eating, consuming), and of the postmodern impetus of such an undertaking that needs to be negotiated, much as the initially rude local Finnish women must overcome their preconceived objections to Sachie's diner.

Ogigami is, then, concerned to put nationhood under a microscope, to satirise the notion that any particular country can be summarised, visualised and indeed understood through reference to any single aspect of its culture, society or in this case cuisine. Christina Zimmermann (2011) has discussed the comedic specific-ity of Ogigami's work as it revolves almost entirely around stereotypes involved in stories of women who travel abroad, and this is apparent in the director's subsequent feature. *Glasses* (*Megane*, 2007) is also about looking and perception, and similarly concerns a group that is tentatively formed, and where most of the members are on a break from their day-to-day lives. The protagonist, Taeko, is a reserved career woman who travels to a small beachfront hotel on an island and is confronted with a small, isolated community whose insularity and quaint way of life initially alienate her. However she increasingly warms to the locals, something depicted in the very form of the film as Ogigami enshrines the (narratively) dead time of the small community simply relaxing and spending time together. The fact that Taeko has to leave her luggage behind when she is given a ride on a bicycle back to her initial hotel after she had left bespeaks the figurative baggage that she needs to rid herself of in order to get along with her new companions and their way of life, to as it were see them properly, see past her urban inculcation. To this end she also loses her glasses in the film's penultimate scene as she leaves the island – a significant point in that everyone at her guest house also wears glasses, as much as to suggest that these people with impaired vision have 'seen' something valuable in this place that had perhaps eluded them elsewhere in their lives (none are locals), something beyond the surfaces that predominate in lives lived within the city and its postmodern capitalist impulses. These tenets of the film build incrementally into an almost allegorical vision. One member of the small community is an elderly lady named Sakura who, we are told, arrives promptly every spring to stay on the island for a short spell. Her name, Sakura (or cherry blossom), along with her punctual seasonal appearance, aligns her directly with this natural phenomenon, so that she may be read as a symbol for a traditional, maybe bygone Japan, one distinct from the hectic urban and modernised (Westernised) country that Taeko has been used to but one that she needs to connect with in order to progress in her life.

A number of modern female filmmakers in Japan have turned their hand to directing from other careers. Kitagawa Eriko is an example of this (she was a television writer), and alongside her is Ninagawa Miwa, a former fashion photographer who made her feature debut with a *jidai-geki* drama written by Tanada Yuki entitled *Sakuran* (2006). This film is not dissimilar to *Memoirs of a Geisha* (1998) in that it details a young girl's forced and at times violent induction into the world of a largely all-female enclave, in this case a brothel. The girl, Kiyoha, eventually reconciles herself to her work as a prostitute, particularly when it becomes clear that her beauty sets her apart and makes her ideal for this particular profession. However romantic travails become central when Kiyoha's close relationship with one particular patron is prohibited, and ultimately she draws ever closer to the man, even when an apparently advantageous marriage is arranged to a samurai lord who is willing to buy her out of her life in the brothel. Another example of a postmodern aesthetic increasingly overrides the generic identity of *Sakuran*. Ninagawa tends to stress the perceived gloss of this hermetic world through

Figure 7.3   The saturated *mise-en-scène* of *Sakuran* comments on the commodification of its women, the spectacle of their sexuality (Kiyoha is third from left).

an exaggerated, saturated *mise-en-scène* (Fig. 7.3) and contemporary soundtrack that offers not only an expressionist vision of life inside a world predicated entirely upon sensory indulgence and female objectification, but also stresses a non-period aesthetic that suggests that the gender imbalances that it dramatises should not necessarily be confined purely to the past. The director also uses this design to thematise spectacle and, by extension, spectatorship. A recurrent motif throughout the film is the use of goldfish. The brothel has several such adornments around its many rooms, and they figure in more than one metaphorical allusion to the life and situation of Kiyoha. Tanada and Ninagawa equate their protagonist with the fish on two separate, rhyming occasions early and later in the narrative, when the knocking over of a goldfish bowl leads to a fish becoming stranded on the floor. On the first occasion the bowl is knocked over by the protagonist as she runs from the brothel in an attempt to escape. The fish perishes, as in a sense does Kiyoha, an aspect of her life and personality dying when she is caught and forcibly returned to the brothel as a proverbial fish out of water. Subsequently a young apprentice (exactly as Kiyoha once was) finds a goldfish stranded outside its bowl; she places it back inside the water and says 'that's the only place you can live, you know', relating it directly to Kiyoha and her decision to remain within the brothel and accept her status as exalted object and the empowerment that it offers her.

Of arguably more significance is the direct correlation between the brothel and the bowl. The former is a space perennially on view, its women always displayed for the consumption of paying male clients. An opening scene in which men look in on the prostitutes in order to decide which of them they would like to buy time with makes this plain, and it is cemented in a subsequent flashback to Kiyoha's first days in the brothel when she wakes to find the woman to whom she has been assigned to learn her trade having sex in an adjacent room. Ninagawa depicts this through a POV shot with the young Kiyoha looking at the act directly through a goldfish bowl beside her futon. It is a reflection both on this particular act and, by extension, the establishment in which it takes place, and thus crystallises the characterisation of the brothel as a figurative goldfish bowl with its 'workers' always on display, always being looked at.

Problems surrounding female spectacle in an age of post-feminism are even more to the fore in Ninagawa's second film. *Helter Skelter* (*Heruta sukeruta*, 2012) is a drama set in the world of models and fashion photography, a milieu obviously well known to the director, and is something of a conceptual horror film in which a popular model named Lilico keeps up with increasing pressure to remain beautiful by repeatedly returning for a radical, illegal new surgical procedure that uses baby organs in order to ensure physical youth. The side effects of this procedure include increasingly unsightly marks like bruises on the skin and a malfunction of internal organs, something that signals the film's debt to the subset of Japanese horror cinema that has stressed bodily decay and transformation as a means of explicating the changes being wrought upon the nation (the national body). Lilico, like Kiyoha in *Sakuran*, is at the top of her profession because of her beauty. Indeed Ninagawa draws an explicit parallel with her feature debut by including an interior shot of a fish tank, which motif, along with *Helter Skelter*'s opening images of eyes, confer upon this picture a sense not only of spectacle but of coded looking, of seeing the world through a particular lens, a prism, which of course has significance with regard to female objectification, of seeing only beauty and youth. As the detective investigating the company responsible for Lilico's surgery says about the protagonist: 'her beauty is a montage of images. The sum total of our desires.' In other words she does not exist beyond her objectification, and (again like Kiyoha) it is through this that she exerts a measure of control and personal agency. In particular there is a scene in which she enters the flat of her meek personal assistant Michiko and proceeds to have sex with her boyfriend whilst Michiko watches in horror, in effect turning the tables on the ostensible subject and underlining the terror and more importantly the helplessness of looking and of seeing.

Lilico's surgery and the ongoing treatments it requires are designed to stem the flow of time, in effect to petrify the subject, as a result of which her trajectory throughout much of the narrative sees her alternate between ecstatic highs and terrifying lows. The former typically entails her asserting her control over others (usually Michiko), whilst the latter sees her breaking down over the pressures inherent in her work. She is trapped in a stylised, glossy, insular world of surfaces

Figure 7.4   Protesting the look in *Helter Skelter*.

that stand as a facade, a cover to mask the lack of anything tenable beneath. In this case this description rather aptly captures Lilico herself, her beautiful visage a mask that must be worn at all times. It transpires that Lilico is entirely a creation, a monster born from her mother's desire to replicate her own youthful dreams of fame and beauty, someone who has undergone cosmetic surgery on her whole body to literally create her looks and figure. She is a synthetic being who, like Frankenstein's monster, is put together, created, and the final scene of the film underlines this point by featuring Lilico being found in the basement of a Tokyo nightclub like another iconic 'monster'. She had previously been thought dead after appearing to commit suicide at a press conference, but instead has become a figure akin to the phantom of the opera, a literal monstrous feminine. The fact that her staged suicide involved stabbing herself in an eye offers a further comment on the theme of looking (Fig. 7.4). She half blinds herself as an (implicit) protest at her status as a purely decorative and objective figure, removing some of her power of sight as a marker of her own increasing disgust at being fixed as a desirable object. This potent image of proto-body horror echoes throughout the canon of Japanese horror cinema. Jay McRoy has demonstrated how images of the 'splattered body' in the film *Naked Blood* (*Nekeddo burāddo: megyaku*, 1996) dramatise 'social anxieties accompanying changes and continuities in gender roles and expectations as they relate to contemporary Japan's transforming social and economic landscape' (2005b, p. 113). *Helter Skelter* does not share this examination of transformation in the gendered social body, of woman in a perceived masculine space; rather it depicts a particularly feminine sphere of action and (compromised) agency, and in so doing reflects anxieties over the extent to which the nominally old, or at least long embedded, socio-cultural paradigm that it dramatises (of objectified women) is an ongoing and relevant feature of contemporary Japan.

There is thus a pervasive ambiguity between victim and aggressor, predator and prey, in *Helter Skelter*, and the extent to which Lilico is an object or a subject is a complex matter. She accrues a measure of power from her exalted status and certainly treats those around her, even those seemingly closest to her, in a despicable manner. Indeed, from this perspective, there is a nascent nihilism in the film as regards its portrait of the various characters, the way that it depicts a societal obsession with beauty and surface perfection. This refers not only to Lilico and her boyfriend (who revels only in having a trophy girlfriend and who becomes involved with another woman as soon as Lilico's looks and status begin to deteriorate), but also to those around the protagonist who are depicted in places as akin to parasites feeding from the life force of a host (even Michiko continues her faithful servitude to the woman whose beauty casts a light that she can somehow bask in). Moreover there are two rhyming scenes at the beginning and end of the film that feature a group of high school girls who act like a narrative chorus. They avidly read the magazines in which Lilico features, and both consume and reject her image, indeed her life, as if it were their property. It is an allusion to how the protagonist is in a sense owned by those around her, those who objectify her, and it is against this simultaneous power and powerlessness, the fact that she is 'better' than most others but at the same time monstrous, a lesser person, that the protagonist must be evaluated and judged. Lilico's cruelty towards those around her is regarded by Ninagawa as symptomatic of her exalted status, the fact that she has been elevated to a social position that is apparently commensurate with her looks and her body but remains as tenuous and subject to sudden change as her physicality – the one attendant on the other. Her excesses of both need and repulsion, of seeking companionship even as she repels those closest to her, bespeak another case of fundamental childishness, another infantilised woman to populate the ambiguous landscape of post-feminism in Japan. It is especially pertinent to the work done by Valerie Wee (2011), Imelda Whelehan (1995) and especially Naomi Wolf (1990), who argued that 'the quality called "beauty" objectively and universally exists' (p. 12), its oppressive but not undesirable imperative concisely reflected by Ninagawa's film. Lilico's position in the narrative as a perennially desired object in search of a concomitant subjectivity places her in a liminal space that echoes that of the similarly childlike protagonists of *Halfway* or of *Dogs and Cats*. It is perhaps crude and simplistic to suggest that these indeterminate textual sites of Japanese femininity reflect any absolute or lived realities on the part of women in Japan in the twenty-first century. But the sense in these films of being caught in an in-between space, a site of indeterminacy, may be seen to reflect a feminine selfhood currently caught or suspended between an overbearing past in the legacy of their patriarchal culture and a potentially problematic future that continues to require negotiation and struggle.

The prevalence of female directors in modern Japanese filmmaking has led Annette Kuhn to state that they have become 'new producers of representation in Japanese cinema' (1994), something Armendariz reiterates by suggesting that Tanada and Iguchi in particular represent a 'new phenomenon in the history of Japanese cinema' (2011, p. 33). Both Joan E. Ericson (1997) and Conrad Totman (2000) have stressed the extent to which post-war female writers have made as much impact as their male counterparts, to which end one may point not only to the directors who have occupied the focus of this chapter but also those who have carved out careers on more mainstream genre films. J-horror and fantasy in particular have seen more than one female director making her mark on the genre in ongoing series, with the films *Organ* (1996) *Ju-on: Black Ghost* (*Ju-on: kuroi shōjo*, 2009) and the first two works of the popular *Eko Eko Azarak* series all directed by women (Fujiwara Kei, Asato Mari and Sato Shimako, respectively). Moreover the international success of directors such as Yokohama Satoko, Inoue Tsuki and Wada Junko further reinforces an acceptance that these filmmakers are a significant force in the industry: that despite the fact that many wish to eschew a gendered reading of their professionalism they nonetheless represent a useful means of` conceptualising a contemporary landscape of Japanese cinema whose female visions of femininity can be contrasted with the male visions of the same that predominated in earlier eras. Part of the interest of films by Iguchi and Nishikawa in particular is their awareness of this intertextual landscape, the ways in which their work implicitly facilitates such a connection in order to throw new light on the imperatives of their own productions. The children of Japanese cinema could in fact be taken as a theme for this book, and it is in evidence in particular in these significant filmmakers.

BIBLIOGRAPHY

REFERENCES

Abe, K., 2003. *beat takeshi vs. takeshi kitano*. Translated from the Japanese by William O. Gardner and Takeo Hori. New York: Kaya Press.

Allison, A., 2000. *Permitted and Prohibited Desires: Mothers, Comic, and Censorship in Japan*. Berkeley and Los Angeles: University of California Press.

Altman, R., 1999. *Film/Genre*. London: British Film Institute.

Anderson, B., 1991. *Imagined Communities: Reflections on the Origin and Spread of Nationalism*. London and New York: Verso.

Armendariz, A., 2011. 'An alternative representation of sexual difference in Japanese cinema made by women directors'. *Journal of Japanese and Korean Cinema*, Vol. 3, No. 1, pp. 21–35.

Aufderheide, P., 2007. *Documentary: A Very Short Introduction*. Oxford: Oxford University Press.

Balmain, C., 2008. *Introduction to Japanese Horror Film*. Edinburgh: Edinburgh University Press.

Barnouw, E., 1993. *Documentary: A History of the Non-Fiction Film*. Second edition. New York: Oxford University Press.

Baudrillard, J., 1988. *America*. London: Verso.

Baudrillard, J., 1994. *Simulacra and Simulation*. Translated from the French by Sheila Faria Glaser. Ann Arbor: University of Michigan Press.

Baudrillard, J., 1995. *The Gulf War Did Not Take Place*. Translated from the French by Paul Patton. Indianapolis: Indiana University Press.

Beasley, W. G., 1995. *The Rise of Modern Japan: Political, Economic and Social Change since 1850*. Second edition. London: Weidenfeld & Nicolson.

Benedict, R., 1946. *The Chrysanthemum and the Sword: Patterns of Japanese Culture*. Boston: Houghton Mifflin Company.

Berra, J., 2012a. Introduction. In: Berra, J., ed. 2012. *Directory of World Cinema: Japan 2*. Bristol: Intellect, pp. 7–10.

Berra, J. 2012b. *Outrage* – Review. In: Berra, J., ed. 2012. *Directory of World Cinema: Japan 2*. Bristol: Intellect, pp. 331–2.

Berry, C., Xinyu, L and Rofel, L., eds. 2010. *The New Chinese Documentary Film Movement: For the Public Record*. Hong Kong: Hong Kong University

Bingham, A., 2009a. 'Kitano Takeshi and Modern Japanese Cinema: Genre, Authorship, Stardom'. PhD, University of Sheffield.

Bingham, A., 2009b. 'Beyond Borders: A Brief Introduction to the Work of Fujiwara Toshi'. *Asian Cinema*. Vol. 20, No. 1, pp. 155–65.

Bingham, A., 2010. 'Original Visions: Female Directors in Contemporary Japanese Cinema'. *Cineaction*, Issue 81, pp. 56–61.

Bingham, A., 2012. 'Shomin-geki/Lower Class Life'. In: Berra, J., ed. 2012. *Directory of World Cinema: Japan 2*. Bristol: Intellect, pp. 303–6.

Bingham, A., 2014. '*Cats and Dogs* and *Wild Berries*: New Female Visions in Japanese Cinema'. In: Kelly, G. and Robson, C., eds. 2014. *Celluloid Ceiling: Women Film Directors Breaking Through*. Twickenham: Supernova Books, pp. 188–204.

Blake, L., 2008. *The Wounds of Nations: Horror Cinema, Historical Trauma, and National Identity*. Manchester: Manchester University Press.

Bloom, C., 2007. *Gothic Horror*. Second edition. Basingstoke and New York: Palgrave Macmillan.

Blouin, M. J., 2013. *Japan and the Cosmopolitan Gothic: Specters of Modernity*. Basingstoke and New York: Palgrave Macmillan.

Booth, A., 1986. *The Roads to Sata: A 2000-mile walk through Japan*. London, New York and Tokyo: Kodansha International.

Booth, A., 1996. *Looking for the Lost: Journeys through a Vanishing Japan*. London, New York and Tokyo: Kodansha International.

Burch, N., 1979. *To the Distant Observer: Form and Meaning in the Japanese Cinema*. Berkeley and Los Angeles: University of California Press.

Buruma, I., 1984. *A Japanese Mirror: Heroes and Villains in Japanese Culture*. Harmondsworth: Penguin Books.

Buruma, I., 2001. *A Japanese Mirror: Heroes and Villains in Japanese Culture*. Second edition. London: Phoenix.

Buruma, I., 2003. *Inventing Japan: From Empire to Economic Miracle, 1853–1964*. London: Weidenfeld & Nicolson.

Carey, P., 2005. *Wrong about Japan*. London: Faber & Faber.

Cartmell, D. and Hunter, I. Q., 2001. 'Introduction: Retrovisions: Historical Makeovers in Film and Literature'. In: Cartmell, D., Hunter, I. Q. and Whelehan, I., eds. 2001. *Retrovisions: Reinventing the Past in Film and Fiction*. London: Pluto Press, pp. 1–7.

Cather, K., 2010. 'Perverting Ozu: Suō Masayuki's Abnormal Family'. *Journal of Japanese and Korean Cinema*, Vol. 2, No. 2, pp. 131–45.

Chanan, M., 2007a. 'Authentic Talking Cinema'. *Sight and Sound*, Vol. 17, No. 9, pp. 27–9.

Chanan, M., 2007b. *The Politics of Documentary*. London: British Film Institute.

Chopra-Gant, M., 2006. *Hollywood Genres and Post-War America: Masculinity, Family and Nation in Popular Movies and Film Noir*. London: I. B. Tauris.

Clarke, D. B., 1997. 'Introduction: Previewing the Cinematic City'. In: Clarke, D. B., ed. 1997. *The Cinematic City*. London and New York: Routledge, pp. 1–18

Clavell, J., 1975. *Shōgun*. London: Hodder & Stoughton.

Clements, J., 2010. *The Samurai: A New History of the Warrior Elite*. London: Robinson.

Colvile, G. M. M., 2006. 'Between Surrealism and Magic Realism: The Early Feature Films of André Delvaux'. *Yale French Studies*, No. 109, pp. 115–28.

Cousins, M., 2004. *The Story of Film*. Edinburgh: BCA.

Cousins, M. and McDonald, K. eds. 1996. *Imagining Reality*. London: Faber & Faber.

Creed, B., 1993. *The Monstrous Feminine: Film, Feminism, Psychoanalysis*. London and New York: Routledge.

D., C., 2005. *Outlaw Masters of Japanese Film*. London and New York: I. B. Tauris.

Davies, R.J. and Ikeno, O. eds. 2002. *The Japanese Mind: Understanding Contemporary Japanese Culture*. Boston: Tuttle Publishing.

Davis, D. W., 1996. *Picturing Japaneseness: Monumental Style, National Identity, Japanese Film*. New York: Columbia University Press.

Davis, D. W., 2001. 'Reigniting Japanese Tradition with *Hana-Bi*'. *Cinema Journal*, Vol. 40, No. 4, pp. 55–81.

Davis, D. W., 2006. 'Japan: Cause for (Cautious) Optimism'. In: Ciecko, A.T., ed. 2006. *Contemporary Asian Cinema*. New York and Oxford: Berg, pp. 193–206.

Davis, D. W., 2007. 'Therapy for Him and Her: Kitano Takeshi's *Hana-Bi* (1997)'. In: Phillips, A. and Stringer, J., eds. 2007. *Japanese Cinema: Texts and Contexts*. Abingdon: Routledge, pp. 284–95.

Davis, D. W. and Yeh, E. Y. Y., 2008. *East Asian Screen Industries*. London: British Film Institute. p. 119.

Degli-Esposti, C., 1998. 'Postmodernism(s)'. In: Degli-Esposti, C., ed. 1998. *Postmodernism in the Cinema*. New York and Oxford: Berghahn Books, pp. 3–18.

De Michiel, H. and Zimmermann, P.R., 2013. 'Documentary as Open Space'. In: Winston, B., ed. 2013. *The Documentary Film Book*. London: British Film Institute, pp. 355–65.

Desser, D., 1988. *Eros plus Massacre: An Introduction to the Japanese New Wave Cinema*. Bloomington and Indianapolis: Indiana University Press.

Desser, D. and Nolletti, Jr, A., eds. 1992. *Reframing Japanese Cinema: Authorship, Genre, History*. Bloomington and Indianapolis: Indiana University Press, pp. 165–92.

Dew, J., 1999. *A Ride in the Neon Sun: A Gaijin in Japan*. London: Little, Brown & Company.

Dimendberg, E., 2004. *Film Noir and the Spaces of Modernity*. Cambridge, MA: Harvard University Press.

Douglas, M., 2012. 'Jidaigeki/Period Drama'. In: Berra, J., ed, 2012. *Directory of World Cinema: Japan 2*. Bristol: Intellect, pp. 224–7.

Dowmunt, T., 2013. 'Autobiographical Documentary – the "Seer and the Seen"'. *Studies in Documentary Film*, Vol. 7, No. 3, pp. 263–77.

Eco, U., 1998. *Faith in Fakes: Travels in Hyperreality*. Translated from the Italian by William Weaver. London: Vintage.

Ericson, J. E., 1997. *Be a Woman: Hayashi Fumiko and Modern Japanese Women's Literature*. Honolulu: University of Hawai'i Press.

Eshelman, R., 2008. *Performatism, or the End of Postmodernism*. Aurora, CO: Davies Group Publishers.

Featherstone, M., 2007. *Consumer Culture and Postmodernism*. London: SAGE Publications.

Fraser, N., 2013. 'Foreword: Why Documentaries Matter'. In: Winston, B., ed. 2013. *The Documentary Film Book*. London: British Film Institute, pp. 10–5.

Fujimura-Fanselow, K., 2011. Introduction. In: Fujimura-Fanselow, K., ed. 2011. *Transforming Japan; How Feminism and Diversity are Making a Difference*. New York: The Feminist Press, pp. 17–31.

Fujiwara, T., 2009. 'Beyond Borders: A Brief Introduction to the work of Fujiwara Toshi'. *Asian Cinema*. Vol. 20, No. 1, pp. 155–65.

Fujiwara, T., 2014. Conversation about Japanese Documentary cinema [email] (personal communication, 4 February 2014).

Gallagher, T., 1996. 'Anhels Gambol Where They Will: John Ford's Indians'. In: Kitses, J. and Rickman, G., eds. 1998. *The Western Reader*. New York: Limelight Editions, pp. 269–76.

Galloway, P., 2005. 'Stray Dogs & Lone Wolves: *The Samurai Film Handbook*'. Berkeley: Stone Bridge Press.

Garcia, H., 2010. *A Geek in Japan: Discovering the Land of Manga, Anime, Zen and the Tea Ceremony*. Clarendon: Tuttle Publishing.

Gellar, T. L., 2008. 'Transnational Noir: Style and Substance in Hayashi Kaizo's *The Most Terrible Time in My Life*'. In: Hunt, L. and Wing-Fai, L., eds. 2008. *East Asian Cinemas: Exploring Transnational Connections on Film*. London and New York: I. B. Tauris. pp. 172–90.

Gerow, A., 1999. 'A Scene at the Threshold: Liminality in the Films of Kitano Takeshi'. *Asian Cinema*, Vol. 10, No. 2, pp. 107–15.

Gerow, A., 2007. *Kitano Takeshi*. London: British Film Institute.

Goldberg, R., 2005. 'The Nightmare of Romantic Passion in Three Classic Japanese Horror Films'. In: McRoy, J., ed. 2005. *Japanese Horror Cinema*. Edinburgh: Edinburgh University Press, pp. 29–37.

Goodwin, J., 1994. *Akira Kurosawa and Intertextual Cinema*. Baltimore and London: Johns Hopkins University Press.

Grigg, R., 2008. *Lacan, Language, and Philosophy*. New York: State University of New York Press.

Grossman, A., 2004. *Tetsuo The Iron Man/Tetsuo 2: Body Hammer*. In: Bowyer, J., ed. 2004. *The Cinema of Japan and Korea*. London: Wallflower Press, pp. 139–50.

Grosz, E., 1990. *Jacques Lacan: A Feminist Introduction*. Florence: Routledge.

Grundy, G., 1998. *Hana-Bi*. Neon, August, pp. 101–2.

Hall, K., 2005. 'Blind Swordsman: *Zatoichi* by Kitano Takeshi: Not a Mere "Entertainment"'. *Asian Cinema*, Vol. 16, No. 2, pp. 45–62.

Hallam, L., 2009. '"100% Sadist": Violence is Sex in Takashi Miike's *Ichi the Killer*'. *Asian Cinema*, Vol. 20, No. 2, pp. 206–16.

Hallam, J. and Marshment, M., 2000. *Realism and Popular Cinema*. Manchester and New York: University of Manchester Press.

Hara, K. and Bingham, A. 2010. 'Report from the Sheffield Documentary Film Festival, 2009'. *Asian Cinema*, Vol. 21, No. 1, pp. 219–22.

Harper, J., 2008. *Flowers from Hell: The Modern Japanese Horror Film*. Hereford: Noir Publishing.

Hart, S., 1983. 'Magical Realism in Gabriel Garciá Márquez's *Cien años de soledad*'. *Revista de literature Hispánica*, No. 16–17, pp. 37–52.

Harvey, D., 1990. *The Condition of Postmodernity*. Oxford: Blackwell.

Hegerfeldt, A. C., 2005. *Lies that Tell the Truth: Magic Realism Seen through Contemporary Fiction from Britain*. Amsterdam: Editions Rodopi.

Hendry, J., 2003. *Understanding Japanese Society*. Third edition. London: RoutledgeCurzon.

High, P. B., 2002. *The Imperial Screen*. Madison: University of Wisconsin Press.

Higson, A., 1989. 'The Concept of National Cinema'. In: Williams, A., ed. 2002. *Film and Nationalism*. New Brunswick, NJ and London: Rutgers University Press, pp. 52–67.

Hill, D., 2010. 'Yakuza/Gangster'. In: Berra, J., ed. 2010. *Directory of World Cinema: Japan 1*. Bristol: Intellect, pp. 266–9.

Hori, H., 2007. 'Migration and Transgression: Female Pioneers of Documentary Filmmaking in Japan'. *Asian Cinema*, Vol. 16, No. 1, pp. 89–97.

Howard, C., 2012. 'Shinjuku Triad Society'. In: Berra, J., ed. 2012. *Directory of World Cinema: Japan 2*. Bristol: Intellect, pp. 338–9.

Huber, C., 2011. *13 Assassins*. Sight and Sound, Vol. 21, No. 6, pp. 57–8.

Hughes-Warrington, M., 2007. *History Goes to the Movies: Studying History on Film*. London: Routledge.

Humm, M., 1997. *Feminism and Film*. Edinburgh: Edinburgh University Press.

Hutchings, P., 2004. *The Horror Film*. Harlow: Pearson Education Limited.

Iaccino, J. F., 1994. *Psychological Reflections on Cinematic Terror: Jungian Archetypes in Horror Films*. Westport, CT, London: Praeger.

Iizuka, T., 2009. 'Filmmaking as a Way of Life: Tsuchimoto, Ogawa, and Revolutions in Documentary Cinema'. *Asian Cinema*. Vol. 20, No. 1, pp. 166–75.

Iles, T., 2008. *The Crisis of Identity in Contemporary Japanese Film: Personal, Cultural, National*. Boston: Brill Academic Publishers.

Inoue, C. S., 2009. 'Yamada Yōji, and the kinder, gentler samurai: *The Twilight Samurai*, *The Hidden Blade*, and *Love and Honor*'. *Journal of Japanese and Korean Cinema*, Vol. 1, No. 2, pp. 157–65.

Ivy, M., 1995. *Discourses of the Vanishing: Modernity, Phantasm, Japan*. Chicago and London: University of Chicago Press.

Izuhara, M., 2006. 'Changing Families and Policy Responses to an Ageing Japanese Society'. In: Rebick, M. and Takenaka, A., eds. 2006. *The Changing Japanese Family*. Abingdon: Routledge, pp. 161–76.

James, N., 2010. 'Cannes 2010'. *Sight and Sound*, Vol. 20, No. 7, pp. 16–22.

Jameson, F., 1986. 'On Magic Realism in Film'. *Critical Inquiry*, 12, Winter 1986, pp. 301–25.

Jancovich, J. ed., 2002. *The Horror Film Reader*. London and New York: Routledge.

Jīngfū, Ā., 1994. 'The Pain of a Half Taoist: Taoist Principles, Chinese Landscape Painting, and King of the Children'. In: Desser, D. and Ehrlich, L.C., eds. 1994. *Cinematic Landscapes: Observations on the Visual Arts and Cinema of China and Japan*. Austin: University of Texas Press, pp. 117–25.

Johnson, G. A., 1998. 'Pyrotechnics from Japanese Mega-star'. *San Francisco Examiner*, 20 March [online], available at: www.sfgate.com/cgi-bin/article.cgi?f=/e/a/1998/03/20/WEEKEND5470.dtl [accessed 2 December 2013].

Kasho, A., 1994. *beat takeshi vs. takeshi kitano*. Translated from the Japanese by William O. Gardner and Takeo Hori. Tokyo: Kaya Press.

Kawakita, N., 1956. 'Japanese Audiences and Foreign Films'. *Japan Quarterly*. Vol. 3, No. 2, pp. 219–22.

Keene, D., 1998. *Dawn to the West: Japanese Literature of the Modern Era*. New York: Columbia University Press.

Kehr, D., 1998. 'Equinox Flower'. *Film Comment*, Vol. 34, No. 2, pp. 31–5.

Keirstead, T. and Lynch, D., 1995. 'Eijanaika: Japanese Modernization and the Carnival of Time'. In: Rosenstone, R. A., ed. 1995. *Revisioning History: Film and the Construction of a New Past*. Princeton: Princeton University Press, pp. 64–76.

Kerr, A., 2001. *Dogs and Demons: The Fall of Modern Japan*. London: Penguin.

Kiyono, P., 2013. *The Samurai's Garden* [e-book]. Astraea Press. Available at: www.amazon.co.uk/Samurais-Garden-Patricia-Kiyono-ebook/dp/B00A2ZGHL4/ref=sr_1_fkmr0_2?s=books&ie=UTF8&qid=1417631621&sr=1-2-fkmr0&keywords=samurai%27s+garden+kiyoni [accessed 14 November 2014].

Knudsen, E., 2008. 'Transcendental Realism in Documentary'. In: Austin, T. and de Jong, W., eds. 2008. *Rethinking Documentary: New Perspectives, New Practices*. Maidenhead: Open University Press, pp. 108–20.

Ko, M., 2006. 'The Break-up of the National Body: Cosmetic Multiculturalism and the Films of Miike Takashi'. In: Vitali, V. and Willemen, P., eds. 2006. *Theorising National Cinema*. London: British Film Institute, pp. 129–37.

Kristeva, J., 1982. *Powers of Horror: An Essay on Abjection*. Translated from the French by L. S. Roudiez. New York: Columbia University Press.

Kuhn, A., 1994. *Women's Pictures: Feminism and Cinema*. Second edition. London: Verso.

Laird, C. A., 2012. 'Directors: Naoko Ogigami'. In: Berra, J., ed. 2012. *Directory of World Cinema: Japan 2*. Bristol: Intellect, pp. 52–4.

Lapsley, R., 1997. 'Mainly in Cities and at Night: Some Notes on Cities and Film'. In:

Clarke, D. B., ed. 1997. *The Cinematic City*. London and New York: Routledge, pp. 186–208.

Lawrence, W., 2005. *When the Last Sword is Drawn* [DVD]. London: Tartan DVD (supplementary essay).

Le Fanu, M., 2005. *Mizoguchi and Japan*. London: British Film Institute.

Lyotard, J.-F., 1984. *The Postmodern Condition: A Report on Knowledge*. Translated from the French by Geoff Bennington and Brian Massumi. Manchester: Manchester University Press.

Mackie, V., 2003. *Feminism in Modern Japan: Citizenship, Embodiment and Sexuality*. Cambridge: Cambridge University Press.

McDonald, K. I., 1992. 'The *Yakuza* Film: An Introduction'. In: Desser, D. and Nolletti, Jr, A., eds. 1992. *Reframing Japanese Cinema: Authorship, Genre, History*. Bloomington and Indianapolis: Indiana University Press, pp. 165–92.

McDonald, K. I., 2000. *From Book to Screen: Modern Japanese Literature in Film*. London and New York: M. E. Sharpe.

McDonald, K. I., 2006. *Reading a Japanese Film: Cinema in Context*. Honolulu: University of Hawai'i Press.

McDonald, K. I., 2007. 'Daring To Be First: The Japanese Woman Director Tazuko Sakane (1904–1971)'. *Asian Cinema*, Vol. 18, No. 2, pp. 128–46.

McRobbie, A., 2004. 'Post-feminism and Popular Culture'. *Feminist Media Studies*, Vol. 4, No. 3, pp. 255–64.

McRoy, J., 2005a. Introduction. In: McRoy, J., ed. 2005. *Japanese Horror Cinema*. Edinburgh: Edinburgh University Press, pp. 1–14.

McRoy, J., 2005b. 'Cultural Transformation, Corporeal Prohibitions and Body Horror in Sato Hisayasu's *Naked Blood*'. In: McRoy, J., ed. 2005. *Japanese Horror Cinema*. Edinburgh: Edinburgh University Press, pp. 107–19.

McRoy, J., 2008. *Contemporary Cinema, Volume 4: Nightmare Japan: Contemporary Japanese Horror Cinema*. Amsterdam: Editions Rodopi.

Marquez, G. G., 1970. *One Hundred Years of Solitude*. Translated from the Spanish by Gregory Rabassa. New York: Harper & Row.

Masao, M., 1991. *Off Center: Power and Culture Relations between Japan and the United States*. Cambridge, MA and London: Harvard University Press.

Masazumi, T. and Yamane, S., 2003. 'Tokyo Story'. In: Cheuk-to, L., Li, H. C. and Lee, M., eds. 2003. *Ozu Yasujiro: 100th Anniversary*. Hong Kong: Hong Kong Arts Development Council. pp. 146–7.

Mason, M. M., 2011. 'Empowering the Would-be Warrior: Bushidō and the Gendered Bodies of the Japanese Nation'. In: Früstück, S. and Walthal, A., eds. 2011. *Recreating Japanese Men*. Berkeley: University of California Press, pp. 68–90.

Masterson, G., 1988. *Tengu*. New York: Time Warner Paperbacks.

Maysles, A., 2013. Foreword. In: Quinn, J., ed. 2013. *This much is True: 14 Directors on Documentary Filmmaking*. London: Bloomsbury, pp. 9–10.

Meikle, D., 2005. *The Ring Companion*. London: Titan Books.

Mellen, J., 1976. *The Waves at Genji's Door: Japan through its Cinema*. New York: Pantheon Books.

Mes, T., 2003. *Agitator: The Cinema of Takashi Miike*. Godalming: FAB Press.

Mes, T., 2005. *A Yakuza in Love* [DVD]. New York: ARTSMAGICDVD (supplementary interview).

Mes, T., 2006. 'Sway. Midnight Eye' [online], available at: www.midnighteye.com/reviews/sway.com [accessed 2 May 2014].

Mes, J. and Sharp, J., 2004. 'The Twilight Samurai. Midnight Eye' [online], available at: www.midnighteye.com/reviews/twilight-samurai/html [accessed 3 January 2014].

Mes, T. and Sharp, J., 2005. *The Midnight Eye Guide to New Japanese Film*. Berkeley: Stone Bridge Press.

Miike, T., 2011. 13 'Assassins' [DVD]. London: Artificial Eye (supplementary interview).

Mills, M. C., 1989. 'Magic Realism and Garciá Márquez's Eréndira'. *Literature Film Quarterly*, Vol. 17, Issue 2, pp. 113–22.

Mishima, Y., 2001 (1956). *The Temple of the Golden Pavilion*. Translated from the Japanese by Ivan Morris. London: Vintage.

Miyao, D., 2003. Foreword. In: Abe, K., 2003. *beat takeshi vs. takeshi kitano*. Translated from the Japanese by William O. Gardner and Takeo Hori. New York: Kaya Press, pp. 9–16.

Miyoshi, M., 1991. *Off Center: Power and Culture Relations between Japan and the United States*. Cambridge, MA and London: Harvard University Press.

Morton, L., 2003. *Modern Japanese Culture: The Insider View*. Oxford and New York: Oxford University Press.

Mulvey, L., 1975. 'Visual Pleasure and Narrative Cinema'. In: Braudy, L. and Cohen, M., eds. 2004. *Film Theory and Criticism: Introductory Readings*. Sixth edition. New York and Oxford: Oxford University Press, pp. 837–48.

Murakami, Y. and Ogawa, N., 1999. *Japan Movies Now*. Tokyo: Sofuto kabā.

Nagib, L., Dudrah, R. and Perriam, C. eds. 2012. *Theorizing World Cinema*. New York: I. B. Tauris.

Napier, S., 2005. *Anime: From Akira to Howl's Moving Castle*. Second edition. Basingstoke and New York: Palgrave Macmillan.

Naremore, J., 1998. *More than Night: Film Noir in its Contexts*. Berkeley and Los Angeles: University of California Press.

Ndalianis, A., 2009. 'Dark Rides, Hybrid Machines and the Horror Experience'. In: Conrich, I., ed. *Horror Zone: The Cultural Experience of Contemporary Horror Cinema*. London: I. B. Tauris, pp. 11–26.

Neale, S., 1980. *Genre*. London: British Film Institute.

Neale, S., 1983. 'Prologue: Masculinity as Spectacle: Reflections on Men and Mainstream Cinema'. In: Cohan, S. and Hark, I.R., eds. 1992. *Screening the Male: Exploring Masculinities in the Hollywood Cinema*. London: Routledge, pp. 9–22.

Nealon, J., 2012. *Post-postmodernism: Or, the Cultural Logic of Just-in-time Capitalism*. Stanford: Stanford University Press.

Nichols, B., 2001. *Introduction to Documentary*. Bloomington: Indiana University Press.

Nolletti, Jr, A., 1992. 'Woman of the Mist and Gosho in the 1930s'. In: Desser, D. and Nolletti, Jr, A., eds. 1992. *Reframing Japanese Cinema: Authorship, Genre, History*. Bloomington and Indianapolis: Indiana University Press, pp. 3–32.

Nornes, A. M., 2003. *Japanese Documentary Film: The Meiji Era through Hiroshima*. Minneapolis: University of Minnesota Press.

Nornes, A. M., 2007a. *Forest of Pressure: Ogawa Shinsuke and Postwar Japanese Documentary*. Minneapolis: University of Minnesota Press.

Nornes, A. M., 2007b. 'The Riddle of the Vase: Ozu Yasujirō's *Late Spring* (1949)'. In: Phillips, A. and Stringer, J., eds. 2007. *Japanese Cinema: Texts and Contexts*. Abingdon: Routledge, pp. 78–89.

Nornes, A. M., 2013. 'Eastwards'. In: Winston, B., ed. 2013. *The Documentary Film Book*. London: British Film Institute, pp. 209–16.

Nowell-Smith, G., 2008. *Making Waves: New Cinemas of the 1960s*. London and New York: Continuum.

Nygren, S., 1993. 'Inscribing the subject: The melodramatization of gender in *An Actor's Revenge*'. In: Dissanayake, W., ed. 1993. *Melodrama and Asian Cinema*. Cambridge: Cambridge University Press, pp. 127–42.

Okri, B., 1991. *The Famished Road*. London: Jonathan Cape.

Osenlund, R. J., 2011. *Still Walking*. Cineaste, Vol. 36, No. 3, pp. 54–5.

Otaka, H., in Morton, L., 2003. *Modern Japanese Culture*. Oxford and New York: Oxford University Press.

Philips, A., 2007. 'Unsettled Visions: Imamura Shōhei's *Vengeance is Mine* (1979)'. In: Philips, A. and Stringer, J., eds. *Japanese Cinema: Texts and Contexts*. Abingdon: Routledge, pp. 229–39.

Pinkerton, N., 2011a. 'The Banality of Evil'. *Village Voice* [online], available at: www.villagevoice.com/2011–04–27/film/the-banality-of-evil-same-old-epic-samurai-showdown-in-13-assassins/html [accessed 5 January 2014].

Pinkerton, N., 2011b. 'Outrage'. *Village Voice* [online], available at: www.villagevoice.com/2011–11–30/film/outrage-film-review/html [accessed 15 February 2014].

Powell, A., 2005. *Deleuze and Horror Film*. Edinburgh: Edinburgh University Press.

Prince, S., 1991. *The Warrior's Camera: The Cinema of Akira Kurosawa*. Princeton: Princeton University Press.

Quinn, J., 2013. Introduction. In: Quinn, J., ed. 2013. *This Much is True: 14 Directors on Documentary Filmmaking*. London: Bloomsbury, pp. 11–13.

Rawle, S., 2009. 'From *The Black Society* to *The Isle*: Miike Takashi and Kim Ki-Duk at the Intersection of Asia Extreme'. *Journal of Japanese and Korean Cinema*, Vol 1, No 2, pp. 167–84.

Rayns, T., 1998. 'Then the Fireworks'. *Sight and Sound*, Vol. 8, No. 8, pp. 32–3.

Rayns, T., 2001. 'To Die in America'. *Sight and Sound*, Vol. 11, No. 4, pp. 26–7.

Rayns, T., 2003. 'Luck of the Drawn Blade'. *Sight and Sound*, Vol. 13, No. 11, pp. 20–3.

Rebick, M. and Takenaka, A., 2006. 'Editors' Preface: The Changing Japanese Family'. In: Rebick, M. and Takenaka, A. eds. 2006. *The Changing Japanese Family*. Abingdon: Routledge, pp. 3–16.

Renov, M., 1993. 'Towards a Poetics of Documentary'. In: Renov, M., ed. 1993. *Theorizing Documentary*. London and New York: Routledge, pp. 12–37.

Richie, D., 1962. 'Japanese Shapes'. In: Silva, A., ed. 2001. *The Donald Richie Reader*. Berkeley: Stone Bridge Press, pp. 42–6.

Richie, D., 1971. *Japanese Cinema: Film Style and National Character*. New York: Anchor Books.

Richie, D., 1974. *Ozu*. Berkeley and Los Angeles: University of California Press.

Richie, D., 1996. *The Films of Akira Kurosawa*. Third edition. Berkley and Los Angeles: University of California Press.

Richie, D., 2001. *A Hundred Years of Japanese Film*. Tokyo, New York, London: Kodansha International.

Roberts, L., 2011. 'Name and Honor': A Merchant's Seventeenth-Century Memoir. In: Frūstück, S. and Walthal, A., eds. 2011. *Recreating Japanese Men*. Berkeley: University of California Press, pp. 48–67.

Robey, T., 2004. *The Twilight Samurai* [DVD]. London: Tartan DVD (supplementary essay).

Romney, J., 2003. *Dolls. Sight and Sound*, Vol. 13, No. 6. p. 42.

Rosenstone, R. A., 1995. *Visions of the Past*. Cambridge, MA and London: Harvard University Press.

Roudinesco, E., 2003. 'The Mirror Stage: An Obliterated Archive'. In: Rabaté, J.-M., ed. 2003. *The Cambridge Companion to Lacan*. Cambridge: Cambridge University Press, pp. 25–34.

Rushdie, S., 1981. *Midnight's Children*. London: Jonathan Cape.

Russell, C., 2011. *Classical Japanese Cinema Revisited*. London and New York: Continuum.

Saeed-Vafa, M. and Rosenbaum, J. 2003. *Abbas Kiarostami*. Urbana and Chicago: University of Illinois Press.

Saint-Cyr, M., 2012. *Ichi the Killer*. In: Berra, J., ed. 2012. *Directory of World Cinema: Japan 2*. Bristol: Intellect, pp. 329–31.

Sato, T., 1987. *Currents in Japanese Cinema*. Second edition. Translated from the Japanese by Gregory Barret. New York and Tokyo: Kodansha International.

Sato, M., 2006. *The Rhetoric of Documentary*. Tokyo: Misuzu shobo.

Saunders, D., 2007. *Direct Cinema: Observational Documentary and the Politics of the Sixties*. New York: Columbia University Press.

Schilling, M., 1997. *The Encyclopedia of Japanese Pop Culture*. New York: Weatherhill.

Schilling, M., 1999. *Contemporary Japanese Film*. New York and Tokyo: Weatherhill.

Schilling, M., 2003. *The Yakuza Movie Book*. Berkeley: Stone Bridge Press.

Schneider, S. J. 2004. 'Introduction: Psychoanalysis in/and/of the Horror Film'. In: Schneider, S. J., ed. 2004. *Horror Film and Psychoanalysis: Freud's Worst Nightmare*. Cambridge: Cambridge University Press, pp. 1–16.

Sharrett, C., 2004. 'Preface: Japanese Horror Cinema'. In: McRoy, J., ed. 2005. *Japanese Horror Cinema*. Edinburgh: Edinburgh University Press, pp. 11–14.

Shikibu, M., 2001. *The Tale of Genji*. Translated from the Japanese by Royall Tyler. London: Penguin.

Shimizu, F., 2012. Chambara/Samurai Cinema. In: Berra, J., ed. 2012. *Directory of World Cinema: Japan 2*. Bristol: Intellect, pp. 144–7.

Shonagon, S., 2006. *The Pillow Book*. Translated from the Japanese by Meredith McKinney. London: Penguin.

Silver, A., 2005. *The Samurai Film*. Revised and expanded edition. Woodstock and New York: Overlook Press.

Skrodzka, A., 2012. *Magic Realist Cinema in East Central Europe*. Edinburgh: Edinburgh University Press.

Soda, K. and Grey, J., 2007. Kazuhiro Soda (interview). *Midnight Eye* [online], available at: www.midnighteye.com/interviews/kazuhiro-soda/html [accessed 15 April 2014].

Sontag, S., 1965. 'The Imagination of Disaster'. In Sontag, S. 2009. *Against Interpretation and other Essays*. London: Penguin, pp. 209–25.

Standish, I., 2005. *A New History of Japanese Cinema*. London and New York: Continuum.

Stevens, B., 2009. *A Gaijin's Guide to Japan: An Alternative Look at Japanese Life, History and Culture*. London: Friday Books.

Stojkovic, J., 2010. 'Alternative Japan'. In: Berra, J, ed. 2010. *Directory of World Cinema: Japan*. Bristol: Intellect, pp. 34–7.

Strain, E., 1998. 'E. M. Forster's Anti-touristic Tourism and the Sightseeing Gaze of Cinema'. In: Degli-Esposti, C., ed. 1998. *Postmodernism in the Cinema*. New York and Oxford: Berghahn Books, pp. 146–66.

Stringer, J., 2007. 'The Original and the Copy: Nakata Hideo's *Ring* (1998)'. In: Philips, A. and Stringer, J., ed. 2007. *Japanese Cinema: Texts and Contexts*. London and New York: Routledge, pp. 296–307.

Sugimoto, Y., 2003. *An Introduction to Japanese Society*. Second edition. Cambridge and New York: Cambridge University Press.

Suzuki, K., 2004. *Ring*. Translated from the Japanese by R. G. Rohmer and G. Walley. London: HarperCollins.

Takakusu, J., 1906. 'The Social and Ethical Value of the Family System in Japan'. *International Journal of Ethics*, Vol. 17, No. 1, pp. 100–6.

Tansman, A., 2001. 'Where's Mama? The Sobbing Yakuza of Hasegawa Shin'. In: Cavanaugh, C. and Washburn, D., eds. 2001. *Word and Image in Japanese Cinema*. Cambridge and New York: Cambridge University Press, pp. 149–73.

Tezuka, Y., 2012. *Japanese Cinema Goes Global*. Hong Kong: Hong Kong University Press.

Tobias, S., 2002. 'Fireworks'. A.V. Club [online], www.avclub.com/content/node/1376 [accessed 3 December 2013].

Totman, C., 2000. *A History of Japan*. Oxford: Blackwell.

Tsutsui, W., 2004. *Godzilla on my Mind*. Basingstoke and New York: Palgrave Macmillan.

Tucker, R. N., 1973. *Japan: Film Image*. London: Studio Vista.

Turnbull, S., 2006. *The Samurai and the Sacred*. Oxford: Osprey Publishing.

Vincendeau, G., 2008. 'Family Ties'. *Sight and Sound*, Vol. 18, No. 8, pp. 16–20.

Wada-Marciano, M., 2008. *Nippon Modern: Japanese Cinema of the 1920s and 1930s*. Honolulu: University of Hawai'i Press.

Wada-Marciano, M., 2012. *Japanese Cinema in the Digital Age*. Honolulu: University of Hawai'i Press.

Wang, Y., 1993. 'Melodrama as Historical Understanding: The Making and the Unmaking of Communist History'. In: Dissanayake, W., ed. 1993. *Melodrama and Asian Cinema*. Cambridge: Cambridge University Press, pp. 73–100.

Wechsler, J., 1985. 'Magic Realism: Defining the Indefinite'. *Art Journal*, Winter 1985, pp. 293–8.

Wee, V., 2011. 'Patriarchy and the Horror of the Monstrous Feminine'. *Feminist Media Studies*, Vol. 11, No. 2, pp. 151–65.

Whelehan, I., 1995. *Modern Feminist Thought: From the Second Wave to 'Post-feminism'*. Edinburgh: Edinburgh University Press.

White, D. J., 2011. *Hanging Garden* – Review. *Japan Cinema* [online], available at: http://japancinema.net/2011/07/05/hanging-garden-review/html [accessed 5 April 2014].

White, E., 2005. 'Case Study: Nakata Hideo's *Ringu* and *Ringu 2*'. In: McRoy, J., ed. 2005. *Japanese Horror Cinema*. Edinburgh: Edinburgh University Press. pp. 38–50.

Williams, A., 2002. Introduction. In: Williams, A., ed. 2002. *Film and Nationalism*. New Brunswick, NJ and London: Rutgers University Press, pp. 1–22.

Williams, L., 2002. 'Mirrors without Memories: Truth, History, and *The Thin Blue Line*'. In: Grant, B. K. and Sloniowski, J, eds. 2014. *Documenting the Documentary*. Third edition. Detroit: Wayne State University Press, pp. 379–96.

Williams, T., 1996. *Hearths of Darkness: The Family in the American Horror Film*. London: Associated University Presses.

Willis, H., 2005. *New Digital Cinema: Reinventing the Moving Image*. London and New York: Wallflower.

Winston, B., 1995. *Claiming the Real: The Documentary Revisited*. London: British Film Institute.

Wolf, N., 1990. *The Beauty Myth: How Images of Beauty are used against Women*. London: Chatto & Windus.

Wood, R., 1986. *Hollywood from Vietnam to Reagan*. New York: Columbia University Press.

Wood, R., 1998. *Sexual Politics and Narrative Film: Hollywood and Beyond*. New York: Columbia University Press.

Wood, R., 2002. *Hitchcock's Films Revisited*. New York: Columbia University Press.

Yomota, I., 2000. *Nihon eiga shi hyakunen*. Tokyo: Shueisha shinsho.

Yoshimoto, M., 1993. 'Melodrama, Postmodernism, and Japanese Cinema'. In: Dissanayake, W., ed. 1993. *Melodrama and Asian Cinema*. Cambridge: Cambridge University Press, pp. 101–26.

Yoshimoto, M., 2000. *Kurosawa: Film Studies and Japanese Cinema*. Durham: Duke University Press.

Zimmermann, C., 2011. 'Juggling with cultural stereotypes: the light humour of Naoko Ogigami'. *Journal of Japanese and Korean Film*, Vol. 3, No. 1, pp. 45–53.

FURTHER READING

Balmain, C., 2012. 'J-Horror/Japanese Horror'. In: Berra, J., ed. 2012. *Directory of World Cinema: Japan 2*. Bristol: Intellect, pp. 194–7.

Clements, J. and Tamamuro, M., 2003. *The Dorama Encyclopedia*. Berkeley: Stone Bridge Press.

Cousins, M., 2007. 'Shaking the World'. *Sight and Sound*, Vol. 17, No. 9, pp. 22–6.

Crawford, A., 2009. '"Oh Yeah!": *Family Guy* as Magical Realism?' *Journal of Film and Video*, 61.2, pp. 52–69.

Ferguson, W., 2003. *Hokkaido Highway Blues: Hitchhiking Japan*. Edinburgh: Canongate Books.

Früstück, S., 2011. 'After Heroism: Must Soldiers Die?' In: Früstück, S. and Walthal, A., eds. 2011. *Recreating Japanese Men*. Berkeley: University of California Press, pp. 91–111.

Gerow, A., 2007. 'Playing with Postmodernism: Morita Yoshimitsu's *The Family Game* (1983)'. In: Phillips, A. and Stringer, J., eds. 2007. *Japanese Cinema: Texts and Contexts*. Oxon: Routledge, pp. 240–52.

Golden, A., 1998. *Memoirs of a Geisha*. London: Vintage.

Holland, M., 2012. 'Yakuza/Gangster'. In: Berra, J., ed. 2012. *Directory of World Cinema: Japan 2*. Bristol: Intellect, pp. 324–7.

Hotes, C. M., 2012, 'Cultural Crossover: Japanese Cinema and Bunraku Puppetry'. In: Berra, J., ed. 2012. *Directory of World Cinema: Japan 2*. Bristol: Intellect, pp. 28–32.

Howard, C., 2010. 'Boiling Point'. In: Berra, J., ed. 2010. *Directory of World Cinema: Japan 1*. Bristol: Intellect, pp. 270–1.

Jacoby, A., 2010. 'Disputed Territories'. *Sight and Sound*, Vol. 20, No. 7, pp. 38–41.

Jameson, F., 1984. 'Postmodernism: Or, the Cultural Logic of Late Capitalism'. *New Left Review*, No. 146, July–August, pp. 59–92.

Jerslev, A. ed., 2002. *Realism and 'Reality' in Film and Media*. Copenhagen: Museum Tusculanum Press, University of Copenhagen.

Kitano, T., 1998. 'Takeshi Kitano, "Respect at last? Hold your Tickets"'. *Japan Quarterly*, Vol. 45, No. 1, pp. 4–9.

McDonald, K. I., 2007. 'Married to Cinema: Actress and Filmmaker Kinuyo Tanaka (1904–1976)'. *Asian Cinema*, Vol. 16, No. 1, pp. 184–204.

Nishikawa, M. and Ogata, M., 2012. Interview: Film Director Miwa Nishikawa. Blouin Artinfo [online], available at: http://enjp.blouinartinfo.com [accessed 1 May 2014].

Nygren, S., 2007. *Time Frames: Japanese Cinema and the Unfolding of History*. Minneapolis: University of Minnesota Press.

Renov, M., 2013. 'Art, Documentary as Art'. In: Winston, B., ed. 2013. *The Documentary Film Book*. London: British Film Institute, pp. 345–52.

Richie, D., 2001. 'Foreword: Outside Views of the Japanese Film'. In: Cavanaugh, C. and Washburn, D., eds. 2001. *Word and Image in Japanese Cinema*. Cambridge and New York: Cambridge University Press, pp. 13–18.

Russell, C., 2008. *The Cinema of Naruse Mikio: Women and Japanese Modernity*. Durham, NC and London: Duke University Press.

Saga, J., 1991. *Confessions of a Yakuza*. Translated from the Japanese by John Bester. Tokyo: Kodansha International.

Sato, M., 1997. *Mirror called Everyday: The World of Documentary Film*. Tokyo: Gaifusha.

Sato, M., 2001. *The Horizons of Documentary Film: To Understand the World Critically*. Tokyo: Gaifusha.

Sato, M. and Nornes, A. M., 2005. Sato Makoto (interview). Yamagata International Documentary Film Festival [online], available at: www.yidff.jp/docbox/25/box25-1-1-e.html [accessed 5 May 2014].

Schneider, S. J. ed., 2004. *Horror Film and Psychoanalysis: Freud's Worst Nightmare*. Cambridge: Cambridge University Press.

Tanada, Y. and Sharp, J., 2009. Yuki Tanada (interview). Midnight Eye [online], available at: www.midnighteye.com/interviews/yuki-tanada.com [accessed 14 April 2014].

SELECT FILMOGRAPHY

Abnormal Family: Older Brother's Bride (*Hentai kazoku Aniki no yomesan*, Suo Masayuki: 1984)
An Actor's Revenge (*Yukinojo henge*, Ichikawa Kon: 1963)
After Life (*Wandāfuru raifu*, Koreeda Hirokazu: 1998)
After the Rain (*Ame agaru*, Koizumi Takashi: 1999)
Ain't no Tomorrows (*Oretachi ni asu wa naissu*, Tanada Yuki: 2008)
Air Doll (*Kūki ningyō*, Koreeda Hirokazu: 2009)
Akitsu Springs (*Akitsu onsen*, Kiju Yoshida: 1964)
Alien (Ridley Scott: 1979)
The Amityville Horror (Stuart Rosenberg: 1979)
Angel Dust (*Enjeru dasuto*, Ishii Sogo: 1994)
Another Heaven (*Anaza hevun*, Iida Joji: 2000)
Another Lonely Hitman (*Shin kanashiki hitman*, Mochizuki Rokuro: 1995)
April Story (*Shigatsu monogatari*, Iwai Shunji: 1998)
Artists in Wonderland (*Mahiru no hoshi*, Sato Makoto: 1998)
Assassination (*Ansatsu*, Shinoda Masahiro: 1964)
Attack of the Mushroom People (*Matango*, Ishiro Honda: 1960)
August Without Him (*Kare no inai hachigatusu ga*, Koreeda Hirokazu: 1994)
Azumi (Kitamura Ryuhei: 2003)
Battles without Honour and Humanity (*Jingi naki tatakai*, Fukasaku Kinji: 1973)
Be Bop High School (*Be bappu haisukuru*, Nasu Hiroyuki: 1985)
The Bird People in China (*Chūgoku no chōjin*, Miike Takashi: 1998)
The Birds (Alfred Hitchcock: 1962)
Black Cat (*Kuroneko*, Shindo Kaneto: 1968)
Black Rain (*Kuroi ame*, Imamura Shohei: 1986)
The Blessing Bell (*Kōfuku no kane*, Sabu: 2002)
Blue Spring (*Aoi haru*, Toyoda Toshiaki: 2001)
Boiling Point (*San tai yon ekkusu jugatsu*, Kitano Takeshi: 1990)

Boy (*Shōnen*, Oshima Nagisa: 1969)
Bright Future (*Akarui mirai*, Kurosawa Kiyoshi: 2003)
The Brood (David Cronenberg: 1979)
Brother (Kitano Takeshi: 2000)
Campaign (*Senkyo*, Soda Kazuhiro: 2007)
Charisma (*Kurisuma*, Kurosawa Kiyoshi: 1999)
Cinema is About Documenting Lives (*Eiga wa ikimono no kiroku de aru: Tsuchimoto Noriaki
    no shigoto*, Fujiwara Toshi: 2007)
Cold Fish (*Tsumetai nettaigyo*, Sono Sion: 2010)
Cops vs. Thugs (*Kenkei tai soshiki bōryoku*, Fukasaku Kinji: 1975)
Crazy Family (*Gyakufunsha kazoku*, Ishii Sogo: 1984)
Crocodile Dundee (Peter Faiman: 1986)
Cruel Story of Youth (*Zangiku monogatari*, Oshima Nagisa: 1960)
Cure (*Kyūa*, Kurosawa Kiyoshi: 1997)
Dear Doctor (*Dia dokutā*, Nishikawa Miwa: 2009)
Dead or Alive (*Dead or Alive: Hanzaisha*, Miike Takashi: 1999)
Death by Hanging (*Kōshikei*, Oshima Nagisa: 1968)
Demon (*Yasha*, Furuhata Yasuo: 1985)
Distance (Koreeda Hirokazu: 2002)
Dodes'ka-den (Kurosawa Akira: 1975)
Dogs and Cats (Inuneko, Iguchi Nami: 2004)
Dolls (*Dōruzu*, Kitano Takeshi: 2002)
Dr Akagi (*Kanzo sensei*, Imamura Shohei: 1998)
Don't Laugh at my Romance (*Hito no sekkusu o warau na*, Iguchi Nami: 2007)
Doppelganger (*Dopperugangā*, Kurosawa Kiyoshi: 2003)
Dora-heita (Ichikawa Kon: 2000)
Dream Girls (Kim Longinotto and Jano Williams: 1994)
Dreams (*Yume*, Kurosawa Akira: 1990)
Drive (*Doraibu*, Sabu: 2001)
Dying at a Hospital (*Byōin de shinu to iu koto*, Ichikawa Jun: 1993)
Early Summer (*Bakushu*, Ozu Yasujiro: 1951)
Eat the Kimono (Kim Longinotto and Jano Williams: 1989)
The Eel (*Unagi*, Imamura Shohei: 1997)
Eijanaika (Imamura Shohei: 1981)
EM Embalming (*EM enbāmingu*, Aoyama Shinji: 1999)
Ending Note: Death of a Japanese Salaryman (*Endengu nōto*, Sunada Mami: 2011)
The End of Summer (*Kohayagawa-ke no aki*, Ozu Yasujiro: 1961)
ET: The Extra-Terrestrial (Stephen Spielberg: 1982)
Even Dwarfs Started Small (*Auch Zwerge haben klein angefangen*, Werner Herzog: 1970)
EXTE: Hair Extensions (*Ecusute*, Sono Sion: 2007)
The Eye (*Gin gwai*, Pang Brothers: 2002)
Eyes of the Spider (*Kumo no hitomi*, Kurosawa Kiyoshi: 1998)
The Family Game (*Kazoku gēmu*, Morita Yoshimitsu: 1983)
Female Yakuza Tale (*Yasagure anego den: sōkatsu rinchi*, Ishii Teruo: 1973)
Fence (*Fensu*, Fujiwara Toshi: 2008)
Fight Club (David Fincher: 1999)
The 47 Killers (*Shijushichinin no shikaku*, Ichikawa Kon: 1994)
The 400 Blows (*Les quatre cents coups*, Francois Truffaut: 1959)
Full Metal Yakuza (*Full Metal Gokudō*, Miike Takashi 1997)
The Funeral (*Osōshiki*, Itami Juzo: 1984)
Gaea Girls (Kim Longinotto and Jano Williams: 2000)
Gate of Hell (*Jigokumon*, Kinugasa Teinosuke: 1953)

Ghost Cat Mansion (*Bōreo kaibyō yashiki*, Nakagawa Nobuo: 1958)
The Ghosts of Kasane Swamp (*Kaidan kasane-ga-fuchi*, Nakagawa Nobuo: 1957)
The Ghost of Yotsuya (*Tōkaidō Yotsuya kaidan*, Nakagawa Nobuo: 1959)
Glasses (*Megane*, Ogigami Naoko: 2007)
The God Suzaku (*Moe no Suzaku*, Kawase Naomi: 1997)
Godzilla (*Gōjira*, Honda Ishiro: 1954)
Gohatto [*Taboo*] (Oshima Nagisa: 1999)
Goodbye CP (*Sayonara CP*, Hara Kazuo: 1972)
Gozu (*Gokudō kyōfu dai-gekijō: gozu*, Miike Takashi: 2003)
Graveyard of Honour (*Jingi no hakaba*, Fukasaku Kinji: 1975)
Graveyard of Honour (*Shin Jingi no hakaba*, Miike Takashi: 2002)
The Grudge 3 (Toby Wilkins: 2009)
The Guard from Underground (*Jigoku no keibīn*, Kurosawa Kiyoshi: 1992)
Guilty of Romance (*Koi no tsumi*, Sono Sion: 2011)
Halfway (*Harufuwei*, Kitagawa Eriko: 2009)
Hana and Alice (*Hana to Arisu*, Iwai Shunji: 2004)
Hana-Bi (*Fireworks*, Kitano Takeshi: 1997)
Hanako (Sato Makoto: 2001)
Hana/Hana – The Tale of a Reluctant Samurai (*Hana yori mo naho*, Koreeda Hirokazu: 2006)
The Hanging Garden (*Kuchu teien*, Toyoda Toshiaki: 2005)
Harakiri (*Seppuku*, Kobayashi Masaki: 1962)
Hara-Kiri: Death of a Samurai (*Ichimei*, Miike Takashi: 2011)
The Haunting (Robert Wise: 1963)
Helpless (*Herepuresu*, Aoyama Shinji: 1995)
Helter Skelter (*Heruta sukeruta*, Ninagawa Mika: 2012)
The Hidden Blade (*Kakushi ken oni no tsume*, Yamada Yoji: 2004)
Himizu (Sono Sion: 2011)
Home from the Sea (*Kokyō*, Yamada Yoji: 1972)
House (*Hausu*, Obayashi Nobuhiko: 1977)
Humanity and Paper Balloons (*Ninjo kami fusen*, Yamanaka Sadao: 1937)
Ichi the Killer (*Koroshiya Ichi*, Miike Takashi: 2001)
I Have to Buy New Shoes (*Atarashī kutsu wo kawanakucha*, Kitagawa Eriko: 2012)
Ikiru [*Living*] (Kurosawa Akira: 1953)
The Insect Woman (*Nippon konchuki*, Imamura Shohei: 1963)
I Walked with a Zombie (Jacques Tourneur: 1943)
I Wish (*Kiseki*, Koreeda Hirokazu: 2011)
Jiro Dreams of Sushi (David Gelb: 2011)
Ju-on: The Curse (*Ju-on*, Shimizu Takashi: 2000)
Ju-on: The Curse 2 (*Ju-on 2*, Shimizu Takashi: 2000)
Ju-on: Black Ghost (*Ju-on: kuroi shōjo*, Asato Mari: 2009)
Ju-on: The Grudge (*Ju-on*, Shimizu Takashi: 2001)
Ju-on: The Grudge 2 (*Ju-on 2*, Shimizu Takashi: 2003)
Ju-on: White Ghost (*Ju-on: shiroi rōjo*, Miyake Ryūta: 2009)
Kakera: A Piece of Our Life (*Kakera*, Ando Momoko: 2009)
Kamome Diner (*Kamome shokudō*, Ogigami Naoko: 2006)
Kamikaze Girls (*Shimotsuma monogatari*, Nakashima Tetsuya: 2004)
The Key (*Kagi*, Ichikawa Kon: 1959)
Kill Bill Volume 1 (Quentin Tarantino: 2003)
Knock Out (*Dotsuitarunen*, Sakamoto Junji: 1989)
Kwaidan (*Kaidan*, Kobayashi Masaki: 1965)
Lancelot du Lac (Robert Bresson: 1974)
The Land of Hope (*Kibo no kuni*, Sono Sion: 2012)

The Last Samurai (Edward Zwick: 2003)
Late Spring (*Banshun*, Ozu Yasujiro: 1949)
Letter from a Yellow Cherry Blossom (*Tsuioku no dansu*, Kawase Naomi: 2003)
Ley Lines (*Nihon kuroshakai*, Miike Takashi: 1999)
Like Father, Like Son (*Soshite chichi ni naru*, Koreeda Hirokazu: 2013)
Living on the River Agano (*Aga ni ikiru*, Sato Makoto: 1993)
Loft (*Rofuto*, Kurosawa Kiyoshi: 2005)
Lost in Translation (Sofia Coppola: 2003)
Love and Honour (*Bushi no ichibun*, Yamada Yoji: 2006)
Love Exposure (*Ai no mukidashi*, Sono Sion: 2008)
Love Letter (*Koibumi*, Tanaka Kinuyo: 1953)
The Lower Depths (*Donzoko*, Kurosawa Akira: 1957)
The Loyal 47 Ronin (*Genroku Chushingura*, Mizoguchi Kenji: 1941/1942)
Maborosi (*Maboroshi no hikari*, Koreeda Hirokazu: 1995)
Manhunter (Michael Mann: 1986)
A Man Vanishes (*Ningen johatsu*, Imamura Shohei: 1967)
Marebito (Shimizu Takashi: 2004)
Marks (*Marks no yama*, Yoichi Sai: 1995)
The Mars Canon (*Kasei no kanon*, Kazama Shiori: 2002)
Max mon amour (Oshima Nagisa: 1986)
Memories of Agano (*Aga no kioku*, Sato Makoto: 2005)
Mental (*Seishin*, Soda Kazuhiro: 2008)
Minamata: The Victims and Their World (*Minamata: kanja-san to sono sekai*, Tsuchimoto Noriaki: 1971)
Mobsters' Confessions (*Gokudo zangeroku*, Mochizuki Rokuro: 1998)
Monday (Sabu: 2000)
Moon and Cherry (*Tsuki to Cherī*, Tanada Yuki: 2004)
Naked Blood (*Nekeddo burāddo: megyaku*, Sato Hisayasu: 1996)
New Clothing (*Hatsu sugata*, Sakane Tazuko: 1936)
Night of the Demon (Jacques Tourneur: 1957)
9 Souls (*Nain sōruzu*, Toyoda Toshiaki: 2003)
Nobody Knows (*Dare mo shiranai*, Koreeda Hirokazu: 2003)
No Man's Zone (*Mujin chitai*, Fujiwara Toshi: 2012)
An Obsession (*Tsumetai chi*, Aoyama Shinji: 1997)
One Million Yen Girl (*Hyakuman-en to nigamushi onna*, Tanada Yuki: 2008)
One Missed Call (*Chakushin ari*, Miike Takashi: 2003)
Onibaba (Shindo Kaneto: 1964)
Onibi: The Fire Within (Onibi, Mochizuki Rokuro: 1997)
Organ (Fujiwara Kei: 1996)
Osaka Story (*Ōsaka monogatari*, Ichikawa Jun: 1999)
Osaka Tough Guys (*Naniwa yukyōden*, Miike Takashi: 1995)
Outrage (*Autoreiji*, Kitano Takeshi: 2010)
Outrage Beyond (*Autoreiji: biyondo*, Kitano Takeshi: 2012)
Owl's Castle (*Fukuro no shiro*, Shinoda Masahiro: 1999)
Panic High School (*Koko dai panikku*, Ishii Sogo: 1978)
Peace (Soda Kazuhiro: 2010)
Peeping Tom (Michael Powell: 1960)
Poltergeist (Tobe Hooper: 1982)
Porno Star (*Poruno sutā*, Toyoda Toshiaki: 1998)
POV – A Cursed Film (*POV: norowareta firumu*, Tsuruta Norio: 2012)
Premonition (*Yogen*, Tsuruta Norio: 2004)
Primary (Robert Drew and Richard Leacock: 1960)

Princess Mononoke (*Mononoke hime*, Miyazaki Hayao: 1997)
The Profound Desire of the Gods (*Kamigami no fukaki yokubo*, Imamura Shohei: 1968)
Pulse (*Kairo*, Kurosawa Kiyoshi: 2001)
Rainy Dog (*Gokudō kuroshakai*, Miike Takashi: 1997)
Ran (Kurosawa Akira: 1985)
Rashomon (*Rashōmon*, Kurosawa Akira: 1950)
The Ravaged House: Zoroku's Disease (*Tadareta ie: Zoroku no kibyo*: Kumakiri Kazuyoshi: 2004)
Reincarnation (*Rinne*, Shimizu Takashi: 2005)
Retribution (*Sakebi*, Kurosawa Kiyoshi: 2006)
Ring (*Ringu*, Nakata Hideo: 1998)
Ring 2 (*Ringu 2*, Nakata Hideo: 1999)
Ring 0: Birthday (*Ringu 0: bāsudei*, Tsuruta Norio: 2000)
Sakuran (Ninagawa Mika: 2007)
Samurai Rebellion (*Joi-uchi: hairyo tsuma shimatsu*, Kobayashi Masaki: 1967)
Samurai Resurrection (*Makai tensho*, Hirayama Hideyuki: 2003)
Sanjuro (*Tsubaki Sanjurō*, Kurosawa Akira: 1962)
Séance (*Kōrei*, Kurosawa Kiyoshi: 2000)
Self and Others (*Serefu ando azazu*, Sato Makoto: 2000)
The Serpent's Path (*Hebi no michi*, Kurosawa Kiyoshi: 1998)
Seven (David Fincher: 1995)
Seven Samurai (*Shichi-nin no samurai*, Kurosawa Akira: 1954)
The Seventh Seal (*Det sjunde inseglet*, Ingmar Bergman: 1957)
Sex and Fury (*Furyō anego den: Inoshika ochō*, Suzuki Norifumi: 1973)
SF: Samurai Fiction (*Esu Efu, Samurai fikushon*, Nakano Hiroyuki: 1998)
The Shadow Warrior (*Kagemusha*, Kurosawa Akira: 1980)
Shall We Dance? (*Sharu we dansu*, Suo Masayuki: 1997)
Shara (Kawase Naomi: 2003)
The Shining (Stanley Kubrick: 1980)
Shinjuku Boys (Kim Longinotto and Jano Williams: 1995)
Shinjuku Triad Society (*Shinjuku kuroshakai*, Miike Takashi: 1995)
Shiranui Sea (*Shiranui-kai*, Tsuchimoto Noriaki: 1975)
The Silence of the Lambs (Jonathan Demme: 1991)
Snake Woman's Curse (*Kaidan hebi-onna*, Nakagawa Nobuo: 1968)
Sonatine (*Sonachine*, Kitano Takeshi 1993)
Still Walking (*Aruitemo aruitemo*, Koreeda Hirokazu: 2008)
Strange Circus (*Kimyo na sakasu*, Sono Sion: 2005)
Street Mobster (*Gendai yakuza: hitokiri yota*, Fukasaku Kinji: 1972)
Sway (*Yureru*, Nishikawa Miwa: 2006)
Sweet Home (*Suīto hōmu*, Kurosawa Kiyoshi: 1989)
Switchblade Romance (*Haute Tension*, Alexandre Aja: 2004)
The Tale of Zatoichi (*Zatōichi monogatari*, Misumi Kenji: 1962)
Tampopo [*Dandelion*] (Itami Juzo: 1986)
Tarachime (Kawase Naomi: 2006)
Tetsuo: The Iron Man (*Tetsuo*, Tsukamoto Shinya: 1989)
They Who Tread on the Tiger's Tail (*Tora no O o fumu otokotachi*, Kurosawa Akira: 1945)
13 Assassins (*Jūsan-nin no shikaku*, Kudo Eiichi: 1962)
13 Assassins (*Jūsan-nin no shikaku*, Miike Takashi: 2010)
Three Outlaw Samurai (*Sanbiki no samurai*, Gosha Hideo: 1964)
Throne of Blood (*Kumonosu-jo*, Kurosawa Akira: 1957)
Tokyo Family (*Tōkyō Kazoku*, Yamada Yoji: 2013)
Tokyo-Ga (Wim Wenders: 1985)

Tokyo Lullaby (*Tōkyō yakyoku*, Ichikawa Jun: 1997)
Tokyo Marigolds (*Tōkyō marigōrudo*, Ichikawa Jun: 2001)
Tokyo Siblings (*Tōkyō kyōdai*, Ichikawa Jun: 1995)
Tokyo Sonata (*Tōkyō sonata*, Kurosawa Kiyoshi: 2008)
Tokyo Story (*Tōkyō monogatari*, Ozu Yasujiro: 1953)
Tokyo Twilight (*Tōkyō boshoku*, Ozu Yasujiro: 1957)
Turtles are Surprisingly Fast Swimmers (*Kami wa igai to hayaku oyogu*, Satoshi Miki: 2005)
The Twilight Samurai (*Tasogare Seibei*, Yoji Yamada: 2004)
Two Punks (*Chinpira*, Aoyama Shinji: 1996)
Ugetsu monogatari (Mizoguchi Kenji: 1953)
Unchain (Toyoda Toshiaki: 2000)
Vengeance is Mine (*Fukushu suru wa ware ni ari*, Imamura Shohei: 1979)
Vertigo (Alfred Hitchcock: 1958)
The Village (*Harakara*, Yamada Yoji: 1975)
Violent Cop (*Sono otoko, kyōbō ni tsuki*, Kitano Takeshi: 1989)
Warm Water under the Red Bridge (*Akai hashi no shita nonuruimizu*, Imamura Shohei: 2001)
When the Last Sword is Drawn (*Mibu gishi den*, Takita Yojiro: 2003)
Why Don't You Play in Hell? (*Jigoku de nazu warui*, Sono Sion: 2013)
Wild Berries (*Hebi ichigo*, Nishikawa Miwa: 2003)
Without Memory (*Kioku ga usinawareta toki*, Koreeda Hirokazu: 1996)
Wolf Creek (Greg McLean: 2004)
Yakuza Apocalypse (*Gokudō daisensō*, Miike Takashi: 2015)
A Yakuza in Love (*Koi gokudo*, Mochizuki Rokuro: 1997)
Yakuza Tale (*Yasagure anego den: sōkatsu rinchi*, Suzuki Norifumi: 1973)
Yojimbo (Kurosawa Akira: 1961)
Young Yakuza (Jean-Pierre Limosin: 2007)
Zatoichi (*Zatōichi*, Kitano Takeshi: 2003)
Zombie Flesh Eaters (Lucio Fulci: 1979)

INDEX